Jewish Cult and Hellenistic Culture

Essays on the Jewish Encounter with Hellenism and Roman Rule

by

John J. Collins

BRILL

LEIDEN • BOSTON

2005

This book is printed on acid-free paper.

Library of Congress Cataloging-in-Publication Data

Collins, John Joseph, 1946–
  Jewish cult and Hellenistic culture : essays on the Jewish encounter with Hellenism and Roman rule / by John J. Collins.
    p. cm. — (Supplements to the Journal for the study of Judaism, ISSN 1384–2161 ; v. 100)
  Includes bibliographical references and index.
  ISBN 90–04–14438–2 (alk. paper)
    1. Judaism—History—Post-exilic period, 586 B.C.–210 A.D. 2. Jews—History—168 B.C.–135 A.D. 3. Jews—Civilization—Greek influences. 4. Hellenism. 5. Bible. O.T. Apocrypha. Wisdom of Solomon—Criticism, interpretation, etc. 6. Philo, of Alexandria. 7. Jews—Rome—Civilization. I. Title. II. Series.

BM176.C645 2005
296'.09'014—dc22

2005046991

ISSN 1384–2161
ISBN 90 04 14438 2

Jewish Cult and Hellenistic Culture

Supplements

to the

Journal for the Study of Judaism

Editor

John J. Collins
The Divinity School, Yale University

Associate Editor

Florentino García Martínez
Qumran Institute, University of Groningen

Advisory Board

J. DUHAIME — A. HILHORST — P.W. VAN DER HORST
A. KLOSTERGAARD PETERSEN — M.A. KNIBB — H. NAJMAN
J.T.A.G.M. VAN RUITEN — J. SIEVERS
G. STEMBERGER — E.J.C. TIGCHELAAR — J. TROMP

VOLUME 100

CONTENTS

PREFACE

Eleven of the twelve essays in this volume have appeared elsewhere over the years 2000 to 2005. (The exception is the first essay, on "Hellenistic Judaism in Recent Scholarship," which appears here for the first time). I have made occasional minor corrections, standardized the style, and updated some references. Otherwise the essays are reprinted as they originally appeared. In the case of chapter 8, "Life after Death in Pseudo-Phocylides," I have added a postscript to respond to a rejoinder to the original essay by P. W. van der Horst.

The original publication information is as follows:

1. "Hellenistic Judaism in Recent Scholarship," not previously published, was delivered as a paper at a conference on "Athens and Jerusalem" at UCLA in March, 2003.
2. "Cult and Culture: The Limits of Hellenization in Judea," in J. J. Collins and G. E. Sterling, ed., *Hellenism in the Land of Israel* (Notre Dame, IN: University of Notre Dame, 2001) pp. 38–61.
3. "Reinventing Exodus: Exegesis and Legend in Hellenistic Egypt," in R. A. Argall, B. A. Bow, and R. A. Werline, ed., *For A Later Generation, The Transformation of Tradition in Israel, Early Judaism and Early Christianity* (Harrisburg, PA: Trinity Press International, 2000) 52–62.
4. "Messianism and Exegetical Tradition. The Evidence of the LXX Pentateuch," in M. A. Knibb, ed., *Messianism and Septuagint* (Leuven: Peeters, 2005).
5. "The Third Sibyl Revisited," in E. Chazon and D. Satran, ed., *Things Revealed. Studies in Early Jewish and Christian Literature in Honor of Michael E. Stone* (Leiden: Brill, 2004) 3–19.
6. "Spells Pleasing to God. The Binding of Isaac in Philo the Epic Poet," in A. Yarbro Collins and M. M. Mitchell, ed., *Antiquity and Humanity, Essays on Ancient Religion and Philosophy presented to H. D. Betz* (Tübingen: Mohr Siebeck, 2001) 3–13.
7. "Joseph and Aseneth. Jewish or Christian?" *Journal for the Study of the Pseudepigrapha* 14(2004) 57–72.

8. "Life after Death in Pseudo-Phocylides," in F. García Martínez and G. P. Luttikhuizen, ed., *Jerusalem, Alexandria, Rome. Studies in Ancient Cultural Interaction in Honour of A. Hillhorst* (Leiden: Brill, 2003) 75–86.

9. "The Reinterpretation of Apocalyptic Traditions in the Wisdom of Solomon" appeared in Italian as "La Reinterpretazione delle Tradizioni Apocalittiche nella Sapienza di Salomone," in G. Bellia and A. Passaro, ed., *Il Libro della Sapienza. Tradizione, Redazione, Teologia* (Rome: Città Nuova, 2004) 157–71. An earlier form of this article appeared as "Apocalyptic Eschatology in Philosophical Dress in the Wisdom of Solomon," in J. L. Kugel, ed., *Shem in the Tents of Japhet. Essays on the Encounter of Judaim and Hellenism* (Leiden: Brill, 2002) 93–107.

10. "The Mysteries of God," in F. García Martínez, ed., *Wisdom and Apocalyptic* (Leuven: Peeters, 2003) 287–306.

11. "The Jewish World and the Coming of Rome," in W. Dever and S. Gitin, ed., *Symbiosis, Symbolism, and the Power of the Past. Canaan, Ancient Israel and Their Neighbors from the Late Bronze Age Through Roman Palestine. Proceedings of the Centennial Symposium, W.F. Albright Institute of Archaeological Research and American Schools of Oriental Research, Jerusalem, May 29–31, 2000.* (Winona Lake, IN: Eisenbrauns, 2003) 353–62.

12. "Anti-Semitism in Antiquity? The Case of Alexandria," in C. Bakhos, ed., *Ancient Judaism in its Hellenistic Context* (Leiden: Brill, 2005) 9–29.

I wish to express my gratitude to University of Notre Dame Press, Trinity Press International, Peeters, Mohr Siebeck, T. & T. Clark International, Eisenbrauns and Brill Academic Publishers for permission to republish.

CHAPTER ONE

HELLENISTIC JUDAISM IN RECENT SCHOLARSHIP

Few episodes in ancient history have had more profound and lasting implications than the encounter of Judaism and Hellenism. The spread of Greek culture to the east was the first great encounter of east and west, the first instance of a clash of civilizations that has been repeated in various forms down to the present. Few people in antiquity could have anticipated that the Jews would be the most enduring representatives of ancient Near Eastern culture. Alexander can scarcely have given Judea a second thought. The eventual importance of Judaism on the world stage would be due in part to the extraordinarily distinctive self-consciousness of the Jewish people, and in part to their historic link to the Christian religion, which would dominate so much of western history. But for the Christian connection, the remarkable corpus of literature produced by Greek-speaking Jews might well have been lost, like the literature of other Near Eastern peoples. Be that as it may, the Jews are the only eastern people of the Hellenistic world who have left behind a substantial literature.[1] Only in the case of Judaism do we have the material to assess the response of an eastern people to Hellenism, and to see how an eastern tradition was adapted in light of the different and dominant culture of the Greeks.

The encounter between Judaism and Hellenism took place in two arenas. In the land of Israel, the majority of the population continued to speak a Semitic language, Aramaic or Hebrew. The initial attempt to turn Jerusalem into a Hellenistic polis met with violent rejection, for reasons that were religious rather than cultural in the

---

[1] For surveys see J. J. Collins, *Between Athens and Jerusalem* (New York: Crossroad, 1983; revised ed. Grand Rapids: Eerdmans, 2000); M. Goodman, "Jewish Literature Composed in Greek," in E. Schürer, *The History of the Jewish People in the Age of Jesus Christ* (rev. and ed. G. Vermes, F. Millar and M. Goodman; 3 vols.; Edinburgh: Clark, 1973–87) 2.470–704; J. M. G. Barclay, *Jews in the Mediterranean Diaspora* (Edinburgh: Clark, 1996); E. Gruen, *Heritage and Hellenism. The Reinvention of Jewish Tradition* (Berkeley: University of California, 1998).

broader sense.[2] But Hellenistic culture, and even pagan religion, continued to have a profound impact in Israel in the following centuries, reaching a high point in the reign of Herod the Great.[3] The dynamic in the land of Israel, however, was different from that in the Diaspora, where Greek was the language of Jew and Gentile alike. My concern here will be with the encounter in the Diaspora, specifically in Egypt, which is the source of most of the Greco-Jewish literature that survives. This literature documents a remarkable attempt to embrace Greek culture while maintaining a distinctive Jewish identity at the same time. It is the peculiar nature of this fusion of horizons that concerns us here.

Apologetic Literature?

Beginning in the nineteenth century, modern scholarship classified the literature of Egyptian Jewry as "apologetic" and propagandistic, on the assumption that it was intended to defend Judaism from attack and win converts from the gentile world.[4] That view of the literature was overturned by Victor Tcherikover in a famous article in 1956, in which he argued that the literature was addressed to the Jewish community itself.[5] Subsequent scholarship has discredited the view that there was any sustained or systematic Jewish proselytism in the Hellenistic period, or the first century of Roman rule.[6] Tcherikover did not deny the existence of any Jewish apologetic literature. The *Contra Apionem* of Josephus is the prime example, and

---

[2] See my essay, "Cult and Culture. The Limits of Hellenization in Judea," in J. J. Collins and G. E. Sterling, *Hellenism in the Land of Israel* (Notre Dame, IN.: University of Notre Dame Press, 2001) 38–61, reprinted in this volume.

[3] M. Hengel, in collaboration with C. Markschies, *The 'Hellenization' of Judaea in the First Century after Christ* (Philadelphia: Trinity Press International, 1989); D. Roller, *The Building Program of Herod the Great* (Berkeley: University of California Press, 1998).

[4] The classic expression of this view can be found in M. Friedländer, *Geschichte der jüdischen Apologetik als Vorgeschichte des Christentums* (Zurich: Schmidt, 1903).

[5] V. Tcherikover, "Jewish Apologetic Literature Reconsidered," *Eos* 48(1956) 169–93. See the reflections of J. Barclay, "Apologetics in the Jewish Diaspora," in J. R. Bartlett, ed., *Jews in the Hellenistic and Roman Cities* (London: Routledge, 2002) 129–48.

[6] See especially M. Goodman, *Mission and Conversion. Proselytizing in the Religious History of the Roman Empire* (Oxford: Clarendon, 1994). L. H. Feldman, *Jew and Gentile in the Ancient World* (Princeton: Princeton University Press, 1993) 288–341, is exceptional among recent authors in arguing for extensive proselytism.

Philo is also known to have composed an apologetic work.[7] Tcherikover's point was simply that the great bulk of Greco-Jewish literature was most likely intended for Jewish readers, and received little attention from Gentiles. This point has generally been accepted, althoug Louis Feldman still continues to detect "missionary motives" in such books as the Sibylline Oracles, the Wisdom of Solomon and the Letter of Aristeas.[8]

While Tcherikover successfully debunked the view that this literature was missionary in purpose, the question of apologetics is somewhat more subtle. To be sure, a writing like the Letter of Aristeas is not apologetic in the explicit sense of Josephus' *Contra Apionem*. But there are also less direct ways of engaging in apologetics, by seeking to rebut criticism of one's religion and affirm its positive features. In fact, Tcherikover's view of Diaspora Judaism was rather defensive. Hellenistic culture presented a temptation "to be like all the peoples."[9] While there were isolated exceptions, he argued that "the Diaspora Jews were closely attached to their nationality and that the overwhelming majority of them did not incline to assimilation."[10] They maintained their communities based on the foundation of "Jewish tradition." This kind of antithetical view of the relationship between "Jewish tradition" and Hellenism has its roots in 2 Maccabees, where the excesses of the so-called Hellenistic reform, in the period before the Maccabean revolt, are described as *akmē tis hellēnismou*, an extreme of Hellenism (2 Macc 4:13). The contrast is polemical and overdrawn. Its problematic character is shown already by the fact that 2 Maccabees, the *locus classicus* for the antithesis, is itself a thoroughly Hellenistic book in many ways.

Tcherikover's view of Hellenistic Judaism has been enormously influential over the last half century, but few scholars to-day would state the antithesis between Judaism and Hellenism in such stark terms. Jews in the Diaspora did not perceive Hellenism as a threat to be resisted. Most scholars, however, would agree that there was

---

[7] Tcherikover, "Jewish Apologetic Literature Reconsidered," 183; Eusebius, *PE* 8.8.19.

[8] Feldman, *Jew and Gentile*, 437.

[9] Tcherikover, *Hellenistic Civilization and the Jews* (Peabody, MA: Hendrickson, 1989, first published in 1959 by the Jewish Publication Society, Philadelphia) 354.

[10] Ibid.

some tension between Hellenistic culture and Jewish tradition, even when both were perceived positively. In the words of Greg Sterling:

> there are two foci which constitute the horizons of Alexandrian Jewish self-identity: the necessity of maintaining allegiance to the ancestral tradition, and the right to participation in Hellenism *de bon coeur*. While the tensions created by these apparently bi-polar foci were resolved in numerous ways within the Alexandrian Jewish community, Jewish self-identity was preserved as long as both horizons were kept in view.[11]

I myself have written of dissonance between Jewish self-perception and the depiction of Judaism by some Hellenistic authors, and also of dissonance in some cases between Greek and Jewish cultural values.[12] Consequently much of the Diaspora literature has an apologetic quality, insofar as it tries to correct Gentile impressions and to show that Judaism was really in accordance with the best in Greek culture.[13] Sterling has written of apologetic historiography, exemplified in authors such as Artapanus.[14] Martin Goodman, in his revision of the relevant section of Schürer's *History*, has characterized this literature as "largely apologetic in the most comprehensive sense of the word" insofar as its chief preoccupations "lay in the praise and aggrandisement of Jewish religion and the history of the Jewish people."[15]

Gruen and Barclay

In recent years there have been two important attempts to modify this view of Hellenistic Jewish literature in significant ways. The apologetic character of the literature, even in the broad sense, has been called in question by Erich Gruen. According to Gruen, Hellenistic Judaism "transcends a Diaspora mentality. The surviving products

---

[11] G. E. Sterling, "'Thus Are Israel': Jewish Self-Definition in Alexandria," *Studia Philonica Annual* 7 (1995) 8.

[12] Collins, *Between Athens and Jerusalem*, 14–16.

[13] Philo is the classic example of this endeavor. See M. Niehoff, *Philo on Jewish Identity and Culture* (Tübingen: Mohr Siebeck, 2001) and on the specific topic of *philanthropia*, K. Berthelot, *Philanthrôpia judaica. Le débat autour de la 'misanthropie' des lois juives dans l'Antiquité* (Leiden: Brill, 2003) 233–321.

[14] G. E. Sterling, *Historiography and Self-Definition. Josephos, Luke-Acts and Apologetic Historiography* (Leiden: Brill, 1992) 103–225.

[15] Goodman, in Schürer, *The History*, 472–3.

do not present a struggle for identity in an alien world, an apologia for strange customs and beliefs, or propaganda meant to persuade the Gentile. The texts instead display a positive quality, bold and inventive, sometimes startling, often light-hearted and engaging, and throughout directed internally to Jews conversant with or altogether inseparable from the culture of the Greeks. The relationships portrayed rarely have an antagonistic or adversarial quality—at least not without reconciliation and a happy ending. The imaginative fictions made political subordination palatable by pointing to the Jewish roots of pagan accomplishments and Jewish involvement in the course of Hellenistic history."[16]

There are, it seems to me, two important insights in this description of the literature. First, Jews in the Diaspora did not view Hellenistic culture as something foreign, much less as a temptation to be resisted.[17] Greek was their native language. They were heirs to Greek literature and philosophy just as much as were their Gentile neighbors.[18] Second, Jewish tradition (or any other tradition for that matter) is not static. It is something that is fashioned and refashioned in every age. Hellenistic Judaism is simply the form taken by Judaism in Greek-speaking environments in the Hellenistic age. Some questions remain, however. To say that tradition is refashioned raises the question of continuity. Are there elements in a tradition that are of its essence? Are some more essential than others to maintaining Jewish identity? Gruen's own comment about political subordination suggests that the relationship of the Jews to the dominant culture may not have been altogether trouble-free. Moreover, Gruen has elsewhere demonstrated that "a strong strain in Jewish literature emphasized the differences in culture and behavior between the two peoples, categorizing the Greeks as aliens, inferiors, even savage antagonists and barbarians."[19] This would seem to call for some

---

[16] Gruen, *Heritage and Hellenism*, 292–93. He develops his argument for "Diaspora Humor" in his more recent book, *Diaspora. Jews amidst Greeks and Romans* (Cambridge, MA: Harvard, 2002) 135–212.

[17] Even though Gruen also speaks of "the temptations and allure of Hellenism," ibid., 292.

[18] A similar point is made by Sterling, "'Thus are Israel,'" 8, in his insistence Jewish participation in Hellenistic culture. That participation is well documented by Feldman, *Jew and Gentile*, 45–83.

[19] See Gruen, "Jewish Perspectives on Greek Culture and Ethnicity," in Collins and Sterling, *Hellenism in the Land of Israel*, 82.

qualification of the happy picture of Hellenistic Judaism painted in *Heritage and Hellenism.*

A rather different approach to the material is advocated by John Barclay, in his book, *Jews in the Mediterranean Diaspora from Alexander to Trajan.* In line with academic trends at the end of the twentieth century, Barclay devoted more space to theoretical concerns than any previous student of Hellenistic Judaism, and called for a more differentiated treatment of the material. Specifically, he distinguished between assimilation, acculturation and accommodation. Assimilation is "the degree to which Diaspora Jews were integrated into, or socially aloof from, their social environment."[20] Acculturation concerns such matters as language, values and intellectual traditions. Accommodation concerns "the use to which acculturation is put, in particular the degree to which Jewish and Hellenistic cultural traditions are merged, or alternatively, polarized."[21] The latter category is especially important. All Jewish literature written in Greek exhibits acculturation to some degree, if only by the use of the Greek language. This does not mean, however, that it has a uniformly positive attitude towards Hellenistic culture. Greek literary forms may be used ironically, to subvert the values of the dominant culture, or to advance a quite traditional form of Judaism.[22] Barclay's formulation of the issue is influenced by post-colonial theory.[23] Of course scholars have always reckoned with the possibility that Greek language and literary genres might cloak unreconstructed Hebraic thought patterns.[24] Barclay's point is different, and allows for a sophisticated use of Hellenistic media for anti-Hellenistic purposes. This is an important insight, and it calls for a nuanced analysis of Hellenistic Jewish literature.

Barclay's analytical categories are constructive and helpful. His application of them in his book is, in my opinion, more problematic, The most controversial aspect of the book is his attempt to distinguish texts that exhibit "cultural convergence" from those "whose

---

[20] Barclay, *Jews in the Mediterranean Diaspora*, 93.

[21] Ibid., 96.

[22] Compare E. R. Goodenough's interpretation of Philo in *The Politics of Philo Judaeus* (New Haven: Yale, 1938).

[23] For a sampling, see B. Ashcroft, G. Griffiths and H. Tiffin, *The Post-Colonial Studies Reader* (London: Routledge, 1995).

[24] For a recent example see E. Puech, "Il Libro della Sapienza e I Manoscritti del Mar Morto: Un Primo Approcio," in G. Bellia and A. Passaro, ed., *Il Libro della Sapienza. Tradizione, Redazione, Teologia* (Rome: Città Nuova, 2004) 131–55.

socio-cultural stance is predominantly oppositional and antagonistic."[25] There are indeed Jewish texts, composed in Greek, that are predominantly antagonistic to the Gentile world. The fifth book of Sibylline Oracles is a case in point.[26] But attitudes to Hellenistic culture are seldom so simple as to admit of simple binary oppositions. Rather, in the words of Erich Gruen, "supposedly different voices coexist in the same texts."[27] Even those documents that are explicitly hostile to some aspects of Hellenism, may be quite enthusiastic about Hellenism in other respects. Many of the examples classified as antagonistic by Barclay are in fact quite complex, and by no means antagonistic to Hellenistic culture *tout court*.

More recently, Barclay has returned to the subject in an essay on "Jewish Identity Strategies under the Hegemony of Hellenism."[28] In agreement with Gruen, he objects to approaches that attribute to this literature an apologetic character, or that see its relationship to Hellenistic culture as one of dissonance, or its objective as "problem-solving." While he admits that there were undoubtedly anxieties and clashes in the cultural encounters, he claims that for many Jews, such as Philo, "social and cultural embeddedness in the Hellenistic world appears to have been wholly unproblematic."[29] As an alternative approach, he proposes to regard Hellenistic Jews as "cultural negotiators." "The question," he writes, "is not how Jews "reached out" to Hellenistic culture, or "struck balances" with it, but how, taking it for granted, they used it for their own cultural purposes."[30] He emphasizes three features of this model. First is a focus on positive strategy: negotiators do whatever best serves the interests of their communities. Jews both used and refused Hellenistic culture, neither adopting it uncritically nor rejecting it outright. Second is the factor of power. Jews in Alexandria had no choice but to adopt

---

[25] Barclay, *Jews in the Mediterranean Diaspora*, 181. He is concerned here with accommodation, or the purpose of the literature, rather than with acculturation.

[26] See Collins, *Between Athens and Jerusalem*, 143–50.

[27] Gruen, "Jewish Perspectives on Greek Culture," 81.

[28] J. M. G. Barclay, "Using and Refusing. Jewish Identity Strategies under the Hegemony of Hellenism," in M. Konradt and U. Steinert, ed., *Ethos and Identität. Einheit und Vielfalt des Judentums in hellenistisch-römischer Zeit* (Paderborn: Schöningh, 2002) 13–25. See also his introductory comments, "Introduction: Diaspora Negotiations," in Barclay, ed., *Negotiating Diaspora* (JSPSup 45; London and New York: T. & T. Clark International, 2004) 1–6.

[29] Ibid. 16.

[30] Ibid.

Greek forms of discourse, but we should allow for the possibility that their use of them contains "hidden transcripts," which subvert, or even mock the dominant culture.[31] Finally, the negotiations involve continual change, "a continuous process of self-refashioning."[32] Here again Barclay echoes and endorses a point made by Gruen: Jewish tradition is not static or unitary. Hellenistic Judaism is simply a phase in its development.

All of this seems to me a distinct improvement over Barclay's earlier attempts to distinguish between culturally convergent and culturally antagonistic forms of Judaism. Whether it is really different from the apologetic model remains to be seen. On the matter of dissonance between Judaism and Hellenistic culture, it seems to me that Barclay has uncovered a source of dissonance that has not received sufficient attention in the past. This is the resentment of a Near Eastern people toward Hellenistic cultural hegemony, even when political and social relations are relatively harmonious. This very insight, however, casts serious doubt on Barclay's assertion that Jews like Philo found their cultural interactions wholly unproblematic.[33] Moreover, it seems to me that cultural negotiation is itself a form of problem-solving, and is, in effect, an attempt to "strike a balance" with Hellenistic culture by using some aspects of it and refusing others. To speak of cultural negotiation requires that there are two foci of Jewish identity, in Sterling's phrase, that have to be balanced and reconciled in some way. However much Jews in the Diaspora took Hellenistic culture for granted, they were very much conscious of being different in some respects, and were at pains to assert both their separate identity and and their common values.

Some Factors in the Diaspora Situation

Before we turn to test these views of Hellenistic Judaism against a particular text, there are a couple of points that should be kept in

---

[31] For the concept of "hidden transcripts" see J. C. Scott, *Domination and the Arts of Resistance* (New Haven: Yale, 1990).
[32] Barclay, "Using and Refusing," 18.
[33] The factor of resentment in Philo's political thought was noted by Goodenough, *The Politics of Philo Judaeus*, who posited a "hidden transcript" in some of Philo's writings, even though he did not have that terminology. See Collins, *Between Athens and Jerusalem*, 131–8.

mind. First, the Jews in Alexandria and Egypt were not victims of colonization. Some had allegedly been taken to Egypt as slaves, but most had gone there freely, and in any case they remained there of their own accord.[34] From their perspective, the Hellenistic world was a world of opportunity. Consequently, their relation with Greek and Roman colonial powers was very different from that of Jews in the land of Israel.[35] Moreover, as Erich Gruen has recently insisted, Jews prospered in Egypt in the Ptolemaic period, and they were not required to sacrifice either their religion or their identity to do so.[36] Jewish synagogues were dedicated to Ptolemaic rulers, but were not for that reason syncretistic.[37] In Gruen's phrase, "this was symbiosis, not syncretism."[38]

The second point to be noted is that from the time of Antiochus the Great onward, both Greeks and Jews consistently affirmed the right of Jews to live in accordance with their own laws.[39] This right entailed some exceptional privileges. Jews could not be compelled to appear in court or to do business on the Sabbath. In some cases they were exempted from military service. They could collect money and send it to Jerusalem.[40] Even after the Jewish revolt, Titus reaffirmed those rights. Only on exceptional occasions (Antiochus Epiphanes, Caligula) was there any attempt by Greek or Roman authorities to interfere with Jewish religious observance. It is hardly true, then, as is sometimes alleged, that the Greco-Roman culture did not allow Jews to be different. It is true, however, that difference often breeds

---

[34] Gruen, *Diaspora*, 68–70. The Letter of Aristeas, 12–14, says that 100,000 Jewish captives were brought to Egypt by Ptolemy I. Josephus attributes to Hecataeus a story about a High Priest Hezekiah who migrated willingly with his followers (*AgAp* 1.186–87), and elsewhere claims that Jews came to Egypt under Alexander (*Ag Ap* 2.35; *JW* 2.487). See V. Tcherikover, *Hellenistic Civilization and the Jews* (Peabody, MA: Hendrickson, 1999) 272–73.

[35] On Hellenism and Roman rule in the land of Israel see J. J. Collins and G. E. Sterling, ed., *Hellenism in the Land of Israel* (Notre Dame, IN: University of Notre Dame, 2001) and Collins, "The Jewish World and the Coming of Rome," in W. G. Dever and S. Gitin, ed., *Symbiosis, Symbolism and the Power of the Past: Canaan, Ancient Israel and their Neighbors from the Late Bronze Age through Roman Palestine* (Winona Lake, IN: Eisenbrauns, 2003) 353–62 (reprinted in this volume).

[36] Gruen, *Diaspora*, 68–70.

[37] For references, see Gruen, *Diaspora*, 283, n. 111.

[38] Gruen, *Diaspora*, 70.

[39] Tcherikover, *Hellenistic Civilization*, 82; M. Pucci Ben Zeev, *Jewish Rights in the Roman World: The Greek and Roman Documents Quoted by Flavius Josephus* (Tübingen: Mohr, 1998).

[40] Tcherikover, *Hellenistic Civilization*, 308.

conflict, for a host of reasons, and that Ptolemaic patronage of (at least some) Jews did not necessarily preclude resentment on the part of the patronized underlings.

The distinct and different character of Judaism was noted by Gentiles from the beginning of the Hellenistic era.[41] Hecataeus of Abdera, in a passage that declares Moses outstanding for his wisdom and for his courage, says that "as a result of their own expulsion from Egypt, he introduced an unsocial and intolerant mode of life."[42] Hecataeus was not especially hostile to Judaism, much less anti-Semitic.[43] He merely records a common Gentile perception of Judaism. Related charges of *amixia* and *xenophobia* appear frequently in comments by pagan authors on the Jews. An account of Jewish origins, found with some variations in Hecataeus and in the Egyptian author Manetho, traced their ancestry to the Hyksos, the foreign rulers who were driven out of Egypt in the middle of the second millennium BCE.[44] Again, this story was exploited with increasingly hostile intent down to the Roman era. I do not think it is helpful to trace these negative comments by Gentile authors to a virus of anti-Semitism that is *sui generis*. Jews were not the only ethnic group in antiquity (or in modernity either) who had to endure ethnic slurs by their neighbors.[45] But these comments show that the integration of Jews into their Hellenistic environment was not problem free, even in the Ptolemaic era, and it would be amazing if they did not sometimes provoke a rather defensive reaction from Jewish authors.

A final preliminary point concerns the changing circumstances of the Jewish community in Egypt over time. In the first century of the common era, the interaction of Jews and Gentiles in Alexandria became violent. There was a pogrom in 38 CE, in the reign of

---

[41] See Feldman, *Jew and Gentile*, 123–76 ("Prejudice against Jews among Ancient Intellectuals"); P. Schäfer, *Judeophobia. Attitudes toward the Jews in the Ancient World* (Cambridge, MA: Harvard, 1997) 15–118.

[42] Hecataeus, *Aegyptiaca*, in Diodorus Siculus, *Bibliotheca Historica* 40.3; M. Stern, *Greek and Latin Authors on Jews and Judaism* (Jerusalem: The Israel Academy of Sciences and Humanities, 1976) 1.28.

[43] Cf. Gruen, *Heritage and Hellenism*, 50–52.

[44] On this story see my essay, "Reinventing Exodus: Exegesis and Legend in Hellenistic Egypt," in R. A. Argall, B. A. Bow and R. A. Werline, *For a Later Generation. The Transformation of Tradition in Israel, Early Judaism, and Early Christianity* (Harrisburg, PA: Trinity Press International, 2000) 52–62 (reprinted in this volume).

[45] See now B. Isaac, *The Invention of Racism in Classical Antiquity* (Princeton: Princeton University Press, 2004).

Caligula. There were riots again in 66 CE, although the Jews of the Diaspora did not join in the revolt against Rome. Finally, there was a revolt in the Diaspora under Trajan, in 115–118 CE, which ended in the virtual extinction of the Jewish community in Alexandria. As Gruen has rightly emphasized, there was no precedent for such conflict in the Ptolemaic era.[46] Something changed with the coming of Rome, however that change is explained. Negative propaganda against Judaism reaches its apex in the first century CE in the work of Apion, and the most explicit work of Jewish apologetics follows later in the century in the work of Josephus.

For the present, however, I will focus my attention on the Ptolemaic era, before the tensions between Greek and Jew in Alexandria came to a head. It was under the Ptolemies that the Hellenistic Jewish culture was shaped, and this culture still persisted in the work of people like Philo, even in the turmoil of the Roman era.

The Letter of Aristeas

Let us begin with the Letter of Aristeas, as a representative example of the literature often dubbed apologetic in the Ptolemaic era.[47] The Letter purports to tell how the Jewish scriptures were translated into Greek by order of Ptolemy II Philadelphus. The entire account is presented as the report of one gentile courtier to another. Aristeas was not the name of an especially famous person. It was sufficient that he was a Greek, and could supposedly report how Judaism, and the Law of Moses were perceived at the Ptolemaic court. At no point in the narrative do these Greeks say anything even mildly critical of Judaism. The Jewish priest Eleazar, in contrast, is quite critical of Greek and Egyptian religion, but his criticisms are reported with apparent approval, and even admiration, by the supposedly

---

[46] Gruen, *Diaspora*, 67–70. The legendary story of persecution under Ptolemy IV in 3 Maccabees, or under Ptolemy VIII in Josephus can bear little historical weight, and is in any case exceptional.

[47] For the older discussion, see Tcherikover, "The Ideology of the Letter of Aristeas," HTR 51(1958) 59–85. The Letter is discussed by Gruen, *Heritage and Hellenism*, 206–222; Barclay, *Jews in the Mediterranean Diaspora*, 138–49; "Using and Refusing," 20–21; Collins, *Between Athens and Jerusalem*, 191–95. See now also S. Honigman, *The Septuagint and Homeric Scholarship in Alexandria: A Study of the Narrative of the Letter of Aristeas* (London: Routledge, 2003).

Greek Aristeas. The criticism, however, is selective, and does not necessarily apply to all Greeks.

Perhaps the most striking thing about this writing is the importance attached to Gentile respect for the Jews. The whole epistle is presented as a Greek appreciation of Judaism. This motif is perhaps most obvious in the table-talk towards the end of the book, when the Jewish sages perform at the royal command and are rewarded with the approval of king, courtiers and philosophers. It would be going too far to say that Judaism derives its self-esteem from the approval of the Greeks, but that approval is obviously wanted and appreciated. Throughout, the superiority of everything Jewish is conceded by the Greeks, but the assessment derives its validity from the fact that it is rendered by Greeks. The Greeks, or at least the Greeks at the royal court, constitute an implied audience by whose standards the Jews feel the need to measure themselves. The claims of Jewish superiority, then, are not necessarily indicative of the self-confidence of the author, but bespeak the anxiety of people who need the affirmation of their superiors. The desire for Gentile approval is obviously a factor in the frequent recourse to Gentile pseudonyms in the Diaspora literature (the Sibyl, Phocylides, Orpheus, etc.). In contrast, the pseudonymous authors in contemporary writings from the land of Israel are invariably drawn from Israelite, biblical, tradition (Enoch, Moses, Ezra, etc.).

The standards by which the Jews are measured, and approved, in the Letter of Aristeas are distinctly Greek. Eleazar, the High Priest, is introduced as a model of *kalokagathia*, "a Greek gentleman" (3). The translators are distinguished in *paideia* (121). They "zealously cultivated the quality of the mean . . . and eschewing a crude and uncouth disposition they likewise avoided conceit and the assumption of superiority over others" (122). The Jewish author, in short adopts the discourse and even the voice of the hegemonic culture, and to a great degree he also affirms its values. All of this fits quite well with Barclay's model of post-colonial analysis. The author is constrained by the power of the hegemonic culture: "under the pressure of the cultural snobbery that regards anything non-Hellenic as *barbaron*, Aristeas wishes to indicate how 'civilized' Jews can be. There is no scope here for presenting the Jewish tradition as a fundamentally different form of 'civilization', independent of Hellenistic definitions."[48]

---

[48] Barclay, "Using and Refusing," 21.

It should be noted, however, that there is no trace of irony in this presentation. Hellenistic ideals are affirmed and embraced, not mocked or subverted.[49]

Nonetheless, the author of the Letter can take issue with aspects of Hellenistic culture when he chooses to do so. The High Priest undertakes an explanation of the Jewish law that tackles directly those aspects that were alien, if not offensive, to Hellenistic sensibilities, the food laws and the prohibition of idols. He begins "by demonstrating that God is one, that his power is shown in everything, every place being filled with his sovereignty" (132). He proceeds "to show that all the rest of mankind *except ourselves* believe that there are many gods, although they are themselves much more powerful than the gods they vainly worship; they make images of stone and wood, and declare that they are likenesses of those who have made some beneficial discovery for their living, and whom they worship even though their insensibility is readily obvious" (134–5). He goes on to say that "those who have invented these fabrications and myths are usually ranked to be the wisest of the Greeks. There is surely no need to mention the rest of the very foolish people, Egyptians and those like them, who have put their confidence in beasts and most of the serpents and monsters, worship them, and sacrifice to them both while alive and dead." This is why Moses surrounded the Jews with fences "to prevent our mixing with any of the other peoples in any matter, being thus kept pure in body and soul, preserved from false beliefs, and worshiping the only God omnipotent over all creation" (139). "So much for the Greeks," says Gruen. "These are strong words and powerful sentiments, not to be obscured or suppressed in the warm glow of some alleged universalism."[50] Yet this speech is reported by the supposedly Greek Aristeas without any suspicion of offence, and ultimately with admiration. It would seem that Aristeas does not take the derogatory remarks about idolatry personally, and while this admiring Greek is a figment of a Jewish imagination, he represents the kind of Greek to whom Eleazar's speech is addressed. Nothing in the text suggests that this speech is either meant or taken to be offensive. It cannot then be

---

[49] In contrast, a good case can be made that imperial ideals are mocked and subverted in the court tales of Daniel. See D. Smith-Christopher, "The Book of Daniel," *NIB* 7(1996) 19–96.

[50] Gruen, *Heritage and Hellenism*, 216.

the comprehensive broadside against the Greeks that Gruen takes it to be.[51]

In fact, the High Priest's speech is an apologia for Judaism, in the sense that it is intended to respond to Gentile criticisms of Jewish practice. In part, the apologia is unapologetic: "You accuse us of *amixia*. Well yes, our laws keep us from mixing with other peoples, but there is good reason for this. Look at what most Greeks are like, not to mention other peoples, like—Egyptians!" The author proceeds, however, to justify the laws of *kashrut*, which are crucial to the separation of Jews from Gentiles, by allegorizing them so that they conform to Greek standards of rationality. Nothing in the law has been set down heedlessly or in the spirit of myth (*mythōdōs*, 168), and the interpretation is based on the *physikē dianoia*. Moses, the lawgiver, is presented as a philosopher, proceeding from principles. The first principle is that God is one and his power is made manifest throughout creation. Hence the attack on idolatry and polytheism. The Letter goes on to offer an allegorical explanation of the laws. Literalism is dismissed with contempt, no less than Egyptian theriolatry: "Do not take the contemptible view that Moses enacted this legislation because of an excessive preoccupation with mice and weasels or suchlike creatures. The fact is that everything has been solemnly set in order for . . . the sake of righteousness" (144). What the Jews really refuse to mingle with are "vain opinions." The significant distinction is between "men of God, a title applicable to none others but only to him who reveres the true God" and "men of food and drink and raiment" (140). The particular, concrete commandments are reinterpreted allegorically to apply to universal human virtues. The birds forbidden by the dietary laws symbolize oppression and violence, animals that part the hoof symbolize discrimination, those that chew the cud symbolize memory, and so forth. The law, in short, is one symbolic expression of the truth which can also be approached in other ways. In the words of the roughly contemporary Jewish philosopher Aristobulus:

---

[51] Even the despised Egyptians are not comprehensively condemned. Eleazar appeals to the testimony of "the leading priests among the Egyptians," who are respected for their careful research and who refer to the Jews as "men of God" (140). Presumably, these priests are not included among the "very foolish people, Egyptians and those like them," who are dismissed so sweepingly a few lines earlier.

All philosophers agree that it is necessary to hold devout convictions about God, something which our school prescribes particularly well. And the whole structure of our law has been drawn up with concern for piety, justice, self-control, and other qualities that are truly good.[52]

Barclay admits an apologetic motif here, insofar as the High Priest refutes the notion that the Jews worship animals that they refuse to eat.[53] But unless one clings to a very narrow understanding of the term, the apologetic motif is much more extensive than this. The whole passage is a defence of Jewish *amixia*, by arguments that should be acceptable to a Greek. The discourse and standards are still those of the hegemonic culture, even though they are used to support distinctive Jewish practices. Barclay is quite right that the author uses "his extensive education in the cause of Jews themselves, portraying their nation, their Scriptures and their Temple in the best possible light, and defending their distinctive, and potentially awkward, practices as wholly admirable in the terms of Hellenistic culture itself."[54] But is this not precisely what it means to engage in apologetics? And if the author "moves without appreciable discomfort in the world of the Alexandrian elite,"[55] why is a defence of distinctive and awkward practices necessary at all?

In fact, the Letter of Aristeas indicates well the most fundamental and persistent cause of discomfort for observant Jews in the Hellenistic world. This was the pervasiveness of idolatry, which was embedded in the very fabric of Hellenistic culture. Here we touch on the criteria by which fidelity to the Jewish tradition was measured. The Greek language was no threat to Jewish identity. It was, so to speak, an *adiaphoron*. Neither was Greek philosophy or literature. Again, Jewish identity was not a matter of political allegiance. As Gruen has observed, in the Letter of Aristeas, "the emphasis again and again is on Ptolemaic patronage, the king bestowing favors that elicit friendship and devotion."[56] There is no Jewish nationalism in evidence here, and this is true of most of the Diaspora literature. Rather, Jewish identity was a matter of religious observance.

---

[52] Aristobulus, Fragment 4; Eusebius, *PE* 13.12.8; C. R. Holladay, *Fragments of Hellenistic Jewish Authors. 3. Aristobulus* (Atlanta: Scholars Press, 1995) 175.
[53] Barclay, "Using and Refusing," 20.
[54] Ibid. 21.
[55] Ibid.
[56] Gruen, *Heritage and Hellenism*, 214.

Almost everything that Hellenism had to offer could be "used" in Barclay's terminology. The things that had to be "refused" were invariably religious in character—the worship of idols, violation of food laws, certain practices, such as homosexuality and abortion, that are deemed to be unethical.[57] The Letter of Aristeas is actually unusual in addressing the food laws explicitly. Most Hellenistic Jewish writings restrict their focus to practices that could be explained more easily by Greek standards.

Idolatry and polytheism were part of the very fabric of Hellenistic society. For most Gentiles, the refusal of the cults by people who otherwise participated fully in Hellenistic society, was difficult to comprehend. Hence the famous question of Apion: "why then if they are citizens do they not worship the same gods as the Alexandrians?"[58] In the cultural context, the question was not unreasonable.[59] In the words of Shaye Cohen, it seemed as if the Jews wanted simultaneously "to be the same as everyone else while also being different from everyone else."[60] More specifically, they were trying to make a distinction between culture and what we would call religion. This distinction has become commonplace, even fundamental, in the modern world, but in the ancient world it was novel indeed, and for some people, incomprehensible. The Jews were not, of course, claiming that religion was irrelevant to culture. They were claiming that their religion was the true complement of Greek culture, and this is what Greeks found not only unacceptable but offensive.

The Jewish writers, however, do not attempt to justify their distinctive practices by appeal to divine command. Rather, for the author of the Letter of Aristeas, and Aristobulus, and Philo, Judaism was a philosophy, which could be justified on rational grounds and appreciated by Gentiles of intelligence and good will. The most striking affirmation of Judaism that is put on the lips of a Greek in this book is attributed to Aristeas, in the course of a petition for the release of the Jewish slaves: "These people worship God the over-

---

[57] The religious character of Jewish distinctiveness is also emphasized by G. Delling, *Die Bewältigung der Diasporasituation durch das hellenistische Judentum* (Göttingen: Vandenhoeck & Ruprecht, 1987) 91–94.

[58] *AgAp* 2.65.

[59] See the remarks of Shaye Cohen, "'Anti-Semitism' in Antiquity: the Problem of Definition," in D. Berger, ed., *History and Hate: The Dimensions of Anti-Semitism* (Philadelphia: The Jewish Publication Society, 1986) 43–47.

[60] Ibid., 46.

seer and creator of all, whom all men worship including ourselves, O King, except that we have a different name. Our name for him is Zeus and Dis" (16). The significance of this statement has been disputed by Barclay and Gruen, because it is spoken by a pagan, not by a Jew.[61] Yet we find an almost identical sentiment expressed by the roughly contemporary Jewish author Aristobulus, who claims that the inherent meaning of the names Dis and Zeus in the Greek poets refers to God.[62] Aristeas is not an actual Gentile, expressing *bona fide* Gentile views, but the mouthpiece for a Jewish apologist.

The argument is that the true God is one and the same, whether worshipped by Greeks or Jews, and that Gentiles can, in principle, know this God, even if they seldom do so in practice.[63]

The whole rhetorical situation of the Letter implies that the kind of argument made by Eleazar could be, and in fact was, appreciated by enlightened Greeks such as Ptolemy Philadelphus, Aristeas and Philocrates. In the case of the Ptolemy, this, no doubt, was wishful thinking, but in fact there was a well-established tradition in Greek philosophy that was critical of mythology and of idolatry. The example of Judaism is sometimes cited positively by pagan authors.[64] Hecataeus noted Moses' prohibition of images without disapproval. Strabo says that Moses' arguments against idol-worship "persuaded not a few thoughtful men."[65] It remained true that polytheism was nearly universal, and that no other people besides the Jews repudiated it. Poets like Homer were counted to be among the wisest of the Greeks, despite philosophical critiques. But it was also quite possible to envision a Greek like Aristeas, for whom the Jewish critique of idolatry was quite reasonable and inoffensive, and who could accordingly be included in the "us" who were exempted in the general charge of polytheism.

Aristeas and the Ptolemy are part of the implied audience of Eleazar's exposition. The real audience of the text was surely Jewish. The message to this audience was that monotheism and rejection of

---

[61] Barclay, *Jews in the Mediterranean Diaspora*, 143; Gruen, *Heritage and Hellenism*, 216.
[62] Aristobulus, Fragment 4; Eusebius PE 13.12.7; Holladay, *Fragments*, 173.
[63] Compare Wis 13:1–9 and see my article "Natural Theology and Biblical Tradition. The Case of Hellenistic Judaism," *CBQ* 60(1998) 1–15.
[64] See Feldman, *Jew and Gentile*, 117–287.
[65] Strabo, 16.2.36; Stern, *Greek and Latin Authors*, 300.

idols was not un-Hellenic; rather it represented the very best of
Hellenistic theology, and was acknowledged as such by eminent
Gentiles, including the king. Monotheism was not just a matter of
revelation or ancestral faith. It was a philosophical tenet, perfectly
rational and coherent. Essentially the same critique of idolatry would
be repeated in the Wisdom of Solomon and Philo, argued on philosophical grounds.[66] We need not assume that the Jewish community
was beset by grave temptations to idolatry. What was at issue was
the coherence of the self-understanding of Hellenistic Jews. If most
of their neighbors thought that the prohibition of images was odd
or un-Hellenic, that was their problem. The best of the Greeks would
appreciate the Jewish position on philosophical grounds. Not all paths
followed by Gentiles are approved, of course, and some, such as
Egyptian theriolatry, are viewed with contempt, but Aristeas, like
Aristobulus, also affirms that gentiles can arrive at the recognition
of "the only God omnipotent over all creation," even if they call
him Zeus or Dis.

Universalism and Jewish Identity

The ideal of universalism, what Daniel Boyarin calls the "Hellenistic
desire for the One,"[67] has come to be regarded with great suspicion
in the post-modern, post-colonial age. Boyarin recognizes that universalism (as represented by Paul) can be viewed as cultural tolerance, but he argues that "it is, however, this very tolerance that
deprives difference of the right to be different, dissolving all others
into a single essence in which matters of cultural practice are irrelevant."[68] Peter Schäfer has gone so far as to suggest that "only the
idea of world-wide Greco-Hellenistic civilization made it possible for
the phenomenon that we call anti-Semitism to emerge," because it
made Judaism appear xenophobic and misanthropic.[69] It is not apparent to me that such charges are justified, or that Greco-Roman civ-

---

[66] See Collins, *Jewish Wisdom in the Hellenistic Age* (Louisville: Westminster John
Knox, 1997) 209–13.
[67] D. Boyarin, *A Radical Jew. Paul and the Politics of Identity* (Berkeley: University
of California Press, 1994) 7.
[68] Ibid., 9.
[69] Schäfer, *Judeophobia*, 206.

ilization was bent on the suppression of cultural differences. The Romans consistently affirmed the right of Jews to live according to their ancestral laws,[70] even if Roman intellectuals sometimes viewed those laws with contempt. My concern here, however, is not with the empire, but with the perspective of Hellenistic Jews, as an eastern minority confronted with an overpowering western culture.

That perspective was essentially the desire to maintain a bi-focal identity. It is probably not quite correct to speak of Diaspora Jews "using" Hellenistic culture as if it were something foreign to them. Rather, it was the medium in which they naturally expressed themselves. But there were aspects of Hellenistic culture which they did not accept. Jewish tradition, viewed as a religious or even philosophical system, required that Jews refuse to participate in idolatrous worship or in some practices that were commonplace in the Hellenistic world but unacceptable in Judaism. In effect, they attempted to distinguish between religion and other aspects of the dominant culture, a distinction that was incomprehensible to many in the ancient world. They did not, however, claim this distinction on the basis of divine revelation, but attempted to justify it on grounds that would be acceptable to enlightened Gentiles, who might appreciate the superiority of monotheism and share the ethical values of the Jews. The distinction, then, could be viewed as one within Hellenistic culture, between the elite culture of the monotheistic few and the vulgar culture of the masses, who were little better than the despised Egyptians. Even the most philosophical Greeks, however, could scarcely arrive at the full perfection of the Jewish law. The cultural negotiation involved in this argument was necessarily and profoundly apologetic, as it required the justification of Jewish religious practice by the canons of the hegemonic Hellenistic culture.[71]

The coming of Rome brought a gradual deterioration of the situation of the Jewish community in Egypt, until eventually it went up in flames in the revolt under Trajan in 115–18 CE. The story of that deterioration has often been told.[72] It has recently been contested by

---

[70] See Pucci Ben Zeev, *Jewish Rights in the Roman World*.

[71] See further Collins, "Culture and Religion in Hellenistic Judaism," in W. D. Edgerton, ed., *The Honeycomb of the Word. Interpreting the Primary Testament with André LaCocque* (Chicago: Exploration Press, 2001) 17–36.

[72] The classic account remains that of Tcherikover, *Hellenistic Civilization and the Jews*, 269–377; idem, "Prolegomena," in V. Tcherikover and A. Fuks, *Corpus Papyrorum*

Gruen, but that is an issue for another day.[73] Educated upperclass
Jews, such as Philo and the author of the Wisdom of Solomon, did
not lightly abandon their commitment to Hellenistic ideals, but continued the project of their Hellenized predecessors of integrating
Jewish religious convictions with Hellenistic culture. The ultimate
failure of this project was not due to the intrinsic imperialism of universalistic ideals but to the social and economic strains of Roman
rule in Egypt and more generally in the Near East.

Judaicarum (3 vols.; Cambridge, MA: Harvard, 1957–64) 1.1–111. Also J. Mélèze
Modrzejewski, *The Jews of Egypt. From Rameses II to Emperor Hadrian* (Princeton:
Princeton University Press, 1995).
   [73] Gruen, *Diaspora*, 54–83.

CHAPTER TWO

CULT AND CULTURE:
THE LIMITS OF HELLENIZATION IN JUDEA

Some time in the early second century BCE, the Jewish sage, Jeshua ben Sira, made the observation that all the works of the Most High come in pairs, one the opposite of the other (Sir 33:15; cf. 42:24). Or at least, that is how we tend to perceive things. In the study of ancient Judaism and early Christianity, two of the more durable binary oppositions have been Hellenism and Judaism, on the one hand, and Hellenistic (meaning Diaspora) and Palestinian Judaism on the other.[1] Both of these oppositions have been criticized repeatedly in recent years. Erich Gruen has argued eloquently that "'Judaism' and 'Hellenism' were neither competing systems nor incompatible concepts. It would be erroneous to assume that Hellenization entailed encroachment upon Jewish traditions and erosion of Jewish beliefs. Jews did not face a choice of either assimilation or resistance to Greek culture." Gruen's book deals primarily with the literature of the Diaspora, but he also points to the extensive Hellenization of Judea under the Hasmoneans, and questions whether Hellenism was ever an issue for the Maccabees.[2] In his classic study of thirty years ago, Martin Hengel argued that Palestinian Judaism too was Hellenistic Judaism.[3] In this regard, Hengel stood in the tradition of J. G. Droysen, who understood Hellenism as a syncretistic blending of Greek and

---

[1] On the various roles of these distinctions in shaping the identity of modern Judaism see Yaacov Shavit, *Athens in Jerusalem. Classical Antiquity and Hellenism in the Making of the Modern Secular Jew* (The Littman Library of Jewish Civilization; London: Vallentine Mitchell, 1997).

[2] Erich Gruen, *Heritage and Hellenism. The Reinvention of Jewish Tradition* (Berkeley: University of California, 1998) xiv, 1–40. Cf. Tessa Rajak, "The Hasmoneans and the Uses of Hellenism," in P. R. Davies and R. T. White, ed., *A Tribute to Geza Vermes. Essays on Jewish and Christian Literature and History* (JSOT Sup 100; Sheffield: Sheffield Academic Press, 1990) 261–80; Lee I. Levine, *Judaism and Hellenism in Antiquity. Conflict or Confluence?* (Seattle: University of Washington, 1998) 33–95.

[3] Martin Hengel, *Judaism and Hellenism. Studies in their Encounter in Palestine in the Early Hellenistic Period* (Philadelphia: Fortress, 1974) 1.103–106.

oriental cultures.[4] But Hengel went on to discuss the "conflict between Palestinian Judaism and the spirit of the Hellenistic Age." He argued that the crisis of the Maccabean era led to a reaction in Judea, that put a brake on syncretism, fixed intellectual development on the Torah and precluded any fundamental criticism of the cult and the law.[5] The manifold evidence of Hellenistic influence in Judea notwithstanding, the corpus of literature that has come down to us from Judea in the Hellenistic era is very different from its counterpart from the Diaspora. Hellenistic culture was a manifold entity, and it was neither absorbed nor rejected whole. Consequently the question of Hellenism in the land of Israel calls for some differentiation between different aspects of Hellenistic culture.[6]

The Concept of Judaism

At the outset, however, it may be well to reflect for a moment on the other term of the pair, Judaism or *ioudaismos*, a term which, like hellenism, first appears in the second book of Maccabees. Just as *hellenismos* refers to a culture and way of life, so also does *ioudaismos*. In the words of Josephus, it is constituted *ou tō genei monon alla kai tē proairēsei tou biou*, not by race alone but also by the choice of way of life.[7] Shaye Cohen has argued that this understanding of Judaism as a *politeia*, or public way of life, dates from the Hasmonean period. Prior to that time, the term *Ioudaios* was an ethnic designation and meant "Judean" rather than "Jew" in the religio-cultural sense. *Ioudaioi* in the Diaspora were similar to other ethnic groups such, as the Idumeans, who associated together and maintained their traditional customs. While our evidence supports a shift in linguistic usage and a corresponding shift in attitudes in the Hasmonean period, however,

---

[4] J. G. Droysen, *Geschichte des Hellenismus* (2 vols.; Hamburg, 1836–43). Note the essay of Arnaldo Momigliano, "J. G. Droysen between Greeks and Jews," in idem, *Essays in Ancient and Modern Historiography* (Oxford: Oxford University Press, 1977) 307–23.

[5] Ibid. 306–309.

[6] John M. G. Barclay, *Jews in the Mediterranean Diaspora* (Edinburgh: Clark, 1996) 82–102, distinguishes seven different aspects of Hellenism: political, social, linguistic, educational, ideological, religious and material. Cf. Martin Hengel, *Jews, Greeks and Barbarians* (London: SCM, 1980) 60, who has a similar list.

[7] *AgAp* 2.210. See Shaye J. D. Cohen, *The Beginnings of Jewishness* (Berkeley: University of California, 1999) 132–35.

the idea of a distinctive Jewish way of life was established long before this. At the beginning of the Hellenistic period, Hecataeus of Abdera wrote his famous account of the inhabitants of Judea, in which he noted that their way of life (*tas kata ton bion agōgas*) differed from that of other peoples, and was somewhat anti-social and hostile to foreigners.[8] The rights of Jews, or Judeans, to live according to their ancestral laws had been confirmed by Hellenistic rulers, most famously by Antiochus III when he took control of Jerusalem at the beginning of the second century BCE.[9] This way of life was, to be sure, that of an *ethnos*, and the ethnic dimension of Judaism has always remained important. The ethnic dimension became less decisive in the Hasmonean period, but the way of life that became known as Judaism was well established long before the term *Ioudaismos* was coined.

Like Hellenism, Judaism was a manifold entity and not all aspects of it were equally important. The way of life survived quite well in the Greek-speaking Diaspora, and was not seriously threatened by the spread of the Greek language in Palestine. Neither was it imperilled by the adoption of Hellenistic style in literature or architecture, for example. In such matters, Erich Gruen is clearly right that

> Jews were not obliged to choose between succumbing or resisting. Nor should one imagine a conscious dilemma whereby they had to decide how far to lean in one direction or other, how much 'Hellenism' was acceptable before they compromised the faith, at what point on the spectrum between apostasy and piety they could comfortably locate themselves.[10]

Conceptions of God

The conception and worship of God, what we would call religion, was a more sensitive area, but here again considerable rapprochement

---

[8] Hecataeus, in Diodorus Siculus 40.3.4. M. Stern, *Greek and Latin Authors on Jews and Judaism* (Jerusalem: Israel Academy of Sciences, 1976) 1.26.

[9] Elias Bickerman, "Le charte séleucide de Jerusalem," in idem, *Studies in Jewish and Christian History* (Leiden: Brill, 1980) 2.44–85; Victor Tcherikover, *Hellenistic Civilization and the Jews* (New York: Atheneum, 1970) 82–9.

[10] Gruen, *Heritage and Hellenism*, xv. Martin Goodman, "Jewish Attitudes to Greek Culture in the Period of the Second Temple," in G. Abramson and T. Parfitt, ed., *Jewish Education and Learning* (Chur, Switzerland: Harwood Academic Publishers, 1994) 169 comments on the "lack of concern about encroaching Hellenism" and suggests that Jews in the Hasmonean period felt that Greek culture was "not really wholly alien."

was possible. Philo's explanation of the first chapter of Genesis is representative of the theology of Alexandrian Judaism: "It consists of an account of the creation of the world, implying, that the world is in harmony with the Law, and the Law with the world, and that the man who observes the law is constituted thereby a loyal citizen of the world, regulating his doings by the purpose and will of Nature, in accordance with which the entire world itself also is administered."[11] There were certainly precedents in the biblical tradition, especially in the wisdom literature, for "creation theology" that held that the will of God is reflected in nature. Hellenistic philosophy, however, especially Stoicism, permitted a much more systematic "natural theology", which was embraced by Jews like Philo and the author of the Wisdom of Solomon, even if it was not fully compatible with biblical ideas of revelation and election.[12] Fundamental to this theology was a belief in the unity of humankind and of the truth, and an acknowledgement that the truth disclosed in biblical revelation could also be approached, even if imperfectly, in other ways by poets and philosophers. A relatively early (second century BCE) formulation of this belief is found in the Letter of Aristeas. Aristeas explains to King Ptolemy: "These people worship God the overseer and creator of all, whom all men worship, but we, o king, address differently as Zeus and Dis" (*Ep. Arist* 16). Aristeas is supposedly a Greek. Some scholars have argued that the identification was acceptable on the lips of a Greek but would not have been endorsed by Jews.[13] But we find an almost identical formulation in the roughly contemporary Jewish author Aristobulus, who emended the divine names Dis and Zeus in the passages he cited from Greek poets, "for their inherent meaning refers to God," and "the Zeus celebrated in poems and prose compositions leads the mind up to God."[14] From an early point, Greeks had sought correspondences between their deities and those of eastern peoples. The god of the Jews was sometimes identified with Dionysus, because the use of

---

[11] *De Opificio Mundi* 3.

[12] J. J. Collins, "Natural Theology and Biblical Tradition: The Case of Hellenistic Judaism," *CBQ* 60(1998) 1–15.

[13] Barclay, *Jews in the Mediterranean Diaspora*, 143; Gruen, *Heritage and Hellenism*, 216.

[14] Aristobulus, fragment 4. Carl R. Holladay, *Fragments from Hellenistic Jewish Authors. III. Aristobulus* (Atlanta: Scholars Press, 1995) 173.

branches at the feast of Sukkoth was associated with the thyrsus in Bacchic festivals.[15] That identification was generally rejected by Jews, except perhaps for some apostates in the Maccabean era. But the high god Zeus, at least in his more philosophical formulations, was deemed a satisfactory counterpart to God Most High, even though Homeric mythology would undoubtedly have been problematic for most Jews.

Cultic Separatism

Jewish willingness to accept Zeus as an alternative name for God did not entail a willingness to participate in pagan cult. One of the most persistent charges against Jews by their gentile opponents was that of atheism, the refusal to worship the gods of the *polis* or state. This refusal, coupled with distinctive observances required by Jewish law, led to the view of Judaism as "somewhat anti-social and hostile to strangers", in the famous phrase of Hecataeus of Abdera. In the Hellenistic world, religion was deeply imbedded in culture and politics. The refusal of Jews to participate in pagan cults, and the frequent denunciations of idolatry in Jewish literature, has sometimes led to the impression that Jews were antagonistic to Hellenistic culture.[16] The impression is mistaken, however. Both Philo and the Wisdom of Solomon are vehement in their denunciations of idolatry,[17] but they none the less embrace Greek philosophy and the concept of a universal wisdom with enthusiasm. Philo famously declared that the Jews, though strangers, differed little from the citizens.[18] Synagogues were dedicated to Ptolemaic kings, and prayers were offered for Roman emperors. The project of Hellenistic Judaism in the Diaspora required that a distinction be made between cult and culture, however difficult it might be for some gentiles to accept it. Hellenistic culture was not an undifferentiated whole. Political allegiance only became problematic for Diaspora Jews in the Roman era, when relations with the rulers deteriorated. The use of the Greek

---

[15] Plutarch, *Quaestiones Conviviales* 4.6; cf. Tacitus, *Hist* 5.5.5.
[16] See especially Barclay, *Jews in the Mediterranean Diaspora*, 181–228.
[17] Philo, *De Decalogo*, 52–81; *De Vita Contemplativa* 3–9; *De Spec. Leg.* 1.13–29; 2.255; Wis 13–15. See J. J. Collins, *Jewish Wisdom in the Hellenistic Age* (Louisville: Westminster, 1997) 209–213.
[18] *De Vita Mosis* 1.34–36.

language, or of Greek literary forms was never a problem. The
author of 4 Maccabees, who preached strict adherence to the Jewish
Law at a time when relations between Jews and Gentiles were at a
low ebb, nonetheless wrote good Greek with a sophisticated rhetorical style. The language was simply a given, for Jews of the Diaspora,
and many Greek ideas and modes of expression were part of the
air they breathed. Cultic conformity, however, was a different matter. The Jews of the Diaspora might be said to have pioneered the
distinction between cult and culture, which would play an important role in western society in much later times.[19]

Despite the general compatibility of Judaism and Hellenistic culture, then, there were occasions on which Jews were confronted with
a decision as to how much 'Hellenism' was acceptable, or how far
traditional practices could be abandoned. Various Jews might draw
the line at different points and customs and institutions that were
innocuous in some situations might take on symbolic significance at
other times. For those who maintained a commitment to "the Jewish
way of life," however, as distinct from apostates like Philo's nephew
Tiberius Julius Alexander, a line was inevitably drawn at some point.

The Hellenistic Reform in Judea

The paradigmatic instance of a conflict between 'Hellenism' and
'Judaism' is the sequence of events that took place in Jerusalem in
the reign of Antiochus IV Epiphanes, in the years 175–164 BCE.[20]
These events entailed cultural changes, but also eventually cultic
changes imposed by the Syrian king, and finally open warfare. This
was clearly a case where a line was drawn and some practices were
deemed unacceptable. It is important for our discussion to consider
the point at which that line was drawn and the causes of the conflict.

The beginning of this sequence of events is described as follows
in 1 Maccabees:

> In those days certain renegades came out from Israel and misled many,
> saying, "Let us go and make a covenant with the Gentiles around us,

---

[19] See further J. J. Collins, *Between Athens and Jerusalem* (revised edition; Grand
Rapids: Eerdmans, 2000).
[20] For the following discussion of the events in the Maccabean era see my essay
"The Hellenization of Jerusalem in the pre-Maccabean Era," (Publications of the
Rennert Center; Ramat Gan: Bar Ilan University, 1999).

for since we separated from them many disasters have come upon us."
This proposal pleased them, and some of the people eagerly went to
the king, who authorized them to observe the ordinances of the Gentiles.
So they built a gymnasium in Jerusalem, according to Gentile custom,
and removed the marks of circumcision, and abandoned the holy
covenant. They joined with the Gentiles and sold themselves to do
evil (1 Macc 1:11–15).

A more detailed account is provided by 2 Maccabees. Here we find
that the instigator was Jason, brother of the High Priest Onias III,
and that he obtained the High Priesthood by promising to pay large
sums of money to the king. He also paid for the privilege of building the gymnasium and registering "the Antiochenes in Jerusalem."
The precise implications of this registration are not clarified. It is
widely thought to entail the constitution of a Greek *polis* in Jerusalem,
with a new list of citizens.[21] His innovations were initially greeted
with enthusiasm, resulting in an extreme of Hellenization (*akmē tis
hellēnismou*) so that priests lost interest in the temple in preference
for the gymnasium. Nonetheless, no conflict arose until Jason was
usurped by Menelaus, whom he had entrusted with the tribute for
the king. Menelaus then drove Jason into exile and had the legitimate High Priest, Onias III, murdered.[22] When Antiochus Epiphanes
was rumored to have died in Egypt, Jason attempted to regain control of Jerusalem. It was at this point, according to 2 Maccabees,
that Antiochus thought that Judea was in revolt and sent in the
troops.[23]

It is clear that Jason and Menelaus were attracted to some things
Hellenistic, and that the gymnasium, the great symbol of Hellenistic
culture and forum of Greek education, was welcomed by many people in Jerusalem.[24] We may agree then with Hengel that Hellenistic
culture must have made considerable inroads in Judea already before
the reform. Whether Jason's innovations reflected a new, Hellenized,
understanding of religion, however, is a controversial question. Elias
Bickerman, in his classic book, *The God of the Maccabees*, argued that

---

[21] Tcherikover, *Hellenistic Civilization*, 161; Hengel, *Judaism and Hellenism* 1.277–8.
[22] Dov Gera, *Judaea and Mediterranean Politics, 219–161 BCE* (Leiden: Brill, 1998)
49, 129–30, regards the murder of Onias III as fictional, but this position is surely
hyper-critical.
[23] 2 Macc 5:11.
[24] On the importance of the gymnasium in Hellenistic culture see Strabo 5.4.7;
Pausanias 10.4; Jean Delorme, *Gymnasion* (Paris: Boccard, 1960).

it did.[25] Greeks were aware that other lawgivers besides Moses had
claimed divine authority, and concluded that all such laws were of
human origin. Jews had not always been separate from Gentiles.
There was a primeval age when separation did not exist. Hecataeus
of Abdera explained the separation as an unfortunate but under-
standable reaction by Moses to his expulsion from Egypt. Other
Greek writers held that separatist laws had been introduced later,
by Moses' inferior successors. "A Hellenized Jew," wrote Bickerman,
"could no more ignore these results of Greek scholarship than can
an enlightened Jew of today ignore the results of scholarly criticism
of the Bible."[26] Even observant Jews like Philo maintained their allegiance to the Mosaic law by understanding it allegorically. Some of
Philo's contemporaries no longer felt the obligation to observe the
letter of the law at all. Bickerman argued that "we have only to
retrace the line of thought of these Jewish Hellenists in order fully
to understand the similar ideology of Jason and Menelaus in Palestine.
They wanted to reform Judaism by eliminating the barbaric separatism, which had been introduced only late, and returning to the
original form of worship, free of any distortion."[27] Writing in Germany
in 1937, Bickerman drew an ominous analogy with modern Judaism:
"The reformers under Epiphanes remind us of the Jewish reform
movement during the forties of the nineteenth century, when men
like G. Riesser, A. Geiger and I. Einhorn proposed the abolition of
the dietary laws and declared circumcision not to be binding. They,
too, were fascinated by the non-Jewish world around them and were
impressed by the hypotheses of (Protestant) scholarship concerning
the origin of the Pentateuch."[28] Bickerman ascribed this ideology not
only to the original reform of Jason but also to Menelaus and the
cultic innovations that followed. In his view "Menelaus and his par-
tisans thus worshipped the heavenly god of their ancestors without
temple and images, under the open sky upon the altar which stood
on Mt. Zion. They were free from the yoke of the law, and in
mutual tolerance they were united with the Gentiles. What could be

[25] Elias Bickerman, *The God of the Maccabees. Studies in the Origin and Meaning of the Maccabean Revolt* (Leiden: Brill, 1979) 85–88.
[26] Bickerman, *The God of the Maccabees*, 86.
[27] Ibid., 87.
[28] Ibid. Bickerman was neither the first nor the last to make such analogies. See Shavit, *Athens in Jerusalem*, 306–314.

more human, what could be more natural, than their desire to force this tolerance also upon those of their coreligionists who were still unenlightened?"[29]

Bickermann's view of the motives of the reformers has not won general acceptance. Isaak Heinemann argued that the Hellenism of the reformers, like that of other "Graeculi des Orients" was superficial and without intellectual foundations.[30] Victor Tcherikover stated bluntly: "The changes in the sphere of religion and culture were not the reason for the reform, but its consequences, and they involved no principles . . ."[31] For him, the reform consisted of converting Jerusalem into a *polis*, primarily with an eye to economic advantage. Martin Hengel, however, rallied to Bickerman's defence on this point.[32] He points to "a whole series of significant philosophers and learned men in the second and first centuries in the Phoenician coastal cities," and notes that even an inland city like Gadara in Trans-Jordan had a significant tradition of Greek education. But there was no such tradition in Jerusalem, prior to Jason's reform. There were, of course, traditions of learning, but they were either concerned with the transmission of sacred literature, or with traditional Near Eastern wisdom. Ben Sira has smatterings of Greek philosophy, but scarcely more. There is no Judean counterpart to the philosophical hermeneutic of Aristobulus, or even to the sporadic allegorizing of Pseudo-Aristeas. No Judean author says that Zeus is another name for the true God.

Hengel's survey of Jewish literature written in Greek in the land of Israel in the Maccabean era yields only three authors, Jason of Cyrene, Eupolemus and an anonymous Samaritan, whose work is attributed to Eupolemus by Eusebius.[33] If we may judge by the

[29] Bickerman, ibid., 88.

[30] Isaak Heinemann, "Wer veranlasste den Glaubenszwang der Makkabäerzeit," *Monatsschrift für Geschichte und Wissenschaft des Judentums* 82(1938) 145–72.

[31] Tcherikover, *Hellenistic Civilization*, 169. Economic motives are also emphasized by Klaus Bringmann, *Hellenistische Reform und Religionsverfolgung in Judäa. Eine Untersuchung zur jüdisch-hellenistischen Geschichte (175–163 v. Chr.)* (Göttinge: Vandenhoeck & Ruprecht, 1983).

[32] Hengel, *Judaism and Hellenism*, 1.299.

[33] Hengel, *Judaism and Hellenism*, 1.88–99. Elsewhere he accepts a Palestinian origin as probable in the case of the epic poets, Philo and Theodotus. (*The Hellenization of Judaea in the First Century after Christ* [Philadelphia: Trinity Press Internatioal, 1989] 26–27), but regardless of their provenance there is no reason to date either of these works to the Maccabean era or earlier.

abbreviation of his work in 2 Maccabees, Jason of Cyrene must have
had a good Greek education, but it is unlikely that he received it
in Jerusalem. As Hengel readily admits, "the very name of Jason of
Cyrene . . . indicates that he was not a real Palestinian but either
came from the Jewish Diaspora in Cyrenaica or at least spent a
good part of his life there."[34] The attribution of the Samaritan work
is disputed.[35] One of the surviving fragments is ascribed to Eupolemus
by Eusebius while the other is said to be from an anonymous work
although it appears to be a briefer summary of the same source. In
any case, Eupolemus is our only example of a Judean author who
wrote in Greek in this period. He is plausibly identified with the
figure mentioned in 1 Macc 8:17 as a Jewish delegate to Rome,
whose father had negotiated the charter of rights for Jerusalem with
Antiochus III. His work "On the kings in Judea" is written in Greek
and uses the LXX. On Hengel's own admission, it has "serious linguistic and stylistic deficiencies,"[36] but it shares an interest common
in Hellenistic historiography in the origins of culture. Moses is portrayed as the first wise man, and is credited with the invention of
the alphabet. Eupolemus also says that Solomon gave a golden pillar to the king of Troy, who set it up in the temple of Zeus. This
latter episode recalls an incident mentioned in 2 Macc 4:18–20, when
Jason sent 300 drachmas for a sacrifice to Hercules at the quad-
rennial games at Tyre, but the envoys requested that the money
be used for triremes instead. Hengel comments: "Perhaps in the
background here is the conception of pre-Maccabean hellenists that
the 'greatest God' (*theos megistos*) to whom Soomon owed his status
as king, the God who gave him the commission to build the temple and whom Suron defined in his answer as 'creator of heaven
and earth,' was in the last resort, as the one god, also identical with
the Zeus of the Phoenicians and the Greeks."[37]

Eupolemus then provides some evidence that the kind of ideas
postulated by Bickerman were current in Jerusalem in the early second century BCE. To say that Jason or Menelaus can be credited
with such ideas remains a gratuitous inference. But the most inter-

---

[34] Hengel, *Judaism and Hellenism*, 1.95.
[35] By Robert Doran, "Pseudo-Eupolemus," *OTP* 2.873–82, who ascribes the fragments in question to the Judean Eupolemus.
[36] Hengel, *Judaism and Hellenism*, 1.92.
[37] Ibid., 1.94.

esting thing about Eupolemus, in any case, is that such a Hellenized figure was chosen by Judas Maccabee for the mission to Rome. And that should hardly surprise us. A major qualification for such a mission was the ability to speak Greek. The quarrel of the Maccabees was not with the Hellenistic understanding of history, nor even with the correlation of Zeus Olympios and the God of Israel.[38]

While it is true that we only see the reformers through the eyes of their detractors, we must still make do with the evidence at our disposal. That evidence shows that both Jason and Menelaus, in turn, were ready to pay large sums of money for the control of Jerusalem. Presumably they hoped to gain enough financially to make the investment worthwhile. The background stories of the Tobiad family in Josephus also show far more interest in unscrupulous profiteering than in any kind of religious reform.[39] Menelaus' betrayal of Jason's trust in outbidding him for the priesthood, and Jason's willingness to plunge Jerusalem into civil war further erode confidence in their intellectual idealism. Moreover, it is not clear that much education went on in Jason's gymnasium.[40] There was considerable curricular variety in the gymnasia of the Near East. 2 Maccabees does not complain that people were reading Homer instead of the Torah, only that they were obsessed with the novelty of Greek athletics. While the account in 2 Maccabees may be distorted, it remains the only account we have. No doubt, the reformers were genuinely attracted to the trappings of Hellenism, but there is little evidence that their deeper motives were cultural or religious. I am inclined, then, with Tcherikover, to doubt that there were any principles involved, other than power and profit.[41] Of course the pursuit of

---

[38] Cf. Levine, *Judaism and Hellenism*, 39: "It has been contended that this revolt came in protest to the process of Hellenization in Judaea, but this was patently not the case."

[39] *Ant* 12.175–85; Hengel, *Judaism and Hellenism* 1.269–72. Gera, *Judaea and Mediterranean Politics*, 36–58, regards this story as a fiction, composed by a Jew in Ptolemaic Egypt, primarily because of biblical parallels with the story of Joseph. But while the story is stylized in light of biblical parallels, it is difficult to believe that it had no factual basis.

[40] Robert Doran, "Jason's Gymnasium," in H. W. Attridge, J. J. Collins and T. H. Tobin, ed., *Of Scribes and Scrolls. Studies on the Hebrew Bible, Intertestamental Judaism and Christian Origins* (Lanham, MD: University Press of America, 1990) 99–109.

[41] *Pace* Hengel, who insists that the the Jerusalem aristocracy must have had some "politisch-religiöser Theorie." See the foreword to the third German edition of *Judentum und Hellenismus* (Tübingen: Mohr, 1988) XII.

power and profit was typical of the Hellenistic world, but it was not in any way peculiar to Hellenistic culture.

Both the books of Maccabees imply that the reforms of Jason were significant violations of the Jewish way of life. 1 Maccabees claims that they "removed the marks of circumcision and abandoned the holy covenant." 2 Maccabees says that Jason set aside the constitution based on the ancestral laws, which had been authorized by Antiochus III and "broke down the lawful manners of life, and introduced new customs forbidden by the law" (2 Macc 4:11). Even the Book of Daniel, which pays minimal attention to the cultural reforms and does not mention the gymnasium, refers to the Jewish leaders in this period as "violators of the covenant" (Dan 11:30: מרשיעי ברית). In the judgment of these authors, a line had been crossed, and the new customs were incompatible with the Jewish way of life. It is not apparent, however, that this judgment was widely shared. The introduction of the gymnasium provoked no revolt. (Curiously, we are never told that it was torn down later, although neither are we ever told that it remained in existence. Herod held athletic contests, apparently in Jerusalem, and also had a hippodrome).[42] There is good reason to believe that Jews of Diaspora in the Ptolemaic era frequented the gymnasium.[43] Philo shows considerable familiarity with the institution,[44] and the education that he and other Diaspora writers had evidently received is most easily explained by their attendance at the gymnasium.[45] Whether the Hellenizers of the Maccabean era removed the marks of their circumcision has been disputed.[46] Such a procedure was certainly not required for participation in a gymnasium and even the putative reason for it, nudity, may not have been *de rigueur*. Such a practice, however, would go some way to explaining Daniel's designation of the reformers as "violators of the covenant" and the polemic against nudity in the Book of Jubilees.[47] But even

[42] *Ant* 15. 268–76. Gruen, *Heritage and Hellenism*, 31, finds a very dubious reference to it in the *xystos* or covered collonade mentioned in Josephus, *JW* 2.344, which was connected to the temple by a bridge.

[43] Louis H. Feldman, *Jew and Gentile in the Ancient World* (Princeton: Princeton University Press, 1993) 57–61.

[44] Feldman, ibid., 60. See *De Agricultura* 111–121, among many other passages.

[45] Alan P. Mendelson, *Secular Education in Philo of Alexandria* (Cincinnati: Hebrew Union College Press, 1982) 25–26. Cf. Philo's description of his education in *De Congressu* 74–76.

[46] Doran, "Jason's Gymnasium," 106; Gruen, *Heritage and Hellenism*, 30.

[47] Jub 3:31.

epispasm, or abandonment of circumcision, was not necessarily tantamount to apostasy. These were instances where Jews may have differed as to what was an acceptable place to draw the line. In any case, the introduction of the gymnasium, while it may have been offensive to many Jews, was not the cause of the Maccabean revolt.

The Ideology of the Persecution

This brings us to the second major issue in the Hellenization of Jerusalem under Antiochus Epiphanes. Was the desecration of the temple by Antiochus Epiphanes integrally related to the program of the Hellenizers? Was the new worship on Mt. Zion a reflection of their theology? Bickerman held that it was: "the form of worship introduced by Epiphanes on Mt. Zion corresponded to the Greek conception of a reasonable religion of nature."[48] The persecution of traditional Jews arose from the desire of Menelaus and his cohorts "to force this tolerance also upon those of their coreligionists who were still unenlightened."[49] Hengel argued that "The cult in the temple was also 'reformed' in syncretistic fashion, presumably following the example of the more strongly Hellenized Phoenicians . . . Honour was given above all to the 'supreme God of heaven,' interpreted in a syncretistic and universalistic way. He was identified with Ba'al Shamem of the Phoenicians and Zeus Olympius of the Greeks. Presumably the radical reformers were influenced by the ideas of the Greek enlightenment, and perhaps they sought to restore the original 'reasonable' form of worship of the deity without 'superstitious' falsification. At the same time they sought the complete dissolution of the characteristics of Judaism and its consistent assimilation to its Hellenistic oriental environment."[50]

There were indeed Jews in the second century BCE who argued that the God of Israel was the same deity who was called Zeus by the Greeks. We have already considered the cases of pseudo-Aristeas and Aristobulus. These instances are somewhat later and in a different

---

[48] Bickerman, *The God of the Maccabees*, 87.
[49] Ibid., 88
[50] Hengel, *Judaism and Hellenism*, 1.305. On the hellenization of the Phoenicians see Fergus Millar, "The Phoenician Cities: A Case-Study of Helllenization," *Proceedings of the Cambridge Philological Society* 209(1983) 55–71; idem, *The Roman Near East. 31 BC to AD 337* (Cambridge, MA: Harvard, 1993) 264–95.

cultural context, in the Diaspora. Bickerman argued that "we have
only to retrace the line of thought of these Jewish Hellenists in order
fully to understand the similar ideology of Jason and Menelaus in
Palestine.[51] It must be emphasized, however, that this identification
did not entail "the complete dissolution of the characteristics of
Judaism and its consistent assimilation to its Hellenistic oriental environment." On the contrary, Aristeas proceeds to denounce polytheism
and idolatry and even to defend the rationality of the Jewish food laws.
A willingness to entertain the legitimacy of some Greek conceptions
of God was by no means tantamount to consistent assimilation.

Another relevant instance of *theocrasia*, or the identification of the
God of Israel with a Greek deity is provided by the action of the
Samaritans. According to 2 Maccabees, when Antiochus Epiphanes
re-named the Jerusalem temple in honor of Olympian Zeus, he also
re-named the temple on Mt. Garizim in honor of Zeus Xenios, or
"Zeus the god of strangers," "just as those who inhabited the place
had requested" (2 Macc 6:2). Josephus, who does not appear to use
2 Maccabees in his account of this period, preserves a copy of the
Samaritans' request, in which they are at pains to distinguish themselves from the Jews, and profess to be Sidonians by origin.[52] (It is
possible that the request came from a group of Hellenized citizens
rather than from the Samaritan people as a whole. The wealthy citizens of the Idumean town of Maresha also identified themselves as
Sidonians).[53] Bickerman has defended the authenticity of the request,
and the king's response, at length, although some doubts about the
reliability of Josephus persist.[54] But here again, the identification
of the God by a Greek name entailed no other changes in the
religion, as far as we know.[55] Moreover, other Near Eastern cults,
in Phoenicia and elsewhere, were given a veneer of Hellenistic names
"without losing their identity or continuity."[56] The "Hellenistic enlight-

---

[51] Bickerman, *The God of the Maccabees*, 87.
[52] *Ant* 12.258–264. In Josephus, the new name of the temple is given as Zeus
Hellenios.
[53] I owe this suggestion to Hanan Eshel.
[54] Bickerman, "Un Document Relatif a la Persécution d'Antiochos IV Épiphane,"
in *Studies in Jewish and Christian History*, 1.105–35. For the doubts, see Fergus Millar,
"The Background of the Maccabean Revolution," *JJS* 29(1978) 6. Josephus wrote
some two and a half centuries after the events.
[55] Seth Schwartz, "The Hellenization of Jerusalem and Shechem," in Martin
Goodman, ed., *Jews in a Greco-Roman World* (Oxford: Clarendon, 1998) 40.
[56] Millar, "The Background of the Maccabean Revolution," 6; Bickerman, "Un

enment," then, which led to the identification of Greek and Semitic deities, does not in itself explain the disruptive events in Jerusalem.

Between the reorganization of Jerusalem by Jason and the reorganization of the cult by royal command some seven years later, several important events intervened. First was the usurpation of the High Priesthood by Menelaus, who was not of the Zadokite line. Menelaus had evidently been an associate of Jason, but his agenda may have been quite different. In any case, he was hard pressed to pay the tribute that he had promised to the king, and resorted to the theft and sale of temple vessels. The first outbreak of fighting was occasioned by a popular demonstration against this plunder (2 Macc 4:39–42). A more serious outbreak followed, when a rumor spread that Antiochus had died in Egypt during his second invasion of that country. Jason, with a force of a thousand men attacked Jerusalem, and wrested control of it from Menelaus, who took refuge in the citadel. Then, "when news of these events reached the king, he thought that Judaea was in revolt" (2 Macc 5:11) and he sent in troops to take the city by storm.[57] The walls of the city were torn down, and a military garrison, the Akra, was established in the City of David. According to 1 Macc 1:34, "they stationed there a sinful people, men who were renegades." This garrison "collected all the spoils of Jerusalem." From this point on, there were open hostilities between Epiphanes and his Jewish subjects.[58]

Up to this point, the actions of the king are quite intelligible. The sacking of Jerusalem and establishment of the Akra were punitive measures, intended to punish Jerusalem for its putative revolt. The

---

Document Relatif," 127–8. Bickerman comments: "En faisant appeler 'Zeus' leur dieu, les Samaritains n'introduisirent donc pas un culte grec dans le temple du Garizim ni changèrent leur religion traditionnelle."

[57] This incident is probably identical with the attack led by Apollonius the Mysarch in 1 Macc 1:29, although 1 Maccabees does not mention Jason's coup. On the chronology of events, see still Bickerman, *The God of the Maccabees*, 104–111; also Bringmann, *Hellenistische Reform*, 39. A different sequence is accepted in Emil Schürer, *A History of the Jewish People in the Time of Jesus Christ (175 BC to AD 135)* (rev. and ed. Geza Vermes and Fergus Millar; Edinburgh: Clark, 1973) 1.151; Jonathan A. Goldstein, *II Maccabees* (AB41A: New York: Doubleday, 1983) 115. Gera, *Judaea and Mediterranean Politics*, 153–57, implausibly dates Jason's revolt to the time of Antiochus' first invasion of Egypt.

[58] According to 2 Maccabees 5:27, Judas Maccabee and his followers withdrew to the wilderness before the outbreak of religious persecution, although 1 Maccabees relates their resistance specifically to the requirement of pagan sacrifice.

severity of the punishment was undoubtedly influenced by the fact
that the king had been humiliated in Egypt by the Roman legate,
Popilius Laenas.[59] This humiliation is clearly linked to the fury of
the king in Dan 11:30: "Ships of the Kittim will come against him
and he will be intimidated. He will return and rage against the holy
covenant."[60] The difficulty arises with what happens next.

According to 1 Macc 1:41, "the king wrote to his whole kingdom
that all should be one people and that all should give up their particular customs." Taken at face value, this statement is quite incred-
ible.[61] As late as 166, Antiochus was still celebrating the multiplicity
of gods worshipped in his dominion, at the great festival at Daphne.[62]
He may have written to urge his subjects to "be one people," but
no people other than the Jews were required to abandon their particular customs, and Jews in the Diaspora were not subjected to this
requirement.[63] The alleged universality of the royal edict, then, must
be rejected as an exaggeration. 1 Maccabees, however, goes on to
describe how "the king sent letters by messengers to Jerusalem and
the towns of Judah; he directed them to follow customs strange to
the land" (1:44) and forbade the observance of the traditional cult.
This statement is paralleled in 2 Maccabees 6, where an Athenian
senator is sent to enforce the edict. This attempt to change the religion of a people is extraordinary in antiquity, and lends itself to no
ready explanation. Some scholars have supposed that the edict was
a punitive response to an escalating Jewish revolt, but the evidence
of the books of Maccabees lends little support to this view.[64]

---

[59] Polybius 29.27; Diodorus Siculus 31.2; Livy 45.12.3–6. See Otto Mørkholm,
Antiochus IV of Syria (Copenhagen: Gyldendal, 1966) 94; Erich Gruen, *The Hellenistic
World and the Coming of Rome* (Berkeley: University of California, 1984) 2.658–60;
Gera, *Judaea and Mediterranean Politics*, 171–74.

[60] J. J. Collins, *Daniel* (Hermeneia; Minneapolis: Fortress, 1993) 384.

[61] Bickerman, *The God of the Maccabees*, 84; Tcherikover, *Hellenistic Civilization*,
181–4; Hengel, *Hellenism and Judaism*, 1.286–7.

[62] Mørkholm, *Antiochus IV*, 99, 131–2; Gruen, *The Hellenistic World*, 660.

[63] 2 Macc 6:8–9 claims that a decree was issued at the suggestion of the citizens
of Ptolemais, ordering the neighboring Greek cities to require their Jewish residents
to adopt "Greek manners," but there is no record of such an initiative in the
Diaspora.

[64] 2 Macc 5:27 says that Judas Maccabee and his followers escaped to the wilderness before the edict of persecution, whereas 1 Maccabees has his father Mattathias
initiate the revolt by refusing to offer pagan sacrifice. Even 2 Maccabees, however,
does not attribute militant action to Judas until after the edict was promulgated.
Nonetheless Tcherikover argued that it was not the revolt which came as a response

In view of the anomalous character of Epiphanes' edict in the context of Hellenistic policies, Bickerman argued that the initiative for the persecution came not from the king but from the Hellenizing Jewish High Priest Menelaus.[65] He found some hints of this solution in the sources. In 2 Macc 13:4, Menelaus is put to death by Antiochus V Eupator, because he is identified by Lysias, a Seleucid general, as "the cause of all the trouble." According to Josephus (*Ant* 12.384–5) Lysias made a more specific accusation: it was Menelaus who persuaded the king's father to compel the Jews to abandon their fathers' religion. Josephus wrote some two and a half centuries after the events, but he does not seem to have used 2 Maccabees as a source. Even if Lysias made the accusation, however, he was not an impartial witness. He wanted to relieve the Seleucid monarchy of responsibility for a disastrous sequence of events, and Menelaus was no longer a useful ally.

Bickerman accepted the view of Lysias, and found another, much less explicit, hint in Dan 11:30, which says that the king would pay heed to those who forsook the holy covenant. This position was endorsed by Hengel:

> Neither the king nor his 'friends', who were certainly very little interested in the Jews, will have conceived such unusual ideas, which presuppose a knowledge of conditions within Judaism. This gives greatest probability to Bickermann's view that the impulse to the most extreme escalation of events in Judea came from the extreme Hellenists in Jerusalem itself. . . . Thus Menelaus and the Tobiads who supported him appear as the authors of the edict of persecution.[66]

One might add that some analogies for violent religious reform could be found in Jewish history, both in the earlier reform of king Josiah (2 Kings 22–23) and in the subsequent policies of the Hasmoneans.

Nonetheless, the fact remains that all our primary sources (Daniel, 1 and 2 Maccabees) ascribe primary responsibility to Antiochus Epiphanes. This is also true of the pagan sources. A letter of Antiochus V Eupator to Lysias, preserved in 2 Maccabees 11, acknowledges

---

to the persecution, but the persecution which came as a response to the revolt" (Tcherikover, *Hellenistic Civilization*, 191). Similarly Gera, *Judaea and Mediterranean Politics*, 227–8, argues that the proscription of Jewish religion was the king's "response to an ever deteriorating relationship between the Seleucid authorities and the Jews."

[65] Bickerman, *The God of the Maccabees*, 83.
[66] Hengel, *Judaism and Hellenism*, 1. 287, 289.

that "the Jews do not agree with my father's plan of converting them
to Hellenic customs, but prefer their own way of life."[67] According
to Diodorus, the king was offended by Jewish separatism and hostility toward Gentiles, and "shocked by such hatred directed against
all mankind, he had set himself to break down their traditional practices."[68] Tacitus says that "King Antiochus endeavored to abolish
Jewish superstition and to introduce Greek civilization" but was prevented by war with the Parthians.[69] There are some parallels for the
prohibition of customs that were perceived as barbaric, such as the
Punic custom of human sacrifice.[70] Some centuries later, Hadrian
would prohibit circumcision. The actions of Hadrian provide the
closest analogy to those of Antiochus,[71] but it is possible that he had
the Seleucid precedent in mind. Epiphanes had no such precedent,
but he was known to be an impulsive character; hence the jibe that
he was not *epiphanes*, a god made manifest, but *epimanes*, mad.[72]
Jerusalem had incurred his wrath by seeming to rebel at the moment
of his humiliation, and the Jews were widely perceived in the Hellenistic
world as misoxenic and anti-social. It is not impossible that in his
anger and wounded pride he took unprecedented measures against
what he perceived as strange and alien people. Whether, or to what
degree, he was encouraged in this by Menelaus is a question that
we may never be able to answer.[73]

What appears to be relatively clear, however, is that the measures
taken by Antiochus amounted to an attempt to suppress traditional

---

[67] 2 Macc 11:22–26. See C. Habicht, "The Royal Letters in Maccabees II,"
Harvard Studies in Classical Philology 80(1976) 1–18.

[68] Diodorus 34–35.1.3.

[69] Tacitus 5.8.2.

[70] Bickerman, *The God of the Maccabees*, 77. The suppression of foreign rites, such
as the Bacchanalia, in Rome, which Goldstein, *1 Maccabees* (AB 41; New York:
Doubleday, 1976) 125–60, invokes as a paradigm, is not a particularly close parallel. Antiochus attempted to suppress a cult in its homeland.

[71] Peter Schäfer argues that the comparison between Antiochus Epiphanes and
Hadrian is "not a misguided one" in Schäfer, "Hadrian's Policy in Judaea and the
Bar Kochba Revolt: A Reassessment," in Davies and White, *A Tribute to Geza Vermes*,
296. See also Schäfer, *Der Bar Kokhba- Aufstand* (Tübingen: Mohr-Siebeck, 1981)
48–9, and Martin Hengel, "Hadrians Politik gegenüber Juden und Christen," in
Ancient Studies in Memory of Elias Bickerman = JANES 16–17(1984–5) 153–82.

[72] Polybius 26.1.1. See Mørkholm, *Antiochus IV*, 181–2.

[73] Bickerman's theory about the role of Menelaus is rejected by Tcherikover,
Hellenistic Civilization, 184; Goldstein, *1 Maccabees*, 159; Millar, "The Background to
the Maccabean Revolution," 17–21.

Jewish observance, not to reform it: "It was impossible either to keep the Sabbath, to observe the ancestral festivals, or openly confess oneself to be a Jew" (2 Macc 6:6). Cultic practices introduced included not only the worship of Zeus Olympius but also of Dionysus, and we are told that many Jews sacrificed to idols. Both Zeus Olympios/Baal Shamem, as the god of heaven, and Dionysus were often taken as the pagan counterparts of the God of Israel, but if either of these cults was understood to continue the worship of the traditional God of Israel, then that worship was completely re-conceived, to a degree that is without parallel elsewhere in Hellenistic Judaism. Some practices, such as eating pork, were apparently demanded precisely because they violated the Jewish law.[74] Tcherikover argued plausibly that the new cult in the temple was simply the cult practiced by the Syrian garrison, and Bickerman himself argued that the new order of worship was entirely un-Greek.[75] But then it can hardly have resulted from an enlightened, Hellenized view of the history of religion,[76] and indeed it can only be taken as a very atypical instance of "Hellenism" at all.

I am inclined then to agree with Heinemann and Fergus Millar that a sharp distinction must be drawn between the Hellenistic reform of Jason, on the one hand, and the religious persecution of Antiochus Epiphanes on the other.[77] It was only the persecution, not the reform as such, that provoked the armed rebellion of the Maccabees. It was quite possible to have a gymnasium in Jerusalem without posing a threat to monotheism. If the survival of Judaism was imperilled in this period, it was not because of athletics or the Greek hat, or even nudity in the gymnasium. Still less was it threatened by enlightened Hellenistic views of history and religion. It was only when the traditional Jewish cult was proscribed and some Jews were compelled

---

[74] Goldstein, *1 Maccabees*, 158, suggests that the the enforced eating of pork was due to the fact that the pig was a favored sacrificial animal of Dionysus.

[75] Tcherikover, *Hellenistic Civilization*, 194–5; Bickerman, *The God of the Maccabees*, 75.

[76] Cf. Tcherikover, *Hellenistic Civilization*, 195: "the Jewish Hellenists, if they had sought, as Bickermann believed, to convert the Jews to another faith, would have imposed on them not a Syrian but a Greek form of worship, in accordance with the education which they are alleged to have received."

[77] Goodman, "Jewish Attitudes," 171, goes farther, suggesting that "there was no connection," and that the authors of the books of Maccabees vilified the Hellenizing High Priests for their own political reasons.

to participate in pagan worship that "Hellenism" (if the policies of
Antiochus Epiphanes can be so described) became unacceptable to
the majority of the Jewish people.

The Distinctiveness of Palestinian Judaism

Nonetheless, the fact remains that the corpus of literature that has
come down to us from Palestinian Judaism is very different from its
counterpart from the Diaspora. Jerusalem produced no philosopher
of the stature of Philo. The Diaspora shows no evidence of the kind
of preoccupation with minutiae of the law that we find in some of
the scrolls from Qumran. In his *magnum opus* thirty years ago, Hengel
suggested that the development of Judaism in the land of Israel could
be explained to some degree as a reaction against Jason's reform
and the subsequent persecution. "The failure of the attempt of the
Hellenistic reformers to abolish the Torah by force in effect *fixed*
intellectual development *on the Torah*," and "this fixation meant that
any fundamental theological criticism of the cult and the law could
no longer develop freely within Judaism."[78] Repudiation of Hellenism
could take other forms besides armed rebellion against the Seleucids.
At the same time, Hengel recognizes that in other respects the process
of Hellenization continued, and indeed he insists that Palestinian
Judaism can also be described as Hellenistic Judaism through the
first century CE and later.[79]

It is clear that cultural hellenization continued apace in Judea
under the "phil-hellene" Hasmoneans and even more so under
Herod.[80] The late Arnaldo Momigliano wrote: "the penetration of
Greek words, customs, and intellectual modes in Judaea during the
rule of the Hasmoneans and the following Kingdom of Herod has
no limits."[81] And yet there were some limits. Josephus tells us of
Herod that "because of his ambition . . . and the flattering attention
which he gave to Caesar and the most influential Romans, he was
forced to depart from the customs (of the Jews) and to alter many

---

[78] Hengel, *Judaism and Hellenism*, 1.308–9.
[79] See especially his book, *The Hellenization of Judea*.
[80] See especially Levine, *Judaism and Hellenism in Antiquity*, 33–95.
[81] Arnaldo Momigliano, "Jews and Greeks," in idem, *Essays on Ancient and Modern Judaism* (Chicago: The University of Chicago, 1994) 22.

of their regulations, for in his ambitious spending he founded cities and erected temples—*not in Jewish territory, for the Jews would not have put up with this, since we are forbidden such things, including the honouring of statues and sculptured forms in the manner of the Greeks,*—but these he built in foreign and surrounding territory."[82] Moreover, "he established athletic contests every fifth year in honour of Caesar, and built a theatre in Jerusalem, and after that a very large amphitheatre in the plain, both being spectacularly lavish but foreign to Jewish custom."[83] He even introduced Roman-style gladiatorial contests. These innovations drew criticism from "the natives" (*epichōrioi*). According to Josephus: "more than all else it was the trophies that irked them, for in the belief that these were images surrounded by weapons, which it was against their national custom to worship, they were exceedingly angry."[84] Herod eventually yielded by removing the ornaments. The pattern that we find here is rather similar to what we found in the Maccabean period. Athletic contest and theatrical performances might offend some people, but they could be tolerated. Idolatry, or the worship of pagan gods in Judean territory was intolerable to many. Again, the line would seem to be drawn between culture and cult. Josephus reports several similar incidents in the Roman era, such as the attempt to pull down the golden eagle from the temple shortly before Herod's death,[85] and Jewish resistance to the introduction of Roman standards into Jerusalem by Pontius Pilate[86] and to the installation of a statue of Caligula in the temple.[87]

The case of Herod shows the duality of Jewish reactions to Hellenism. On the one hand, the upper classes in Jerusalem, including many priests, embraced Hellenistic culture as enthusiastically as their counterparts in Alexandria, even if they left no comparable intellectual achievements (with the arguable exception of Josephus).[88]

---

[82] *Ant* 15. 328–9, trans. Ralph Marcus, in the Loeb edition, emphasis added. See the comments of Aryeh Kasher, *Jews and Hellenistic Cities in Eretz Israel* (Tübingen: Mohr, 1990) 204–5. On Herod's building program see Duane Roller, *The Building Program of Herod the Great* (Berkeley: University of California, 1998).

[83] *Ant* 15.268–9.

[84] *Ant* 15. 276.

[85] *JW* 1.648–50.

[86] *JW* 2.169–74.

[87] *JW* 2.184–203.

[88] The Hellenization of the upper classes in Herodian Jerusalem is vividly shown by the archeological remains in the Jewish quarter. See N. Avigad, *Discovering Jerusalem* (Jerusalem: Shikmona, 1980) 81–202; Levine, *Judaism and Hellenism*, 48–51.

On the other hand, the people that Josephus calls "the natives", who presumably constituted the larger part of the population, looked on cultural innovations with suspicion, and sometimes with revulsion. Only idolatry or pagan worship would provoke a militant reaction, but there is also evidence for broader cultural aversion in Judea, in a way that is not attested in the Diaspora.[89] It is significant that Herod is not said to have built a gymnasium in Jerusalem. Presumably this institution had acquired negative associations for the "natives" after the debacle of the Maccabean era.

The negative reaction of some Jews against Hellenistic mores cannot be ascribed entirely to the experiences of the Maccabean era. Consider, for example, a passage in the *Book of the Watchers*, which is one of the oldest sections of the Book of Enoch and was almost certainly written before the Maccabean revolt.[90] There we are told that the fallen angels taught many things to human beings, including the making of weaponry and "the things after these, and the art of making them: bracelets, and ornaments and the art of making up the eyes and of beautifying the eyelids, and the most precious and choice stones, and all kinds of coloured dyes. And the world was changed. And there was great impiety and much fornication and they went astray, and all their ways became corrupt" (*1 Enoch* 8:1–2). It is tempting to see in this passage an allegory of the cultural innovations of the Hellenistic age. The reaction of apocalyptic literature, such as we find in the book of Enoch, is first to hope for a great judgment to cleanse the earth, and second to accompany Enoch in imagination in his ascent to heaven and his journey to the ends of the earth; in short to look for salvation in some other realm that has not been polluted.[91] Similarly the Dead Sea sect withdrew to the wilderness to prepare the way of the Lord, since the temple was judged to be defiled, not only by Jason and Menelaus, but more immediately by the Hasmonean priests.[92] Whether the reaction of

---

[89] See Albert Baumgarten, *The Flourishing of Jewish Sects in the Maccabean Era. An Interpretation* (Leiden: Brill, 1997) 81–113 ("The Encounter with Hellenism and its Effects").

[90] See James C. VanderKam, *Enoch and the Growth of an Apocalyptic Tradition* (CBQMS 16; Washington, D.C.: Catholic Biblical Association, 1984) 111–114.

[91] See John J. Collins, *The Apocalyptic Imagination* (revised edition; Grand Rapids: Eerdmans, 1998) 47–59.

[92] See John J. Collins, *Apocalypticism in the Dead Sea Scrolls* (London: Routledge, 1997).

such people can reasonably be described as a "fixation on the Law" is debatable. The concerns of the Dead Sea sect certainly included halachic observance in great detail, and this was also true of their sectarian rivals, the Pharisees.[93] But they had other concerns too, and their religion cannot be reduced to an obsession with the Law.

Perhaps the most penetrating insight in Hengel's great book, however, is that even those forms of Judaism that seem most resolutely anti-Hellenistic are nonetheless often influenced by Hellenistic culture in profound ways.[94] Both the Dead Sea sect and the Pharisees can be seen as variants of the voluntary associations that proliferated throughout the Hellenistic world.[95] The apocalyptic literature, while by no means typical of Hellenistic thought, has some significant analogues in the Hellenistic world.[96] Most importantly, it introduced into Jewish tradition the hope for individual salvation after death, which was typically Hellenistic, even if it was conceived here in new ways.[97] The world was indeed changed, and neither Judaism nor any other way of life in the ancient Near East could avoid the changes entirely.

Nonetheless, I submit that the most striking thing about the Jewish encounter with Hellenism, both in the Diaspora and in the land of Israel, was the persistence of Jewish separatism in matters of worship and cult. There was a limit to Hellenization, which is best expressed in the distinction between cult and culture. That distinction was extraordinary in the ancient world, but it would be paradigmatic for both Judaism and Christianity in later phases of Western history.

---

[93] Momigliano, "Jews and Greeks," 22–23, regarded "apocalyptic" and Pharisaism as the "two forces that combined, or in contrast with each other, draw a line between Judaism and Hellenism."

[94] See especially Hengel, *Judaism and Hellenism*, 1.175–254.

[95] For a perceptive discussion of both the similarities and the differences between Jewish sects and Greco-Roman voluntary associations see Albert Baumgarten, "Greco-Roman Voluntary Associations and Jewish Sects," in Goodman, ed., *Jews in a Graeco-Roman World*, 93–111.

[96] See Hubert Cancik, "The End of the World, of History and of the Individual in Greek and Roman Antiquity," in J. J. Collins, ed., *The Encyclopedia of Apocalypticism. Volume 1. The Origins of Apocalypticism in Judaism and Christianity* (New York: Continuum, 1998) 84–125.

[97] John J. Collins, "Apocalyptic Eschatology as the Transcendence of Death," in idem., *Seers, Sibyls and Sages* (Leiden: Brill, 1997) 75–97.

CHAPTER THREE

REINVENTING EXODUS:
EXEGESIS AND LEGEND IN HELLENISTIC EGYPT

The story of the Exodus occupies a central and foundational place
in the Hebrew Bible and in Jewish tradition. While the ultimate origin of that story has been called into question in recent years,[1] it
was certainly well established in the Hellenistic period. The re-telling
of the story has been viewed in two distinct, though not necessarily
incompatible, ways in recent scholarship. On the one hand, James
Kugel has argued that the return of the Jewish exiles in the Persian
period ushered in "the age of interpretation," which came to full
bloom in the Hellenistic and Roman periods.[2] Where Louis Ginzberg
in an earlier generation wrote of *The Legends of Jews*, Kugel writes
of interpretations of biblical texts—interpretations of the Jews, so to
speak. On the other hand, Erich Gruen has noted the frequency
with which Hellenistic-Jewish authors "simply rewrote scriptural nar-
ratives, inventing facts or attaching fanciful tales." He concludes that
"the Bible served here less as a text for exegesis than as a spring-
board for creativity."[3] That creativity drew on many sources from
the Gentile world in addition to the Bible. Gruen does not deny
that exegesis plays a part in the process, nor does Kugel claim that
it is the only factor. Their work can be viewed as complementary,
but their perspectives are distinct and both are necessary.

---

[1] See especially E. Blum, *Studien zur Komposition des Pentateuch* (BZAW 189; Berlin:
de Gruyter, 1990); H. Shanks, ed., *The Rise of Ancient Israel* (Washington, D.C.:
Biblical Archaeology Society, 1992).

[2] J. L. Kugel, *The Bible as It Was* (Cambridge, MA: Harvard, 1997) 2; for interpretations of the Exodus see pp. 285–460. See also his more detailed volume,
Traditions of the Bible (Cambridge, MA: Harvard University Press, 1998).

[3] E. Gruen, *Heritage and Hellenism. The Reinvention of Jewish Tradition* (Berkeley:
University of California, 1998) 137.

The Exodus in Artapanus

The most colorful and creative account of the Exodus from an ancient Jewish author is undoubtedly that of Artapanus. Artapanus is known to us only from fragments preserved by Eusebius and Clement,[4] who cited them from the work of Alexander Polyhistor, a native of Miletus who was brought to Rome by Sulla and given his freedom about 80 BCE.[5] Alexander wrote a work "On the Jews" which was a compilation of quotations from Hellenistic Jewish authors. The authors cited must have written no later than the early first century BCE. The fragments of Artapanus deal with Abraham, Joseph and Moses. All, including the Abraham fragment, are set in Egypt, and there can be little doubt that this is where Artapanus wrote. He certainly belonged to the Ptolemaic era rather than the Roman, and he may have written as early as the end of the third century.[6] It is his account of the Exodus that will concern us here.

Artapanus' account agrees with the biblical story in several details. Moses is introduced as a Jewish child, adopted into the family of an Egyptian ruler. He kills an Egyptian, but in self-defence, and flees to Arabia, where he marries the daughter of Raguel. He witnesses miraculous fire "kindled from the earth" that burns without wood, and he hears a divine voice from the fire. He returns to Egypt and performs signs for the king, including the transformation of a rod into a snake, and afflicts the Egyptians with plagues. He notes that the Jews despoiled the Egyptians, and crossed the Red Sea when

---

[4] Three fragments of Artapanus are preserved by Eusebius in PE 9.18, 23 and 27, dealing with Abraham, Joseph, and Moses respectively. The Moses fragment is partially paralleled in Clement, *Stromateis*, 1.23.154, 2–3. See C. R. Holladay, *Fragments from Hellenistic Jewish Authors. Volume 1. Historians* (Chico, CA: Scholars Press, 1983) 199–232. Annotated translations can also be found in J. J. Collins, "Artapanus," *OTP* 2.889–903 and N. Walter, *Fragmente jüdisch-hellenistischer Historiker* (JSHRZ 1/2; Gütersloh: Mohn, 1976) 121–43.

[5] On Alexander Polyhistor see the classic work of J. Freudenthal, *Hellenistische Studien, 1–2, Alexander Polyhistor und die von ihm erhaltenen Reste judäischer und samaritanischer Geschichtswerke* (Breslau: Skutsch, 1875); J. Strugnell, "General Introduction, with a Note on Alexander Polyhistor," *OTP* 2.777–79 and G. E. Sterling, *Historiography and Self-Definition. Josephos, Luke-Acts and Apologetic Historiography* (Leiden: Brill, 1992) 144–52.

[6] On the date of Artapanus see Collins, "Artapanus," 890–91; M. Goodman, "Jewish Literature Composed in Greek," in E. Schürer, *The History of the Jewish People in the Age of Jesus Christ. Volume 3* (rev. and ed. G. Vermes, F. Millar and M. Goodman; Edinburgh: Clark, 1986) 523–4.

Moses struck it with his rod and divided it. From the form of the
proper names (e.g. *Ragouēlos*, Raguel) and verbal echoes it is apparent that he knew the biblical story of the Exodus in its Septuagintal
form.[7] He tells it, however, with numerous embellishments, and adds
stories about the early career of Moses that have no basis in the
biblical text. Moses is identified with Mousaeus and teacher of
Orpheus. He is credited with various inventions for the benefit of
the Egyptians, including most notably the cult of various animals,
including the Apis bull. His successes arouse the envy of the king,
Chenephres, who sends him on a campaign against Ethiopia with a
make-shift army. Moses nonetheless succeeds and even teaches the
Ethiopians circumcision. The continued plotting of Chenephres, however, eventually causes Moses to flee to Arabia, and this is the occasion of the killing of the Egyptian. At first he restrains Raguel from
invading Egypt, but eventually he is instructed to by the divine voice
from the fire to wage a campaign and rescue the Jews. From this
point on, Artapanus' narrative is closer to that of Exodus, but there
are still numerous embellishments. For example, the Egyptians ded-
icate the rod to Isis because of the wonders that Moses works with
his rod.

Gruen has rightly celebrated the ingenuity of this concoction, which
transfers to Moses exploits elsewhere attributed to Semiramis, Sesostris
and other legendary heroes.[8] Indeed, it is so creative that Gruen
feels obliged to reassure us that "Jews would certainly not take it
seriously."[9] But this is to dismiss the evidence of the text without
warrant. We do not know where in Egypt Artapanus lived or what
kind of Judaism he represents, except insofar as that Judaism is
revealed in his text. The idea that Moses created the animal cults
for the benefit of the Egyptians would undoubtedly have been as
offensive to many Jews as it surely would have been to Egyptians,
but Artapanus was clearly not constrained by Deuteronomic ortho-
doxy. Indeed it is striking that he fails to credit Moses with the
accomplishment for which he was most famous in the Hellenistic

---

[7] For the correspondences see Sterling, *Historiography and Self-Definition*, 174.
[8] Gruen, *Heritage and Hellenism*, 158. On the "competitive historiography" of
Artapanus see J. J. Collins, *Between Athens and Jerusalem. Jewish Identity in the Hellenistic
Diaspora* (revised ed.; Grand Rapids: Eerdmans, 2000) chapter 1; Sterling, *Historiography
and Self-Definition*, 176–80.
[9] Gruen, *Heritage and Hellenism*, 158.

world, the giving of the law. However difficult it may be for a modern scholar to take it seriously, the claim that Moses founded the
Egyptian animal cults was for Artapanus a source of ethnic pride,
and this was evidently more important to him than scruples about
violating the Torah.

It is also apparent that Artapanus "worked with more than scripture and his imagination."[10] Much light is shed on his account by
comparison with a passage attributed to Manetho by Josephus.[11]
Manetho claimed that Jerusalem was built "in the land now called
Judaea" by the Hyksos, after they had been expelled from Egypt,
and the claim is accepted by Josephus, who says that "up to this
point he followed the chronicles."[12] But then "by offering to record
the legends and current talk about the Jews, he took the liberty of
interpolating improbable tales in his desire to confuse with us a
crowd of Egyptians, who for leprosy and other maladies had been
condemned to banishment from Egypt." According to this account,
a king named Amenophis "conceived a desire to behold the gods"
and was advised by a sage, also named Amenophis, that this would
be possible "if he cleansed the whole land of lepers and other polluted persons." The king assembled some 80,000 of these people,
including some learned priests, and set them to work in the stone-
quarries, segregated from the ordinary Egyptians. After they had
suffered there for a considerable time they were allowed to occupy
the deserted city of the Hyksos, Avaris, which was dedicated to
Typhon (the Egyptian Seth) according to religious tradition. They
appointed one of the priests of Heliopolis, named Osarseph, as their
leader. He made a law "that they should neither worship the gods
nor refrain from any of the animals prescribed as especially sacred
in Egypt, but should sacrifice and consume all alike, and that they
should have intercourse with none save those of their own confederacy." He then rebelled against the king and summoned the Shepherds
(Hyksos) to his aid from Jerusalem. The Shepherds then invaded

---

[10] Sterling, *Historiography and Self-Definition*, 181. Cf. P. W. van der Horst, "The
Interpretation of the Bible by the Minor Hellenistic Jewish Authors," in idem, *Essays
on the Jewish World of Early Christianity* (Göttingen: Vandenhoeck & Ruprecht, 1990)
187–219 (200–205 on Artapanus).

[11] *AgAp* 1.228–52; M. Stern, *Greek and Latin Authors on Jews and Judaism* (Jerusalem:
The Israel Academy of Arts and Sciences, 1974) 1.78–86.

[12] A separate account of the Hyksos, their expulsion from Egypt and occupation
of Judaea, is found in *AgAp* 1.73–91; Stern, *Greek and Latin Authors*, 1.68–9.

Egypt. King Amenophis gathered the sacred animals to protect them
and hid the images of the gods. Instead of engaging the Hyksos in
battle, he withdrew to Ethiopia. While he was in exile, "the Solymites
made a descent along with the polluted Egyptians and treated the
people so impiously and savagely that the domination of the Shepherds
seemed like a golden age to those who witnessed the present enor-
mities. For not only did they set towns and villages on fire, pillaging the temples and mutilating images of the gods without restraint,
but they also made a practice of using the sanctuaries as kitchens
to roast the sacred animals which the people worshipped; and they
would compel the priests and prophets to sacrifice and butcher the
beasts, afterwards casting the men forth naked." The leader, concludes Manetho, was "named Osarseph after the god Osiris, worshipped at Heliopolis, but when he joined this people, he changed
his name and was called Moses." Eventually Amenophis and his son
returned from Ethiopia and drove the Shepherds and the lepers out
of Egypt, as far as the borders of Syria.

Most students of Artapanus have agreed that his account of Moses
is a rebuttal of this unflattering account attributed to Manetho.[13]
Manetho had alleged that Moses forbade his people to worship the
gods or abstain from the flesh of the sacred animals. Artapanus
claimed that it was Moses who established these cults. Manetho
alleged that Moses had instigated the Hyksos to invade Egypt.
Artapanus claimed that Moses restrained Raguel and the Arabs from
invading and only launched a campaign when he was directly commanded by a divine voice. According to Manetho, the pharaoh had
to protect the sacred animals from Moses. Artapanus claims that the
pharaoh buried the animals which Moses had made sacred, since
he wished to conceal Moses' inventions. In Manetho's account, the
pharaoh sought refuge in Ethiopia from Moses and his allies. In
Artapanus, Moses conducted a campaign against Ethiopia on behalf
of the pharaoh. Artapanus responds to the charge that Moses and
his followers were lepers by claiming that an Egyptian, Chenephres,
was the first to die of elephantiasis and insisting that Moses was
physically impressive. Gruen objects that "this was no somber contest for supremacy between Jewish and pagan intellectuals"[14] and

---

[13] See especially Sterling, *Historiography and Self-Definition*, 182–83, and the literature there cited.
[14] Gruen, *Heritage and Hellenism*, 158.

claims that the Jewish author "did not enlist in a deadly serious encounter to advance Jewish values against the claims of competing nations and cultures."[15] Artapanus was certainly not somber, whether he was "deadly serious" or not, but competitive historiography did not have to be somber. For all its exuberance, Artapanus's account served a serious purpose: to defend the ancestors of his people from gentile slander and to extol them above the heroes of other peoples. The refutation of writers such as Manetho is only the negative side of his work. On the positive side he claimed for Moses the accomplishments of various heroes. The correspondences with Sesostris are especially striking. Sesostris was credited with being the first Egyptian to divide the country into nomes and organize Egyptian religion. These accomplishments are claimed for Moses by Artapanus.[16] The motif of a campaign against Ethiopia was widespread. Semiramis was said to have subdued it. The Persian king Cambyses had tried and failed. Sesostris was said to have been the first man to conquer Ethiopia and the only Egyptian to rule over it. The Moses of Artapanus conquers it with a non-professional army. Moses even outshines the pagan gods. He is identified with Hermes, the supreme culture-bringer, and subordinates Isis, who is identified with the earth. He is also the teacher of Orpheus.[17]

The rationale underlying Artapanus' narrative, then, is clear enough, however unconventional the view of Judaism that it embodies. In this enterprise, the biblical account provided a starting point, but did not constrain the Hellenistic author to any significant degree. He draws freely on pagan legends, sometimes to borrow motifs, sometimes to invert and refute them. We may agree with Gruen that he shows wit and ingenuity, but this is not an exercise in humor or caprice.[18] It is a skirmish in the battle for the view of a people's origins that would have huge repercussions for their status and reputation in the Hellenistic age.

---

[15] Ibid., 160.

[16] Sterling, *Historiography and Self-Definition*, 177.

[17] See further Collins, *Between Athens and Jerusalem*, chapter 1. For the exploits of Sesostris, Semiramis and other legendary heroes of the Hellenistic Near East see M. Braun, *History and Romance in Graeco-Oriental Literature* (Oxford: Blackwell, 1938).

[18] Pace Gruen, *Heritage and Hellenism*, 160.

The Origin of Manetho's Account

But what of the account attributed to Manetho? Josephus presents
this account as the fountain-head of a tradition of anti-Jewish slander, and some modern authors follow this assessment.[19] Similar
accounts of Jewish origins, with increasingly vitriolic variations, are
found in such authors as Lysimachus, Chaeremon and Apion, who,
according to Josephus, carried on a vehement polemic against the
Jews in Alexandria in the early Roman period. The bitter hostility
of Jews and Alexandrian Greeks in the first century CE is well-
known. Manetho, however, wrote under Ptolemy I or Ptolemy II,
in the first half of the third century BCE, and we have no evidence
of such hostility at that early time.[20] Consequently, many scholars
have argued that Manetho's account has suffered interpolation.[21]
Specifically, the identification of Osarseph, leader of the lepers, with
Moses in *AgAp* 1.250 seems to be added as a gloss, and is surely
secondary, as there is no hint of it in the main narrative.[22] Nonetheless,
the marauding invaders in the story come from Jerusalem, and are
presumably the ancestors of the Jews.[23] It is often assumed that
Manetho was giving an Egyptian rejoinder to the story of the Exodus.[24]

It is also widely agreed, however, that the basic narrative reflects
old Egyptian traditions, some of which related to the expulsion of

---

[19] Stern, *Greek and Latin Authors*, 64; P. Schäfer, *Judeophobia. Attitudes toward the Jews
in the Ancient World* (Cambridge, MA: Harvard University Press, 1997) 17–21. See
especially J. W. van Henten and Ra'anan Abusch, "The Depiction of the Jews as
Typhonians and Josephus' Strategy of Refutation in *Contra Apionem*," in L. H. Feldman
and J. R. Levison, ed., *Josephus' Contra Apionem* (Leiden: Brill, 1996) 272–309, who
point out that both the Hyksos and the Jews are consistently associated with Seth-
Typhon, the mythical enemy of the royal god Horus.

[20] On Manetho, see G. P. Verbrugghe and J. M. Wickersham, *Berossos and Manetho,
Introduced and Translated. Native Traditions in Ancient Mesopotamia and Egypt* (Ann Arbor:
University of Michigan, 1996); Sterling, *Historiography and Self-Definition*, 117–36;
P. Fraser, *Ptolemaic Alexandria* (3 vols.; Oxford: Clarendon, 1972) 1.505–11.

[21] E. Meyer, *Aegyptische Chronologie* (Leipzig: Hinrichs, 1904) 71–9; J. G. Gager,
Moses in Greco-Roman Paganism (SBLMS 16; Nashville: Abingdon, 1972) 118. See
Verbrugghe and Wickersham, *Berossos and Manetho*, 116.

[22] This is agreed even by Schäfer, *Judeophobia*, 20, who nonetheless insists that
Manetho's original account was hostile to the Jews.

[23] This was pointed out by V. Tcherikover, *Hellenistic Civilization and the Jews* (New
York: Atheneum, 1970) 362; also Stern, *Greek and Latin Authors*, 64.

[24] E.g. Tcherikover, *Hellenistic Civilization*, 363; Stern, *Greek and Latin Authors*, 64.
A. Kasher, *The Jews in Hellenistic and Roman Egypt* (Tübingen: Mohr, 1985), 328,
argues that the rejoinder was prompted by the translation of the Book of Exodus
into Greek.

the Hyksos in the sixteenth century BCE and some of which derived from the upheaval caused by the religious revolution of Akhenaten in the Amarna period.[25] The story of the lepers may reflect some historical memory of a plague that had swept the country in the second millennium, and was known as "the Asiatic illness."[26] The association with Avaris, city of Typhon or Seth, the mythical adversary of Osiris, represents the demonization of the Hyksos in Egyptian memory.[27] Gruen concludes that "the Manethonian tale does not derive from the Exodus or some garbled form of it. In its essentials, it has nothing whatever to do with Jews."[28] The question then is how it came to be applied to the Jews? Here Gruen has a novel suggestion: "that introduction of the Jews into Manetho's narrative . . . came from Jewish sources themselves."[29] More specifically, "one can envision an earlier layer slanted to the benefit of the Jews."[30] There are two strands in Manetho's account, one the tale of the lepers and the other the story of Jerusalemites who invaded and pillaged Egypt. The latter strand, claims Gruen, "could easily derive from a Jewish construct."[31] In support of this claim he argues that Jewish origins was a question of far greater importance to Jews than to gentiles, that the destruction of pagan cults had a long and favorable history in Israel and that Artapanus "provides direct testimony for a Jewish tradition of mobilization against Egypt."[32]

In order to assess the plausibility of this highly original suggestion we must take into account another gentile narrative of Jewish origins, that of Hecataeus of Abdera who wrote under Ptolemy I and so was probably an older contemporary of Manetho.[33] Josephus claims that Hecataeus wrote a book entirely about the Jews, and cites it at

---

[25] D. B. Redford, "The Hyksos Invasion in History and Tradition," *Orientalia* 39(1970) 1–51; J. Assmann, *Moses the Egyptian* (Cambridge, MA: Harvard University Press, 1997) 23–44.

[26] Assmann, *Moses the Egyptian*, 27; H. Goedicke, "The 'Canaanite Illness,'" *Studien zur Altägyptischen Kultur* 11(1984) 91–105.

[27] van Henten and Abusch, "The Jews as Typhonians."

[28] Gruen, *Heritage and Hellenism*, 61.

[29] Ibid., 63.

[30] Ibid.

[31] Ibid., 65.

[32] Ibid.

[33] Stern, *Greek and Latin Authors*, 20–45; B. Bar-Kochva, *Pseudo-Hecataeus On the Jews. Legitimizing the Jewish Diaspora* (Berkeley: Univrsity of California Press, 1996) 7–43; Sterling, *Historiography and Self-Definition*, 55–91.

length (*AgAp* 1.183–204) but this book has been shown decisively to be a Jewish forgery.[34] There is no doubt, however, about the authenticity of Hecataeus's excursus on the origin of the Jews in his *Aegyptiaka*, which is preserved in the *Bibliotheca* of Photius, who excerpted it from Diodorus Siculus.[35] According to Hecataeus:

> When in ancient times a pestilence arose in Egypt, the common people ascribed their troubles to the workings of a divine agency; for indeed with many strangers of all sorts dwelling in their midst and practising different rites of religion and sacrifice, their own traditional observances in honor of the gods had fallen into disuse. Hence the natives of the land surmised that unless they removed the foreigners, their troubles would never be resolved. At once, therefore, the aliens were driven from the country, and the most outstanding and active among them banded together and, as some say were cast ashore in Greece and certain other regions . . . But the greater number were driven into what is now called Judaea, which is not far distant from Egypt and was at that time utterly uninhabited. The colony was headed by a man called Moses, outstanding both for his wisdom and for his courage. On taking possession of the land he founded, besides other cities, one that is now the most renowned of all, called Jerusalem.[36]

Hecataeus goes on to give a remarkably positive account of Moses' legislation, including the prohibition of images. He notes, however, that "as a result of their own expulsion from Egypt he introduced a somewhat unsocial and intolerant mode of life" (*apanthrōpon tina kai misoxenon bion*). Hecataeus should not be regarded as either pro- or anti-Jewish. His interest in Judaism was incidental. Gruen has rightly noted that the account is a mixture of accurate and inaccurate information, and that Hecataeus had probably some Jewish informants to supplement his general reliance on Egyptian priests.[37] The more accurate information is found in his brief description of Mosaic legislation. The passage quoted above, however, about the expulsion of foreigners in response to a pestilence was presumably derived from Egyptian sources. This passage is a variant of the story of the lepers in Manetho. Hecataeus presents his account with the detachment of a neutral observer. Manetho makes no pretence of such detachment but reflects Egyptian tradition in all its animosity towards the outcasts.

---

[34] Bar-Kochva, *Pseudo-Hecataeus*.
[35] Gager, *Moses*, 26–37; Schäfer, *Judeophobia*, 15–17.
[36] Stern, *Greek and Latin Authors*, 27–28.
[37] Gruen, *Heritage and Hellenism*, 53–54.

Hecataeus shows that the ancestors of the Jews were identified with the expelled foreigners already at the dawn of the Hellenistic age, even before the work of Manetho. His account of Jewish origins bears only superficial similarity to the biblical story of the Exodus. The main point of resemblance is simply that the Jewish forebears were foreigners resident in Egypt, who migrated from there to the land later known as Israel. The circumstances of the migration, however, are entirely different. Plagues figure in both accounts, but again they function in very different ways. It is not necessary to suppose that the account found in Hecataeus was dependent in any way on the story of Exodus. Egyptian tradition from the second millennium BCE remembered the Hyksos as foreigners from Syria who were eventually expelled. The idea that Jerusalem had been founded by these people provided answers to two questions that would have been raised with no great urgency by the Egyptian tradition. Where did the Hyksos go? and who established the city and people in Judea, just beyond Egypt's borders? Given the negative portrayal of the Hyksos in Egyptian tradition, a derogatory view of the Jews was implied, but this was no more than the typical Egyptian contempt for "the vile Asiatics," that is well attested from the second millennium on.[38] Gruen, who recognizes that the impetus for this part of Hecataeus's account does not come from the book of Exodus objects that "it will not do to ascribe to Jewish informants only those details of Hecataeus' text that are accurate, while assigning the rest to malicious Egyptians, Hellenic formulas, or Hecataeus' own errors."[39] Hence his proposal that Diaspora Jews had a hand in fashioning the whole account. It is surely unlikely, however, that Jews would have invented a story that said that their ancestors had been driven from Egypt because they were blamed for a pestilence. We should have to suppose that Hecataeus had altered the hypothetical Jewish account considerably.

In fact, Hecataeus combines two motifs that appear separately in Manetho, the founding of Jerusalem by foreigners expelled from Egypt and the association of Moses and his followers with pestilence, identified as leprosy in Manetho. These motifs may have circulated independently in Egyptian tradition, deriving respectively from the

---

[38] See Redford, "The Hyksos in History and Tradition."
[39] Gruen, *Heritage and Hellenism*, 54.

expulsion of the Hyksos and the monotheistic revolution of Akhenaten.[40] Granted that no Jewish author is likely to have associated his fore-fathers with leprosy or pestilence, is it plausible that the identification with the Hyksos was a Jewish invention?

It is true that Josephus appears to endorse Manetho's initial account of the Hyksos or Shepherds who occupied Egypt but were subse-quently expelled and founded Jerusalem in the land of Judea.[41] For Josephus, the claim that his ancestors had once ruled Egypt was a source of pride.[42] But Josephus is working from Manetho's account and trying to turn it to the advantage of the Jews. He cites no Jewish author in support of the claim. The only other Jewish author that Gruen can cite for a campaign by Moses against Egypt is Artapanus. But Artapanus is also responding to the account of Manetho, as we have seen, and he is ambivalent about the alleged attack on Egypt. He is at pains to make clear that Moses was opposed to attacking at first, and only did so in obedience to a divine voice. His conduct towards the Egyptian cults stands in direct contrast to that of the lepers in Manetho. Although it is true that "taking action against rival cults and abhorrent practices had a long tradition among Jews,"[43] there was no tradition of an invasion of Egypt among the Jews of the Diaspora. The Jewish settlers in Egypt in the Ptolemaic period sought the patronage of the Greek rulers, who in turn assumed much of the ideology of the Pharaohs.[44] While Jewish writers condemned idolatry, it is only in the Roman period, in the context of the great Diaspora revolt under Trajan, that they exulted in the destruction of pagan shrines.[45] The Septuagint famously translated Exod 22:27

---

[40] On the derivation of the story of the lepers from traditions about the Amarna age, see Redford, "The Hyksos Invasion," 49–50; Assmann, *Moses the Egyptian*, 29–44.

[41] *AgAp* 1.73–91. Josephus concludes with the comment that the most remote ancestors of the Jews lived a nomadic life and were called Shepherds. In *AgAp* 2.228 he says that this part of Manetho's account was in accordance with the chronicles.

[42] Cf. *AgAp* 1.224, where he says that the Egyptians hated and envied the Jews because of "the domination of our ancestors over their country."

[43] Gruen, *Heritage and Hellenism*, 64.

[44] See Collins, *Between Athens and Jerusalem*, chapters 1–2. On the appropriation of Pharaonic ideology by the Ptolemies see especially L. Koenen, "Die Adaptation Ägyptischer Königsideologie am Ptolemäerhof," in W. Peremans, ed., *Egypt and the Hellenistic World* (Studia Hellenistica 27; Leuven: Leuven University Press, 1983) 174–90.

[45] E.g. Sib Or 5:484–8. J. M. G. Barclay, *Jews in the Mediterranean Diaspora. From Alexander to Trajan (323 BCE–117 CE)* (Edinburgh: Clark, 1996) argues for a tradition

(LXX 22:28) *'elōhîm lō' t^eqallēl*, "thou shalt not revile God" as "thou shalt not revile gods." Philo explained this text by saying that Moses commanded the Israelites not to "revile with unbridled tongue the gods whom others acknowledge, lest they on their part be moved to utter profane words against Him who truly is."[46] Josephus also says that "our legislator has expressly forbidden us to deride or blaspheme the gods recognized by others, out of respect for the very word 'God.'"[47] Artapanus is exceptional in claiming that Moses founded the animal cults, but he is typical of Hellenistic Jewish literature in presenting the Jewish forefathers as bringers of culture and benefactors of humankind.

Manetho's account of the Hyksos as marauding invaders drew on a long-standing tradition, which reverberated through Egyptian literature from the second millennium down to the Hellenistic age, reinforced by the more recent invasions of the Assyrians and Persians.[48] To be associated with the memory of the Hyksos was to invite execration in Egypt. At least some Jews were aware of the negative associations of Semitic invasion. Sib Or 3:611–14 prophecies that a great king will come from Asia and fill everything with evils and overthrow the kingdom of evil. This disaster will lead to the conversion of Egypt, but the Sibyl makes no suggestion that this king is Jewish. There were several prototypes for this figure, from the Hyksos to Cambyses and Antiochus Epiphanes. No Jewish author in Ptolemaic Egypt, however, would cast a Jewish king in such a hostile and aggressive role. The suggestion that the identification of the Jews with the expelled Hyksos was a Jewish invention remains unsupported and implausible.

Gruen is right, however, that Manetho's account was not a rejoinder to the biblical story of the Exodus, a story that Manetho is unlikely to have known. There are, to be sure, a couple of details

---

of "cultural antagonism" already in Sib Or 3 but this is a misreading of the rhetoric of the Sibyl, which culminates in an appeal for conversion. See the comments of Gruen, *Heritage and Hellenism*, 287, who notes the Sibyl's positive appeal to the Greeks.

[46] Philo, *De specialibus legibus* 1.53. See also *Quaestiones in Exodum* 2.5 and *Vita Mosis* 2.203–5. See P. W. van der Horst, "'Thou shalt not revile the gods.' The LXX translation of Exod 2:28(27), its background and influence," in idem, *Hellenism—Judaism—Christianity. Essays on their Interaction* (Kampen: Kok Pharos, 1994) 112–21.

[47] *AgAp* 2.237.

[48] F. Dunand, "L'Oracle du Potier et la Formation de l'Apocalyptique en Égypte," in F. Raphaël et al., *L'Apocalyptique* (Paris: Geuthner, 1977) 47–67;

that might suggest otherwise. In Manetho's account, the lepers are forced to work in stone-quarries. This is not an exact parallel to the forced labor of the Israelites, but it is somewhat reminiscent of the biblical story. Forced labor in ancient Egypt, however, was not reserved for the Hebrews. The similarity may be mere coincidence. More intriguing is the notice that Osarseph made a law for his followers that they should neither worship the gods nor refrain from sacred animals, and "should have intercourse with none save those of their own confederacy."[49] This notice recalls Hecataeus' reference to the "somewhat anti-social" laws of Moses. Peter Schäfer has argued that this is specifically an anti-Jewish charge, not grounded in the older Egyptian tradition about the Hyksos.[50] This is not necessarily so. The Hyksos had remained in Egypt a race apart, who preserved their Canaanite cult and were always regarded as foreigners, Asiatics.[51] Even if Manetho is alluding to Jewish customs, however, we need not conclude that he knew the book of Exodus in any form. Jews who adhered to their traditional laws were notoriously reluctant to mingle with other races and this social *amixia* underlies the comment of Hecataeus. Manetho required no knowledge of Jewish traditions to observe this reluctance. Manetho evidently identified the ancestors of the Jews with the Hyksos, even apart from the identification of Osarseph with Moses, which appears to be a secondary gloss. His portrayal of these people, however, was primarily an adaptation of Egyptian tradition, that owed little or nothing to any Jewish source.

Conclusion

Most Hellenistic Jewish accounts of the origin of Israel follow the biblical story of the Exodus, even if they embellish it in various ways.[52] But the Bible was not the only source of traditions about the origin of the Jews. Egyptian tradition associated the settling of Judea

---

[49] *AgAp* 1.239.
[50] Schäfer, *Judeophobia*, 19.
[51] Redford, "The Hyksos Invasion," 8.
[52] See P. Enns, *Exodus Retold. Ancient Exegesis of the Departure from Egypt in Wis 10:15–21 and 19:1–9* (HSM 57; Atlanta: Scholars Press, 1997); S. Cheong, *The Exodus Story in the Wisdom of Solomon. A Study in Biblical Interpretation* (JSPSup 23; Sheffield: Sheffield Academic Press, 1997).

and the founding of Jerusalem with the expulsion of the Hyksos.[53] This association had unfortunate consequences for the Jews of Egypt, since it entailed negative stereotypes that were deeply entrenched in the Egyptian psyche. Both Artapanus and Josephus, in their very different ways, tried to adapt this tradition and turn it to their advantage. The blending and free adaptation of traditions finds its most colorful expression in Artapanus, but Manetho may have been just as creative in his re-shaping of Egyptian traditions, quite independently of the biblical story. Both accounts, Egyptian and Jewish, were quite fantastic in their details, and not without entertainment value for their readers. But they were also profoundly serious in their implications for the nature of the Jewish people and the relations between Jew and Gentile in Hellenistic Egypt.

---

[53] It is quite unlikely that this tradition had any historical value as far as the origin of Israel was concerned, despite some modern suggestions to the contrary (e.g. B. Halpern, "The Exodus and the Israelite Historians," *Eretz Israel* 24(1993) 89*–96*.

CHAPTER FOUR

MESSIANISM AND EXEGETICAL TRADITION: THE EVIDENCE OF THE LXX PENTATEUCH

The issue of messianism in the Septuagint is a point of intersection for two distinct debates in contemporary scholarship. The first concerns the nature of the Greek translation, and the relative weight to be given to translation technique as against possible theological or ideological considerations.[1] The second concerns the currency of messianic beliefs in Second Temple Judaism, and the likelihood that such ideas were part of the cultural landscape of the translators.[2] My own interest in the topic arises primarily from the second of these debates, but the currency or absence of messianism in other Jewish literature of the time cannot be determinative here. The question whether the LXX attests to messianic beliefs can only be answered by examination of specific texts and forming an assessment of the Greek translation and its implications.

---

[1] See J. Schaper, *Eschatology in the Greek Psalter* (WUNT 2/76; Tübingen: Mohr-Siebeck, 1995) 16–25. Schaper argues for the importance of "paratextual factors," and criticizes the scholars of the "Finnish School" (I. Soisalen-Soininen, R. Sollamo, A. Aejmelaeus) for neglecting them. For the Finnish approach see I. Soisalen-Soininen, *Beobachtungen zur Arbeitsweise der Septuaginta-Übersetzer,"* in A. Rofé and Y. Zakovitch, ed., *Isac Leo Seeligmann Volume. Essays on the Bible and the Ancient World* (Jerusalem: Rubinstein, 1983) vol. 3 (non-Hebrew Section) pp. 319–29; A. Aejmelaeus, *On the Trail of the Septuagint Translators* (Kampen: Kok, 1996). See also the essays in R. Sollamo and S. Sipilä, ed., *Helsinki Perspectives on the Translation Technique of the Septuagint. Proceedings of the IOSCS Congress in Helsinki 1999* (Publications of the Finnish Exegetical Society 82; Göttingen: Vandenhoeck & Ruprecht, 2001) notably J. Cook, "Ideology and Translation Technique: Two Sides of the Same Coin?" pp. 195–210.

[2] For the range of positions see W. Horbury, *Jewish Messianism and the Cult of Christ*, (London: SCM, 1998) (maximalist), J. Neusner, W. Green and E. Frerichs, *Judaisms and Their Messiahs* (Cambridge: Cambridge University Press, 1987) (minimalist), J. J. Collins, *The Scepter and the Star. The Messiahs of the Dead Sea Scrolls and Other Ancient Literature* (Anchor Bible Reference Library; New York: Doubleday, 1995) (minimalist for the period prior to the Dead Sea Scrolls).

Messianism

By messianism I mean the expectation of a figure who will act as God's designated agent in the eschatological time.[3] Messianism, as distinct from the broader phenomenon of eschatology, is focused on the expectation of a particular figure or figures.[4] These figures are not necessarily designated by the term משיח or translation equivalents (χριστός, משיחא), but are recognized as filling the same functions as figures who are so designated.[5] We know from the Dead Sea Scrolls that a range of messianic figures was expected in the end-time, priestly and prophetic as well as kingly.[6] For purposes of this discussion, however, we can restrict our focus to the royal messiah, the form of messianic expectation that was most widespread in ancient Judaism.[7]

Royal messianism was essentially the hope for the restoration of native kingship in Judah, specifically, the restoration of the Davidic line.[8] This hope was based on the promise to David, recorded in 2 Samuel 7, which was certainly part of the received scriptures throughout the Second Temple period. According to that promise, David's house and kingdom were made sure forever, and his throne was established. After the Babylonian Exile, however, there no longer was a Davidic king in Jerusalem, and so we might expect that pious Judeans would look for the fulfillment of the promise.

---

[3] Collins, *The Scepter and the Star*, 11–12.

[4] Schaper, *Eschatology in the Greek Psalter*, 26–30.

[5] Pace J. A. Fitzmyer, "Qumran Messianism," in idem, *The Dead Sea Scrolls and Christian Origins* (Grand Rapids: Eerdmans, 2000) 73–110.

[6] Collins, *The Scepter and the Star*; J. Zimmermann, *Messianische Texte aus Qumran* (WUNT 2/104; Tübingen: Mohr Siebeck, 1998); G. G. Xeravits, *King, Priest, Prophet. Positive Eschatological Protagonists of the Qumran Library* (STDJ 47; Leiden: Brill, 2002).

[7] W. Horbury, *Messianism among Jews and Christians* (London/New York: Continuum, 2003) 63, argues that the diversity of messianism in the Pseudepigrapha is qualified by the fact that "much of their material has an underlying unity arising from its roots in biblical tradition on the king." But the distinct priestly and prophetic messianic traditions can not be denied.

[8] K. E. Pomykala, *The Davidic Dynasty Tradition in Early Judaism. Its History and Significance for Messianism* (SBLEJL 7; Atlanta: Society of Biblical Literature, 1995) 231–64, argues that there were also "other royal messianic figures" such as the "messiah of Israel" in the Dead Sea Scrolls, who were not Davidic, but it is far more likely that the messianic status of these figures was also based on the promise to David. On the history of the interpretation of that promise see W.S. Schniedewind, *Society and the Promise to David. The Reception History of 2 Samuel 7:1–17* (New York/Oxford: Oxford University Press, 1999).

There is indeed some evidence of such expectation after the Exile. In Jeremiah 23:5–6, the Lord promises to raise up for David a righteous Branch (צמח צדיק). Since the previous chapter ends with a ringing declaration that no descendant of Jehoiachin would ever again sit on the throne of David, there is some reason to doubt whether the oracle in chapter 23 comes from Jeremiah. In any case, the reaffirmation of this prophecy in Jer 33:15–16 is clearly a secondary addition to the book, as it is not found in the Greek.[9] When it was added, we do not know. There was a flurry of messianic excitement centered on Zerubbabel in the period of the restoration. Zerubbabel was proclaimed as the צמח, the fulfillment of the prophecy in Jeremiah, by Zechariah,[10] and as YHWH's signet ring by Haggai.[11] But Zerubbabel disappears abruptly from history, leaving the High Priest Joshua as the recipient of two crowns, one of which was intended for the צמח, in Zechariah 6. Several messianic prophecies are of disputed date. Isaiah 11 is a case in point. The reference to the stump of Jesse may well imply that the tree of the royal line had been cut down, that the line of succession had been broken, although many commentators still assign the passage to the eighth century prophet.[12] There are a few messianic passages in Zechariah 9–14, but they are of uncertain date. The most important of these is in Zechariah 9, which envisions a king entering Jerusalem, "humble and riding on a donkey." This oracle is often related to the campaign of Alexander the Great, because of Zech 9:13: "I will arouse your sons, O Zion, against your sons, O Greece." This reading, however, is suspect on textual grounds. It disrupts the meter and parallelism and it can

---

[9] Collins, *The Scepter and the Star*, 25–6.

[10] Zech 3:8; 6:12. See J. J. Collins, "The Eschatology of Zechariah," in L. L. Grabbe and R. D. Haak, ed., *Knowing the End from the Beginning. The Prophetic, the Apocalyptic and their Relationships* (London/New York: T & T Clark International, 2003) 74–84.

[11] Hag 2:23.

[12] See H. Wildberger, *Isaiah 1–12*. (A Continental Commentary; Minneapolis: Augsburg Fortress, 1991) 465–6. Wildberger attributes the passage to the eighth century prophet. Also H. G. M. Williamson, "The Messianic Texts in Isaiah 1–39," in J. Day, ed., *King and Messiah in Israel and the Ancient Near East* (JSOTSup 270; Sheffield: Sheffield Academic Press, 1998) 258–64, who also inclines to defend the originality of the passage.

easily be explained as resulting from dittography.[13] Without the reference to Greece, the date of this passage is quite uncertain.[14]

These scattered passages show that there was some messianic expectation in the Persian period, but the fact that they are so scattered, and lack context, suggests that messianic expectation was a marginal phenomenon. The more historically oriented books from this period, Ezra and Nehemiah, are devoid of any hint of messianic expectation. William Horbury argues that the Chronicler is "tinged with messianism,"[15] and even Hugh Williamson, who rejects the label "messianic," credits the Chronicler with "a continuing expectation of the re-emergence of a ruling Davidic household."[16] But in fact there is no reference in Chronicles to the future rule of a Davidic king. There are several references to an everlasting kingdom, given to the line of David (1 Chron 17:14; 2 Chron 13:5; 21:7). But while the promise to David in 2 Samuel 7 had said "your house and your kingdom shall be made sure forever before me," 1 Chronicles 17:14 reads: "but I will confirm him in my house and in my kingdom forever." The focus is changed from the dynasty to the temple.[17] The Chronicler seems to have believed that the promise was being fulfilled even when he wrote, and he shows no expectation of a greater fulfillment to come.

Some scholars have argued that messianic expectation remained marginal throughout the Second Temple period.[18] This position, however, can no longer be maintained. The Dead Sea Scrolls provide evidence of the messianic interpretation of several biblical texts which were also taken as messianic prophecies in other strands of Judaism. Isa 11:1–5, Balaam's oracle in Numbers 24, Genesis 49

---

[13] Paul D. Hanson, "Zechariah 9 and an Ancient Ritual Pattern," in *JBL* 92 (1973) 45. בניך יון lacks only one letter of בניך ציון.

[14] J. J. M. Roberts, "The Old Testament's Contribution to Messianic Expectations," in J. H. Charlesworth, ed., *The Messiah. Developments in Earliest Judaism and Christianity*, (Minneapolis: Augsburg Fortress, 1992) 44–5, dates it to the eighth century BCE.

[15] Horbury, *Jewish Messianism*, 45.

[16] H. G. M. Williamson, "The Dynastic Oracle in the Books of Chronicles," in A. Rofé and Y. Zakovitch, ed., *Isac Leo Seeligmann Volume. Essays on the Bible and the Ancient World* vol. 3 (non-Hebrew Section) pp. 305–18 (318).

[17] See Schniedewind, *Society and the Promise to David*, 130–1.

[18] See for example Neusner, Green and Frerichs, *Judaisms and their Messiahs*; J. H. Charlesworth, "From Messianology to Christology: Problems and Prospects," in idem, ed., *The Messiah*, 5.

and 2 Samuel 7 are the most prominent examples. The use of these texts around the turn of the era provides a consistent picture of the character and role of the royal messiah. He is expected to be a warrior, who will kill the wicked with the breath of his lips. He is the messiah of righteousness, who will usher in an era of peace and justice. He is presumably a human figure, although he is endowed with the spirit of the Lord. He is expected to re-establish a dynasty, rather than rule forever himself. In the Dead Sea Scrolls he is often linked with a priestly messiah who would restore the legitimate priesthood, and sometimes with a prophet, who would herald the coming of the final deliverance. But the most basic and widespread expectation in this period was for a royal, Davidic, messiah, who would restore the kingdom of Israel.[19]

In the early Hellenistic period, before the Dead Sea Scrolls, however, evidence for messianic expectation is lacking. The absence of messianic expectation is most conspicuous in the Maccabean era, when it might have been expected. Not only do the books of Maccabees stop short of claiming messianic status for their heroes, but Daniel and the early apocalypses of Enoch do not envision a restoration of the monarchy.[20] The "one like a son of man" in Daniel 7 would later be interpreted as a messiah in both Judaism and Christianity. Scholarly opinion is divided as to whether the original reference was to an angelic figure or to the Jewish people symbolized corporately.[21] Only a few scholars have argued for a messianic interpretation, and their argument is undercut by the absence of messianic expectation elsewhere in the book.[22] When we find reference to "anointed ones" in Daniel 9:25–6, the reference is to anointed

---

[19] Collins, *The Scepter and the Star*, 49–73.

[20] The "white bull" in 1 Enoch 90:37 has sometimes been regarded as a messiah, but he does not function like a messiah, and is more plausibly identified as an Adamic figure. See P. A. Tiller, *A Commentary on the Animal Apocalypse of 1 Enoch* (SBLEJL 4; Atlanta: Society of Biblical Literature, 1993) 384. See also the discussion by G. W. E. Nickelsburg, *1 Enoch 1. A Commentary on the Book of 1 Enoch, Chapters 1–36, 81–108* (Hermeneia; Minneapolis: Fortress, 2001) 406–7, who is more sympathetic to the messianic interpretation, but concludes that the figure might be seen as a new Adam.

[21] For full discussion see J. J. Collins, *Daniel. A Commentary on the Book of Daniel* (Hermeneia; Minneapolis: Augsburg Fortress, 1993) 304–10. I argue for the angelic interpretation.

[22] Horbury, *Jewish Messianism*, 34, states without argument that "the early messianic interpretation is more likely to be right."

High Priests. There is no firm evidence of messianic expectation in the Hellenistic period before the mid-second century BCE, arguably even before the first century.

This view of the evidence has been challenged, however, by William Horbury, in his book, *Jewish Messianism and the Cult of Christ*.[23] Horbury takes a decidedly maximalist view of the messianic implications of such texts as Chronicles and Daniel. Most importantly for our present topic, he claims that "this judgment (i.e. that a 'messianological vacuum' can be identified between the early fifth and the late second century) seems to leave out of account the implications of the LXX Pentateuch."[24] The Pentateuch, by general consensus, was translated in the third century BCE, precisely the "dark age" of messianism. It "attests Jewish interpretation current in the Diaspora," but "according to legend it was translated by Judaeans, and is not without significance for Judaean views."[25] Horbury argues that the Pentateuch itself was understood as "a document of Jewish monarchy," in the Greek period, and that the Greek rendering of three Pentateuchal prophecies, in the mouths of Jacob (Gen 49), Balaam (Num 24) and Moses (Deut 33) "form fundamental but often neglected documents of Jewish kingship and messianism."[26] These are the claims that we will evaluate in the remainder of this paper.

The Septuagint

There is a fundamental problem that arises in the attempt to treat the LXX as a theological document in its own right. Many, perhaps most, scholars of the LXX in recent years have argued that the translators were primarily concerned to reproduce accurately the meaning of the Hebrew text.[27] Some have gone so far as to argue

---

[23] Above, note 2. See also his essay, "Messianism in the Old Testament Apocrypha and Pseudepigrapha," in idem, *Messianism among Jews and Christians*, 35–64.

[24] Horbury, *Jewish Messianism*, 37.

[25] Ibid., 46.

[26] Ibid., 48. Others have detected messianic implications in the translation of Gen 3:15. See J. Lust, "Septuagint and Messianism, with a Special Emphasis on the Pentateuch," in H. G. Reventlow, ed., *Theologische Probleme der Septuaginta und der hellenistischen Hermeneutik* (Gütersloh: Kaiser, 1997) 37–8 (reprinted in Lust, *Messianism and the Septuagint* (BETL 178; Leuven, University Press Peeters: 2004) 129–51.

[27] H. M. Orlinsky, "The Septuagint as Holy Writ and the Philosophy of the Translators," in *HUCA* 46 (1975) 89–114: "It is the literal word-for-word rendering

for an "interlinear" model of translation, on the assumption that the Greek was not meant originally to be read independently, but as an aid to understanding the Hebrew text.[28] This view of the translation, specifically with reference to the subject of messianism, has been challenged by Joachim Schaper, in his study of the LXX Psalter. Schaper argues that the proponents of this view "tend to overlook the relative autonomy of the Septuagint translation units inasmuch as they ignore the fact that the Hellenistic background and a political and socio-economic situation entirely different from that of Israelite religion were bound to leave their unmistakable imprint on a translation even of sacred scriptures."[29] Few scholars would deny that translators may be influenced by their own culture. We should be wary, however, of attributing cultural significance to features of a translation that can be explained by considerations of translation technique. With this caution in mind, we turn to the texts in the LXX Pentateuch that Horbury has singled out as documents of Jewish messianism.

Genesis 49:10

The first of these is the blessing of Judah in Gen 49:8–12. The blessing begins by lauding Judah's military prowess and comparing him to a lion. It ends with a vision of fertility and prosperity. ("He washes his garments in wine, and his robe in the blood of grapes"). In between come the crucial lines for our topic:

לֹא יָסוּר שֵׁבֶט מִיהוּדָה וּמְחֹקֵק מִבֵּין רַגְלָיו
עַד כִּי יָבֹא שִׁילֹה וְלוֹ יִקְּהַת עַמִּים

The first of these lines is easily translated:

The scepter will not depart from Judah
And the ruler's staff from between his feet.

---

that prevailed in the Septuagint rendering of the Torah" (103). Compare the "Finnish School" mentioned in note 1.

[28] So especially A. Pietersma, "A New Paradigm for Addressing Old Questions: The Relevance of the Interlinear Model for the Study of the Septuagint," in J. Cook, ed., *Bible and Computer. The Stellenbosch AIBI Congress—From Alpha to Byte—Proceedings of the 6th AIBI Congress. 17–21 July, Stellenbosch, 2000* (Leiden: Brill, 2002) 337–64.

[29] Schaper, *Eschatology*, 17.

The second line, however, has a famous crux, in the word שִׁילֹה.[30] This word is variously translated as

"Shiloh," the city in northern Israel,[31]
"tribute for him," construing the letters as two words, שַׁי לֹו,[32]
"that which belongs to him," or "the one to whom it belongs,"[33] taking the word as equivalent to אֲשֶׁר לֹו,
"his ruler," taking it as a defective form of מֹשְׁלֹו,[34]

or even as a personal name, perhaps an abbreviation of Solomon.[35] Each of these translations encounters problems. The only place where Judah (the tribe) is said to come to Shiloh in the biblical text is in Joshua 18, in connection with the allotment of the land. It is not apparent what sense a reference to this incident would make in the context of Genesis 49. "Until he comes to Shiloh" might be taken to refer to the extension of Judah's power to the northern kingdom, but Shiloh was destroyed before the rise of David, and never figures in the stories of the rise of the monarchy.[36] Tribute can scarcely be said to "come," or be the subject of the verb. Shiloh is not otherwise attested as a personal name, until it is explained as the name of the messiah in the Talmud. Such phrases as "that which belongs to him," or "the one to whom it belongs" are obscure, and while obscurity is endemic to predictive texts, this does not help us to understand the meaning of the word. "Ruler" requires emendation.

---

[30] See Lust, "Septuagint and Messianism," 39–41 (= *Messianism and the Septuagint*, 145–6). Compare J.-D. Macchi, *Israël et ses tribus selon Genèse 49* (OBO 171; Fribourg, Suisse: Editions Universitaires/ Göttingen, Vandenhoeck & Ruprecht, 1999) 99–109.

[31] So J. A. Emerton, "Some Difficult Words in Genesis 49," in P. Ackroyd and B. Lindars, ed., *Words and Meanings* (Cambridge: Cambridge University Press, 1968) 83–88.

[32] W. L. Moran, "Gen 49,10 and its use in Ez 21,32," in *Biblica* 39 (1958) 405–25.

[33] G. von Rad, *Genesis. A Commentary* (OTL; Philadelphia: Westminster, 1972) 420, 422; H. Cazelles, "Shiloh, The Customary Laws and the Return of the Ancient Kings," in J. I. Durham and J. R. Porter (ed.), *Proclamation and Presence. Old Testament Essays in Honour of Gwynne Henton Davies* (Macon, GA: Mercer University Press, 1983) 239–51.

[34] So Westermann, *Genesis 3. Genesis 37–50* (BKAT I/3; Neukirchen-Vluyn: Neukirchener Verlag, 1982) 262. Alternatively, this meaning may be derived by taking שִׁילֹה as an Akkadian loan word, šēlu or šīlu (ibid.).

[35] A. Caquot, "La parole sur Juda dans le Testament lyrique de Jacob (Gen 49, 8–12)." in *Semitica* 26 (1976) 5–32.

[36] H. Gunkel, *Genesis übersetzt und erklärt* (HAT 1; Göttingen: Vandenhoeck & Ruprecht, 1901) 435, declares a reference to Shiloh "sinnlos."

There is no consensus in modern scholarship about the meaning of the word.[37]

The final phrase of Gen 49:10 reads: "and the obedience of the peoples is his." The word יקהה is attested only here and in Prov 30:17, and is usually emended in the latter passage. The consensus translation of modern scholarship is based on Akkadian and other Semitic parallels, but we should not be surprised if it presented difficulties to ancient commentators.

The scepter and the staff in the first line of Gen 49:10 are usually taken as symbols of pre-monarchical tribal authority, since מחקק is never used for royal insignia. The "obedience of the peoples," however, surely points to the idealized picture of the Davidic monarchy, such as we find in Psalm 2. Gunkel argued that the passage presupposed an eschatological hope for a ruler who would establish a world kingdom, and noted that messianic prophecies are typically cast in an obscure, allusive, style.[38] (The entire blessing of Jacob is introduced as relating to what will happen באחרית הימים). More plausibly, the passage can be taken as an *ex eventu* prophecy of the rise of the Davidic monarchy. In any case, it is not difficult to see why this passage would lend itself to messianic interpretation in later times.

In fact, the messianic interpretation of this passage is attested already in the Dead Sea Scrolls, in 4Q252, a text that is part paraphrase, part commentary on Genesis. Column 5 of this fragmentary text reads as follows:

> The scepter shall [no]t depart from the tribe of Judah. When Israel rules, [there will not] be cut off one who occupies the throne of David. For 'the staff' is the covenant of the kingship, the [thousa]nds of Israel are 'the standards' until the messiah of righteousness comes, the shoot of David. For to him and his seed has been given the covenant of the kingship of his people for everlasting generations, which he kept . . .[39]

The Qumran text does not cite the text that is being interpreted in the manner of the Pesharim. It seems clear, however, that "until the

---

[37] Westermann, *Genesis 37–50*, 263. Macchi, *Israël et ses tribus*, p. 107, declares that the word is a *hapax legomenon*, and suggests that it means "peace," or "tranquillity."

[38] Gunkel, *Genesis*, 436.

[39] Trans. G. Brooke, "252. 4QCommentary on Genesis A," in G. Brooke et al., ed., *Qumran Cave 4. XVII. Parabiblical Texts, Part 3* (DJD XXII; Oxford: Clarendon, 1996) 205–6.

messiah of righteousness comes" is an interpretation of the phrase
עד יבוא שילה. We do not know exactly how the interpreter construed
the disputed word, but this line of interpretation stands in continuity with the much later Talmudic view that Shiloh was the name of
the messiah. The preserved text of 4Q252 does not indicate how
the word יקהת in the last phrase of the verse was understood.

Essentially the same interpretation is found in Targum Onkelos:

> The ruler shall never depart from the house of Judah, nor the scribe
> from his children's children, for evermore, until the Messiah comes,
> whose is the kingdom, and him shall the nations obey.[40]

In this case the full verse is represented. יקהת is understood as referring to obedience, as it is in modern scholarship, except that it is
rendered by a verb, ישתמעון.

Likewise Targum Pseudo Jonathan:

> Kings and rulers shall not cease from those of the house of Judah,
> nor scribes teaching the Law from his descendants, until the time the
> King Messiah comes. In this case יקהת is understood as "cease," or
> "pine away."[41]

We have already mentioned the Talmudic interpretation of this verse
in Sanhedrin 98b:

> Rab said: The world was created only on David's account. Samuel
> said: On Moses' account; R. Joḥanan said: For the sake of the Messiah.
> What is his [the Messiah's] name?—The School of R. Shila said: His
> name is Shiloh, for it is written, *until Shiloh come*.

The passage goes on to list other views on the name of the Messiah.
We have then a widespread exegetical tradition, attested in the Dead
Sea Scrolls, Targum and Talmud, according to which the phrase
עד יבא שילה is understood to refer to the coming of the messiah.

This tradition, however, is not supported by the majority reading
of the LXX:

οὐκ ἐκλείψει ἄρχων ἐξ Ιουδα
καὶ ἡγούμενος ἐκ τῶν μηρῶν αὐτοῦ

---

[40] M. Aberbach and B. Grossfeld, *Targum Onkelos to Genesis* (New York: Ktav, for
the Center for Judaic Studies, University of Denver, 1982) 284. See also S. H.
Levey, *The Messiah. An Aramaic Interpretation. The Messianic Exegesis of the Targum*
(Cincinnati: Hebrew Union College, 1974) 7.

[41] M. Maher, M.S.C., *Targum Pseudo-Jonathan: Genesis* (The Aramaic Bible 1B;
Collegeville, MN: Liturgical Press, 1992) 159. Compare Levey, *The Messiah*, 9.

ἕως ἂν ἔλθῃ τὰ ἀποκείμενα αὐτῷ
καὶ αὐτὸς προσδοκία ἐθνῶν

Here שילה is not construed as a messianic reference but as equivalent to אשר לו, that which belongs to him. This is not an unreasonable way of making sense of a difficult phrase, but it shows that the translator was either not familiar with, or did not accept, the messianic understanding of שילה.

There is a variant reading, found in several manuscripts, "until he comes to whom it belongs," ᾧ ἀπόκειται. In this case, the accent is shifted to the expectation of an individual, presumably a ruler. (The antecedent is unclear). Justin Martyr argued that this was the correct reading,[42] but he obviously preferred it because it lent itself to a messianic interpretation, whereas the majority reading accepted by Jews did not. The variant reading is at best doubtful evidence for the original Septuagintal understanding of the passage.

A few other details merit consideration here. Jacob's blessing predicts what will happen באחרית הימים. The LXX translation of Gen 49:1 renders this as ἐπ' ἐσχάτων τῶν ἡμερῶν. This phrase is the standard translation of the Hebrew, but it definitely has eschatological overtones. Nonetheless, the eschatological motif is not developed as clearly as it is later in the Targumim.[43]

Gen 49:9 reads in the Hebrew: מטרף בני עלית: from the prey, my son, you have gone up. The LXX renders: ἐκ βλαστοῦ υἱέ μου ἀνέβης: from the shoot, my son you have gone up. The Hebrew root can also mean "leaf," or "foliage." Martin Rösel suggests that this translation was influenced by the imagery of Isa 11:1 (a shoot from the stump of Jesse) or the shoot of David.[44] This is possible, but hardly necessary. In any case, the one that has risen from a shoot here is Judah, not some future ruler.

The rendering of שבט and מחקק as ruler and leader shows that the majority LXX reading understood the passage to refer to a future

---

[42] Justin, *Dial* 120.2. He has the same reading in 1 Apol 32,1; 54,5, but follows the usual reading in Dial 52.2. Lust, "Septuagint and Messianism," 41 (= *Messianism and the Septuagint*, 147.)

[43] M. Rösel, "Die Interpretation von Genesis 49 in der Septuaginta," in *Biblische Notizen* 79 (1995) 54–70 (57). See also his article, "Jakob, Bileam und der Messias. Messianische Erwartungen in poetischen Texten" in M. A. Knibb, ed., *The Septuagint and Messianism* (Leuven: Peeters, 2005).

[44] Rösel, "Die Interpretation von Genesis 49," 61–2.

ruler or rulers. מחקק was evidently read as a participle, and שבט was then given a metaphorical interpretation. (שבט occurs two other times in Genesis 49, in vss. 16 and 28, in the sense of "tribe," and is rendered as "tribe" and "sons.")The future rulers are not designated as kings, but the word ἄρχων, ruler, is sometimes used for נשׂיא, prince, a word that can have messianic associations.[45] Moreover, the fact that the ruler and leader are said to come from Judah's loins suggests dynastic continuity.[46] By the time of the translator, the rulers of Judah were no longer kings, and had not been kings for several centuries. It may be that the translator chose the general terms "ruler" and "leader" to affirm that the promise was nonetheless unbroken. The ruler and leader, however, are not a specific eschatological figure, but rather interim figures, who will not be lacking until "that which is laid up" *for Judah* shall come.[47] The expectation that something is laid up for Judah at the end of days is eschatological, but the neuter plural ἀποκείμενα cannot refer to a messianic king.[48] Rösel suggests tentatively that the reference is to the coming of the kingdom of God, as envisioned in Daniel 2 and 7.[49] But the phrase τὰ ἀποκείμενα αὐτῷ does not suggest a kingdom at all, and whatever is laid up belongs to Judah, and so can hardly be a transcendent kingdom. The phrase is quite vague, and this is probably deliberate on the part of the translator. There is an eschatological destiny in store for Judah, but it is NOT specified as a messianic kingdom.

Horbury, however, advances two other considerations in favor of a messianic interpretation.[50] The verb προσκυνέω is used in 49:8 for the obeisance of Judah's brothers. Horbury compares the use of *proskynesis* in connection with Alexander the Great, and with Christ

---

[45] Gen 25:16; Exod 16:22; 22:28; 34:31; 35:27; Lev 4:22 etc.

[46] Rösel, "Die Interpretation von Genesis 49," 63. This connotation may already be present in the Hebrew. See Macchi, *Israël et ses tribus*, 97.

[47] Contra Rösel, "Die Interpretation von Genesis 49," 64, who takes the "ruler and leader" as the antecedent of αὐτῷ. But the ruler and leader are indefinite, so Judah must be the antecedent. Note that while Judah is addressed in the second person in vss. 8–9, he is referred to in the third person in vs. 10a.

[48] *Pace* L. Monsengwo and L. Pasinya, "Deux textes messianiques dans la Septante: Gn 49, 10 et Ez 21,32," in *Biblica* 61 (1980) 357–76.

[49] Rösel, "Die Interpretation von Genesis 49," 63.

[50] Horbury, *Jewish Messianism*, 129.

in the New Testament. But this verb is a rather literal translation of the Hebrew השתחוה. The translators do not appear to have heightened the adulation beyond what was implied in the Hebrew text. The second consideration is the translation of ולו יקהת עמים as αὐτὸς προσδοκία ἐθνῶν. This phrase has often been understood by modern scholars to imply messianic expectation.[51] Horbury makes much of the αὐτός, comparing Virgil Aeneid 6.791, "this is the man, this is he, whom you have often heard of as promised to you," and the question to Christ in the Gospels: "are you he that is to come, or should we expect (προσδοκῶμεν) another?,"[52] parallels that are admittedly several centuries later than the translation of the Torah. The antecedent of αὐτός is Judah, rather than a later individual ruler.[53] The expectation of the nations, then, is focused on the leadership of Judah, and while we naturally tend to assume that this leadership would be exercised through the Davidic kingship, this assumption was not necessarily obvious in the third century BCE. It is noteworthy that the LXX does not use a word meaning "king," in this passage. This is not a decisive objection against a messianic interpretation. The future ruler is often called a נשיא, prince, in Hebrew texts from the Second Temple period. But the avoidance of explicitly royal language tells against Horbury's view that the LXX was influenced by "the general importance of kingship in the Greek world."[54] There are indeed passages that reflect the Hellenistic ideal of kingship, as when Abraham is called a βασιλεύς by the Hittites, where the Hebrew has נשיא. In contrast, when the Hebrew text uses מלך in the "law of the king" in Deut 17: 4–10, the LXX uses the more general term ἄρχων, ruler, and this is also the case in Deut 33:5. It is difficult, then, to argue that the Greek translation shows a clear or consistent expectation of a messianic king.

We have already noted that the word יקהת, is a rare word in the Hebrew Bible, most probably a hapax legomenon. The Greek translation presupposes a different Hebrew reading: והוא תקות עמים, "and

---

[51] So P. Volz, *Die Eschatologie der jüdischen Gemeinde im neutestamentlichen Zeitalter* (Tübingen: Mohr Siebeck, 1934) 183; J. W. Wevers, *Notes on the Greek Text of Genesis* (SBLSCS 35; Atlanta, Scholars Press, 1993) 826.

[52] Matt 11:3, Luke 7:19. Horbury, *Jewish Messianism*, 129.

[53] Again, contra Rösel, "Die Interpretation von Genesis 49," 64, who takes the "ruler and leader" as the antecedent, and sees a parallel to the Servant of the Lord in Isa 42:6; 49:1–6; 52:15.

[54] Horbury, *Jewish Messianism*, 47.

he is the hope of the nations." We cannot be sure whether the translator found this reading in his Vorlage. It is surely a correction, an
attempt to make sense of a difficult Hebrew text, whether it was
made by the translator or by an earlier scribe. To be sure, this reading would only have made sense on the assumption that some eschatological significance should be attached to the tribe of Judah. The
Hebrew text, on any reading, foretold a glorious future for Judah
and its rulers. The translation affirms the prediction that Judah was
destined to play a leadership role not only for the tribes of Israel,
but also for the nations. It does not, however, tie that role to the
expectation of a messianic king, and it does not seem to be informed
by the exegetical tradition found in the Dead Sea Scrolls and the
later Hebrew and Aramaic traditions.

Balaam's Oracles

In the case of Balaam's oracle, Horbury's argument focuses on three
passages, Num 23:21, Num 24:7 and Num 24:17.

Num 23:21

In Num 23:21 the Hebrew reads:

יהוה אלהיו עמו ותרועת מלך בו, literally,

YHWH his God is with him, and there is a shout of a king in him.

The meaning of the latter phrase is not immediately clear. The
NRSV translates: "acclaimed as a king among them," with reference to YHWH.[55] Baruch Levine, in his commentary, translates "the
battle cry of the king is in his midst."[56] In either case, the king is
clearly YHWH.

The LXX translation reads:

Κύριος ὁ θεὸς αὐτοῦ μετ αὐτοῦ
τὰ ἔνδοξα ἀρχόντων ἐν αὐτῷ.

This differs from the Hebrew in two significant respects:

---

[55] Similarly P. J. Budd, *Numbers* (Word Biblical Commentary 5; Waco: Word,
1984) 21.
[56] B. A. Levine, *Numbers 21–36* (Anchor Bible 4A; New York: Doubleday, 2000)
165.

> Instead of "shout," we read of "glorious things," and instead of "king," in the singular, we have "rulers," in the plural.

It is not immediately clear how these divergences are to be explained. The note in BHS suggests that the translators read ותורעת, from the root ירע, to be apprehensive or quiver with fear, and construed the word as "majesty," a unique rendering.[57] Rösel suggests a cross-reference to the mention of "glorious things" in Exod 34:10, where the context is the covenant with Moses.[58] Most interesting for our inquiry is the change from singular "king" to plural "rulers." Wevers takes this rendering as "an intentional avoidance of the notion of a king in Israel."[59] We could, however, construe the passage as a prediction of the rise of Judah's royal line, rather than as a reference to God as king. The reference is not necessarily eschatological, and it does not focus on an individual messiah. In contrast, Targum Ps. Jonathan paraphrases:

"The Memra of the Lord their God is their help, and the trumpet-call of the King Messiah echoes in their midst."[60]

Num 24:7

Num 24:7 reads:

יזל מים מדליו וזרעו במים רבים
וירם מאגג מלכו ותנשא מלכתו

The NRSV translates:

> Water shall flow from his buckets,
> and his seed shall have abundant water,
> his king shall be higher than Agag,
> and his kingdom shall be exalted.

Levine plausibly translates "boughs" rather than "buckets," although דליות is only attested as a feminine plural (cf. Ezek 17:6,7; 31:7, 9, 12).[61] The imagery is of a tree planted by abundant water, and

---

[57] J. W. Wevers, *Notes on the Greek Text of Numbers* (SBLSCS 46; Atlanta: Scholars Press, 1998) 396.
[58] Rösel, "Jakob, Bileam und der Messias."
[59] Wevers, *Notes on the Greek Text of Numbers*, 396.
[60] Levey, *The Messiah*, 19.
[61] So also J. Lust, "The Greek Version of Balaam's Third and Fourth Oracles.

accordingly enjoying luxurious growth. Agag is the Amalekite king killed by Samuel in 1 Sam 15.[62]

The Greek renders this verse as follows:

ἐξελεύσεται ἄνθρωπος ἐκ τοῦ σπέρματος αὐτοῦ
καὶ κυριεύσει ἐθνῶν πολλῶν
καὶ ὑψθήσεται ἢ Γωγ βασιλεία αὐτοῦ
καὶ αὐχιξηθήσεται ἡ βασιλεία αὐτοῦ.

As Johan Lust has remarked, this translation is remarkable. Lust provides an ingenious explanation for the first part of the verse.[63] The translator will have read יזל as the Aramaic verb אזל, to go, and then supplied ἄνθρωπος as the subject. The first occurrence of מים is overlooked, or perhaps dismissed as a mistake, and the translator skips to the mem before דליו.[64] Lust suggests that he understood the "boughs" as the progeny of Israel, and read זרע, seed, as זרוע, arm or power, hence "he will rule." This explanation partially follows that proposed by Geza Vermes.[65] Vermes proposes a more complex exegetical tradition. In his view the phrase יזל מים recalled יזלו צדק in Isa 45:8, where righteousness is symbolically expressed as water, as in Amos 5:24. Further, צדק is associated with the messiah in Jer 23:5 and 33:15 (צמח צדקה). "In short, water = righteousness = Messiah."[66] This exegetical tradition would also underlie the messianic interpretation in the Targums: "their king shall arise from among them, and their deliverer shall be of them and with them."[67] The Targums, however, do not give a close exegesis of the verse,

---

The ἄνθρωπος in Num 24:7 and 17. Messianism and Lexicography," in L. Greenspoon and O. Munnich (eds.) *VIII Congress of the International Organization for Septuagint and Cognate Studies* (SBSSCS 41; Atlanta: Scholars Press, 1992) 235, reprinted in Lust, *Messianism and the Septuagint*, 69–86 (71).

[62] Lust, ibid., suggests that the original reading may have been הגנ, "(higher than) the roof."

[63] J. Lust, "Septuagint and Messianism," 43, and, in more detail, "The Greek Version of Balaam's Third and Fourth Oracles," 236–8 (= *Messianism and the Septuagint*, 70–74).

[64] A. Van Der Kooij, "Perspectives on the Study of the Septuagint. Who Are The Translators?" in F. García Martínez and E. Noort, ed., *Perspectives in the Study of the Old Testament and Early Judaism. A Symposium in Honour of Adam S. van der Woude on the Occasion of his 70th Birthday* (Leiden: Brill, 2000) 214–29 (224), followed by Rösel, "Jakob, Bileam und der Messias," suggests that מים was understood as "seed" and hence translated as "man."

[65] G. Vermes, *Scripture and Tradition in Judaism* (2nd ed., Leiden: Brill, 1972) 159–60.

[66] Vermes, *Scripture and Tradition*, 160.

[67] Vermes, *Scripture and Tradition*, 159, Levey, *The Messiah*, 20.

and may have arrived at the messianic interpretation simply by inference from the scepter. Lust is probably right to reject Vermes's complex explanation.[68]

Again, the argument that זרע was read as זרוע, arm, and rendered, "will rule," does not seem compelling. It seems easier to suppose that the LXX translator took זרע with the first part of the
verse, hence ἐκ τοῦ σπέρματος αὐτοῦ. מים רבים was taken as a metaphorical expression for many nations, and "will rule" was supplied to fill
out the sense.[69] Either the translator was working from a defective
manuscript, from which some of the Hebrew words (מים מדליו) were
missing, or, more plausibly, he was puzzled by the verse and simplified
it by dropping some words. Lust concludes that "the Greek "man"
does not receive any emphasis. It is only the explicit expression of
an implicit subject in the Hebrew."[70]

The issue is complicated, however, by a few considerations. First,
as Lust himself admits, the translation of Agag as Gog, the mythical adversary in Ezekiel 39, "turns the oracle as a whole into a
prophecy about the final days."[71] This is true even if we suppose
that the change was already made in the Hebrew *Vorlage*. Further,
the man is now the natural antecedent of "his kingdom," in the
third line of the verse. This reading is itself a variant from the
Hebrew: it implies a reading of מלכתו rather than the MT מלכו,
"his king." Wevers interprets this translation as intentional avoidance
of a reference to any king other than the Lord.[72] Nonetheless, a
figure who has a kingdom can reasonably be assumed to be a king.

Philo evokes the "man" of Balaam's oracle in his tractate "On
Rewards and Punishments":

> For 'there shall come forth a man,' says the oracle, and leading his
> host to war he will subdue great and populous nations, because God
> has sent to his aid the reinforcement which befits the godly.
>
> (*Praem* 95).[73]

---

[68] Lust, "The Greek Version of Balaam's Oracles," 236 (= *Messianism and the Septuagint*, 72).

[69] Pseudo-Jonathan, cited by Vermes, *Scripture and Tradition*, 160, reads "the seed of the sons of Jacob will rule." In that case, at least, זרע is not read as זרוע.

[70] Lust, "Septuagint and Messianism," 43 (= *Messianism and the Septuagint*, p. 148).

[71] Ibid. (*Messianism and the Septuagint*, 149).

[72] Wevers, *Notes on the Greek Text of Numbers*, 405.

[73] Compare *Mos* 1.290, where the emphasis is on the future power of the people rather than on the individual "man."

The eschatological interpretation of this passage in Philo is remarkable, as Philo otherwise shows very little messianic or eschatological expectation.[74] Lust infers that "this makes it *a priori* probable that the 'man' envisaged in it has no royal messianic connections.[75] But the man functions in the same way that the messiah functions in other texts of the time. And finally the "man" reappears in Num 24:17, where the Hebrew text has שבט.

Num 24:17

The assessment of Num 24:7 is closely bound up with the interpretation of Num 24:17. This is the famous prophecy of the scepter and the star:

דרך כובב מיעקב וקם שבט מישראל:

a star shall come out of Jacob, and a scepter shall rise out of Israel.

The Greek reads:

ἀνατελεῖ ἄστρον ἐξ Ιακωβ
καὶ ἀναστήσεται ἄνθρωπος ἐξ Ισραηλ

The translation of שבט by ἄνθρωπος is a clear case of interpretation; it cannot be explained as rote translation. The significance of the interpretation is disputed. Lust notes correctly that the Hebrew text uses the star and scepter as symbols to foretell the rise of the monarchy in Israel. (The prophecy was probably written after the fact). He continues: "The Septuagint replaces the sceptre-symbol by the vague term ἄνθρωπος. This appears to do away with the royal character of the expected figure."[76] Wevers, similarly, claims that "by substituting ἄνθρωπος for sceptre, Num avoids the notion that the person is a royal figure, a king."[77] Against this, it must be granted that the "man" in Num 24:7 is explicitly said to have a kingdom, and so the royal character is not incompatible with the use of

---

[74] R. D. Hecht, "Philo and Messiah," in Neusner, Green and Frerichs, ed., *Judaisms and their Messiahs*, 139–68; P. Borgen, "There Shall Come Forth a Man, Reflections on Messianic Ideas in Philo," in Charlesworth, ed., *The Messiah*, 341–61.

[75] Lust, "The Greek Version of Balaam's Oracles," 246 (= *Messianism and the Septuagint*, 81).

[76] "The Greek Version of Balaam's Oracles," 241 (= *Messianism and the Septuagint*, 76).

[77] Wevers, *Notes on the Greek Text of Numbers*, 413.

ἄνθρωπος. Nonetheless, it is noteworthy that the translators refrained from calling the individual in question a king.

The messianic interpretation of Num 24:17 around the turn of the era is well attested. Perhaps the most famous messianic interpretation of this passage is in the legend of Akiba's recognition of Bar Kochba: "Rabbi Akiba interpreted, 'A star has come forth out of Jacob' as '[Kosiba] has come forth out of Jacob.' When Rabbi Akiba saw Bar Kosiba he said: 'This is the King Messiah.'"[78] In CD 7:19, the scepter is interpreted as the Prince of the Congregation, who is elsewhere identified with the Branch of David. The verse is cited without interpretation in the War Scroll (1QM 11:5–7) and in the Testimonia, and is likely to have messianic connotations in both contexts. Another possible allusion is found in the blessing of the prince of the congregation in 1QSb 5:27, which says "for God has raised you as a scepter." In the Testament of Judah 24:1–6 we read:

> And after this a star will come forth for you out of Jacob in peace, and a man will rise from among my descendants like the sun of righteousness . . . then will the scepter of my kingdom shine forth, and from your root will come a stem. And from it will spring a staff of righteousness for the Gentiles, to judge and to save all that invoke the Lord.

The Targumim also interpret the verse with reference to the messiah: "a king shall arise out of Jacob, and be anointed messiah out of Israel."[79] In view of this widespread interpretation, no great significance can be attached to the lack of specific Davidic attributes in LXX Numbers.[80] We are dealing, after all, with a translation, which enjoys only limited freedom to depart from the source text.

While the prevalence of the messianic interpretation of this verse might seem to argue in favor of a messianic sense in the LXX, it is not quite correct to speak of a common exegetical tradition. Of the passages we have cited, only the Testament of Judah designates the messianic figure as a "man," and it is probably influenced by the LXX. (Among the Church Fathers, Justin and Irenaeus read ἡγούμενος and *dux*, "leader," instead of the LXX's ἄνθρωπος).[81] In

---

[78] Ta'anith 68d.
[79] So Targum Onkelos. There are minor variations in Ps. Jonathan and the Fragmentary Targum. See Levey, *The Messiah*, 21–25.
[80] *Pace* Rösel, "Jakob, Bileam und der Messias."
[81] Lust, "The Greek Version of Balaam's Oracles," 241 (= *Messianism and the*

other passages where "man" may have a messianic meaning, such as Zech 6:12, the LXX uses ἀνήρ rather than ἄνθρωπος.[82] While words for "man" are sometimes used to refer to messianic figures around the turn of the era,[83] ἄνθρωπος is certainly not a technical term for "messiah" in the LXX.[84] Again in Num 24:7, the Targums identify Agag as the king of Amalek, rather than as Gog, the eschatological enemy: "He shall be stronger than Saul, who showed mercy to Agag king of Amalek, and the kingdom of the King Messiah shall be exalted.[85] We do not find close correspondence in detail between the LXX and the Hebrew and Aramaic interpretations of Balaam's oracle.[86]

I am skeptical, then, as to whether any common exegetical tradition underlies the LXX translation of Balaam's oracle, and the later Hebrew and Aramaic interpretations. Nonetheless, it does seem to me that the Greek of this passage enhances the messianic implications of the Hebrew. The enhancement is qualified. The translator does not use such words as "king," or "anointed." But he does take the passage to refer to a future savior figure, who has a kingdom.[87] Whether, or how far this enhancement reflects live messianic expectation at the time of the translation, either in Judea or in the Diaspora, is another question.

Septuagint, 77). Justin *Dial* 106.4; *1 Apol* 32.12; Irenaeus, *Demonstr* 58. Lust argues that Justin was using a revised Greek text.

[82] Lust, "The Greek Version of Balaam's Oracles," 249 (= *Messianism and the Septuagint*, 84).

[83] See especially Horbury, "The Messianic Associations of 'The Son of Man,'" in idem, *Messianism among the Jews and Christians*, 125–55 (144–51). While Horbury gives a maximalist account of the evidence, some of his examples are clearly valid, e.g. *Sib Or* 5:414.

[84] Lust, "The Greek Version of Balaam's Oracles," 250 (= *Messianism and the Septuagint*, 85): "In the LXX in general, ἄνθρωπος is a more neutral term without messianic connotations."

[85] Vermes, *Scripture and Tradition*, 161, citing the Fragmentary Targum and Neofiti. Compare Lust, "The Greek Version of Balaam's Oracles," 248 (= *Messianism and the Septuagint*, 82).

[86] The use of ἐξελεύσεται in Isa 11:1 may be a deliberate echo of Num 24:7, but this does not require that the translator of Numbers was acquainted with a tradition of messianic interpretation.

[87] Since the reference is to "his kingdom," the scenario envisioned is closer to classical messianism than to the concept of the eschatological kingdom in Daniel (contra Rösel, "Jakob, Bileam und der Messias"). I understand the analogy between LXX Numbers and 4Q246 differently from Rösel, since in my view the "Son of God" figure in the latter text should be interpreted as the messiah. See Collins, *The Scepter and the Star*, 154–72.

Deut 33:5

The third passage adduced by Horbury, the blessing of Moses in
Deut 33:5, is the weakest of the three. The key phrase in Hebrew reads:

ויהי בישדון מלך

There arose a king in Jeshurun.

The passage comes at the end of a description of the theophany of
Yahweh as the Divine Warrior, and so the king in question is usually assumed to be the Lord himself, who reigns in Israel (Jeshurun)
through the law given by Moses.[88] Targum Pseudo-Jonathan and the
midrash on Psalms (on Psalm 1:1) identify the king as Moses.[89] The
Greek renders the waw consecutive of the Hebrew (ויהי) as a future:

Καὶ ἔσται ἐν τῷ ἠγαπημένῳ ἄρχων

and there shall be a ruler in the beloved.

Horbury comments: "The LXX interpretation thus makes Moses
here predict either the rule of God himself (the Greek can be rendered 'and he shall be ruler . . .') or an emperor-like ruler in Israel,
a figure at the centre of the unity of Israel and the nations."[90] He
finds some support for this messianic interpretation in Targum Neofiti
and in the Fragmentary Targum, but his main argument is that "the
latter (i. e. the messianic) interpretation seems preferable, for it accords
with the emphasis laid in Gen. 49:11 and in Num 23:21 LXX on
the future presence of rulers in Israel."[91] At this point, the reasoning is circular: The presence of messianic expectation in the Pentateuch is supported by only three passages, and the third passage is
so interpreted because it would then accord with the other two.
Moreover, as we have seen, the messianic interpretation of Gen 49:11
LXX is implausible, and even the messianic interpretation of the
verses in Numbers is somewhat ambivalent. It is possible to read the
Greek of Deut 33:5 as predicting a future human ruler, but that
interpretation is by no means certain, and can lend no support to

---

[88] See the classic commentary of S. R. Driver, *Deuteronomy* (ICC; New York,
Scribners, 1909) 394. Also R. D. Nelson, *Deuteronomy* (OTL; Louisville, Westminster
John Knox, 2002) 389, who admits that "emerging as king 'in Jeshurun' seems like
an odd thing to say of universal, divine kingship."

[89] Horbury, *Jewish Messianism*, 50.

[90] Ibid., 50–51.

[91] Ibid., 51.

the disputed thesis about messianism in the LXX Pentateuch. It is also noteworthy that here again the Greek translators chose not to use the word 'king,' Βασιλεύς, despite the Hebrew מלך.

Messianism in the Hellenistic Diaspora

The argument for the view that the translators introduced new meanings into the biblical text rests in part on the reasonable assumption that they could not avoid reflecting the beliefs and ideas of their time. But there is in fact no evidence that messianic expectation was part of the cultural milieu of Ptolemaic Egypt when the Torah was translated. We have a substantial corpus of Jewish literature written in Greek, that can be attributed to Ptolemaic Egypt.[92] There is only one passage in this corpus that has been thought by scholars to express the hope for a Jewish messiah. This is in Sib Or 3:252–3:

> And then God will send a king from the sun
> who will stop the entire earth from evil war.[93]

The imagery of a king from the sun, however, is steeped in Egyptian tradition, and elsewhere in this book the sibyl associates the turning point of history with "the seventh reign, when a king of Egypt, who will be of the Greeks by race, will rule" (Sib Or 3:193, compare 318, 608). I have argued at length elsewhere that the "king from the sun" is not a Jewish messiah, but precisely this "seventh king" from the Ptolemaic line (probably either Ptolemy Philometor or his son and anticipated successor).[94] In fact, the hope of Jews in the Diaspora was typically focused on a benevolent Gentile ruler rather than on a Jewish messiah, as can be seen in the Diaspora stories of Esther, Daniel 1–6 and 3 Maccabees. Nowhere else in the Jewish literature written in Greek in the Ptolemaic era (apart from the Greek translation of the Bible) is there even a possible reference to a messiah.

---

[92] For a review, see J. J. Collins, *Between Athens and Jerusalem* (revised edition; Grand Rapids, Eerdmans, 2000).

[93] Trans. J. J. Collins, "The Sibylline Oracles," in J. H. Charlesworth, *The Old Testament Pseudepigrapha* (2 vols.; New York, Doubleday, 1983–1985) 376.

[94] See most recently J. J. Collins, "The Third Sibyl Revisited," in E. Chazon and D. Satran, ed., *Things Revealed: Studies in Early Jewish and Christian Literature in Honor of Michael E. Stone* (JSJSup 89; Leiden, Brill, 2004) 3–19 (reprinted in this volume). Also *Between Athens and Jerusalem*, 92–95.

Even in the early Roman era, Philo is exceptional in ascribing importance to an eschatological "man," and as we have seen, that reference is unique in the corpus of Philo's writings. Only after the failure of the first Jewish revolt against Rome and the deterioration of relations between Jew and Gentile in Egypt, do we find a messianic movement in the Diaspora, and the expression of messianic expectations in the fifth book of the Sibylline Oracles, which dates to the early second century of the common era.[95] Insofar as the translators of the Pentateuch in the third century BCE reflected the beliefs and aspirations of their time, we should not expect to find much by way of messianic expectation in their work.

Conclusion

Of the passages adduced by Horbury as evidence of Messianism in the LXX translation of the Pentateuch, the blessing of Jacob affirms a glorious future for Judah but fails conspicuously to associate that future with an individual ruler, while the blessing of Moses does not speak unambiguously about a human ruler at all. Only Balaam's oracle enhances the role of an eschatological "man" in the Greek translation. This man has a kingdom, and may reasonably be understood as a messiah. Even in this case, however, the translators did not refer to this man as a king, and they never speak of an anointed one who is to come.

These findings are consistent with what we know of Second Temple Judaism in general, prior to the period represented by the Dead Sea Scrolls. Jews in this period were familiar with the scriptural promises to the line of David, found in such passages as 2 Samuel 7 and Isaiah 11. These promises were still affirmed in some sense, but they played only a marginal role in the lives of Jews. One or two possible messianic allusions in all of the Pentateuch is a fair representation of this marginality. Messianic hope was even more marginal in the Greek speaking Diaspora than it was in the land of Israel. There would be a revival of messianism in Judea in the last century before the turn of the era, in reaction to the non-Davidic kingship of the Hasmoneans and then to Roman rule. In the Diaspora, messianism

---

[95] Collins, *Between Athens and Jerusalem*, 140–50.

would only become attractive after relations with the Gentile rulers had been undermined by pogroms in Alexandria, the failure of the first Jewish revolt and the general deterioration of the situation of the Jews in Egypt in the late first and early second centuries of the common era.

CHAPTER FIVE

THE THIRD SIBYL REVISITED

The third book of *Sibylline Oracles*, in the standard collection, runs to 829 verses, and is one of the longer texts that can be attributed to Hellenistic Judaism outside of Philo's writings. The attention it has received in recent scholarship is hardly proportional to its length. To my knowledge, the recent dissertation of Rieuwerd Buitenwerf[1] is the first full monograph devoted to this text since that of Valentin Nikiprowetzky, more than thirty years ago.[2] There have, of course been several other treatments in the intervening years, in connection with other Sibylline books or with Hellenistic Jewish literature.[3] Nonetheless, the Sibyl has not been very prominent in recent scholarship, and has evidently fallen from the lofty perch that won her a place on the ceiling of the Sistine Chapel.

Ironically, when the Sibyl was at the height of her fame in the Middle Ages, the books attributed to her were known only from scattered quotations. One may fairly say that the recovery and subsequent analysis of these books, beginning in the mid-sixteenth century, went hand in hand with the decline of her reputation. Medieval Christianity had venerated her as a pagan prophetess. Critical scholarship concluded that her oracles were Jewish or Christian forgeries, and often tedious besides.[4]

---

[1] R. Buitenwerf, *Book III of the Sibylline Oracles and its Social Setting, With an Introduction, Translation and Commentary* (SVTP 17; Leiden: Brill, 2003).

[2] V. Nikiprowetzky, *La Troisième Sibylle* (Études juives 9; Paris: Mouton, 1970).

[3] J. J. Collins, *The Sibylline Oracles of Egyptian Judaism* (SBLDS 13; Missoula, Mont.: Scholars Press, 1974); "The Sibylline Oracles," in *OTP*, 1:354–80; *Between Athens and Jerusalem: Jewish Identity in the Hellenistic Diaspora* (2d ed.; Grand Rapids: Eerdmans, 2000) 83–97, 160–65; M. Goodman, "The Sibylline Oracles," in E. Schürer, *The History of the Jewish People in the Age of Jesus Christ (175 BC–AD 135)* (3 vols.; rev. ed.; Edinburgh: T & T Clark, 1987) III.1:618–53; J.M.G. Barclay, *Jews in the Mediterranean Diaspora: From Alexander to Trajan (323 BCE–117 CE)* (Edinburgh: T & T Clark, 1996) 216–28; E. S. Gruen, *Heritage and Hellenism: The Reinvention of Jewish Tradition* (Berkeley: University of California Press, 1998) 269–91; H. Merkel, *Die Sibyllinen* (JSHRZ 5.8; Gütersloh: Mohn, 1998) 1057–1080; J.-D. Gauger, *Sibyllinische Weissagungen* (Darmstadt: Wissenschaftliche Buchgesellschaft, 1998).

[4] Buitenwerf, *Book III*, 5–64, provides an excellent history of research.

Among the Sibylline books of the standard collection, Book Three has received more attention than any other, partly because it has been deemed to be the oldest book in the collection. In this case, there has been a significant degree of consensus on the major critical issues regarding its literary character and the time and place of its composition. This consensus was worked out in the nineteenth century and solidified above all in the work of Johannes Geffcken at the beginning of the twentieth.[5] While there have been many variations in detail, the great majority of commentators have held that it is a composite work, but that it is possible to identify an original core, composed in Egypt in the middle of the second century BCE. Nikiprowetzky challenged this consensus, by claiming that the book was a unity, composed in the first century BCE in the time of Cleopatra.[6] His assertion did not win much acceptance. Recently, however, the identification of a core composition from the second century BCE has been challenged vigorously by Erich Gruen.[7] Buitenwerf, in his dissertation, goes farther, rejecting not only the core composition and second century date, but also the Egyptian provenance.[8]

Revisionism is the life-blood of scholarship, and these new proposals have the advantage of revitalizing the discussion of a neglected pseudepigraphon. In my opinion, however, the challenges are not well founded, and the consensus that prevailed for most of the last century still provides the most plausible context for the study of this Sibylline book.

The Composition of the Book

The oldest manuscripts of the Sibylline Oracles date from the fourteenth and fifteenth centuries CE. It is generally acknowledged that the first 92 verses of the third book originally constituted the end of a different book, the second, while *Sib. Or.* Fragments i and iii were

---

[5] J. Geffcken, *Komposition und Entstehungszeit der Oracula Sibyllina* (TUGAL n.F. 8.1; Leipzig: Hinrichs, 1902) 1–17. Geffcken also produced the standard edition of the *Sibylline Oracles, Die Oracula Sibyllina* (GCS 8; Leipzig: Hinrichs, 1902).

[6] Nikiprowetzky, *La troisième Sibylle*, 206–17.

[7] Gruen, *Heritage and Hellenism*, 269–79.

[8] Buitenwerf, *Book III*, 124–34.

probably part of the now missing beginning of Book Three.[9] Lactantius
(ca. 250–317 CE) cites several passages from these fragments and
from Book Three, and attributes them to the Erythrean Sibyl, "since
she inserted her true name into the book and foretold that she would
be called the 'Erythrean' although she was of Babylonian descent."[10]
Passages cited, in addition to those from the fragments, are *Sib. Or.*
3:228–29, 618, 619–623, 741–43, 763–66, 775, 788–92 and 815–18.
It would seem then that Lactantius knew the book in substantially
its present shape, but it should be noted that lengthy sections of the
book are not attested. Clement of Alexandria (ca. 150–215 CE) cites
Sib. Or. 3:586–88 and 590–94. Theophilus of Antioch (second century) cites *Sib. Or.* 3:97–103 and 105. The passage about the tower
of Babylon, in *Sib. Or.* 3:97–107, was cited by Alexander Polyhistor,
who compiled his work in the period between 80 and 40 BCE.[11]

On the basis of these attestations, Buitenwerf claims that "*Sib. Or.*
III must have existed before 40 BCE," and that it can be concluded
"that *Sib. Or.* III was written by a Jew sometime between 80 and
40 BCE."[12] Both conclusions are blatant *non-sequiturs*. Only a small
passage (*Sib. Or.* 3:97–107) is attested before the second century of
the Common Era. We may reasonably infer that this passage was
part of a larger Sibylline book, and even that that book was a form
of what we now know as Book Three, but not that the book already
existed in its present form. Buitenwerf offers no argument whatever
for the *terminus a quo*. Presumably he relies on the fact that some
passages in *Sibylline Oracles* 3 are universally acknowledged to date
from the first century BCE. But if Polyhistor knew the work, or part
of it, between 80 and 30 BCE we should expect that it was composed some time earlier than that. Buitenwerf's conclusion assumes
that *Sibylline Oracles* 3 was composed *ab initio* as a literary unity, by
an author who had an integral view of the whole. He grants that
this author drew on earlier sources but argues that "in establishing
the meaning of the author's final text, however, it is methodologi-
cally unwarranted to separate passages which can be seen to be
based on earlier sources from other passages, since from the author's

[9] Ibid., 65–91.
[10] Lactantius, *Divinae Institutiones* I.6.13–14. Cf. *Sib. Or.* 3:813–14.
[11] J. Strugnell, "General Introduction, with a Note on Alexander Polyhistor,"
OTP, 2:777–79.
[12] Buitenwerf, *Book III*, 130.

point of view all of these passages formed an integral part of the literary unity he was creating."[13] Buitenwerf's demonstration of the supposed literary unity, however, is an outline of "structure" which is little more than a table of contents.[14] He offers no explanation of the supposed coherence of the book.

Buitenwerf's claim of literary coherence in *Sibylline Oracles* 3 contrasts sharply with other recent assessments of the book. According to Martin Goodman in Schürer's revised *History of the Jewish People in the Age of Jesus Christ*, "it is unfortunately not the case that each Book formed an original whole; individual Books also in part comprised an arbitrary number of individual passages. . . . Obviously, much was at first in circulation as isolated pieces and the collection in which they subsequently found a place is fortuitous."[15] According to Erich Gruen, "it seems clear that the third Book of the *Sibylline Oracles* constitutes a conglomerate, a gathering of various prophecies that stem from different periods ranging from the second century BCE through the early Roman Empire."[16] While these judgments may be extreme, they raise the serious possibility that the book may be a collection of oracles, analogous to Biblical prophetic books such as Isaiah or Jeremiah, rather than the unified composition of a literary author. Pagan Sibylline oracles in antiquity were very brief, often consisting of a verse or two.[17] These oracles were distributed by *chrēsmologoi*, who adapted them constantly to changing historical circumstances. If these pagan oracles served at all as a model for the Jewish sibyllist, we should hardly expect a coherent work of more than 800 verses. Buitenwerf's assumption of literary coherence is implausible, and in any case cannot be taken as a default position.

The literary structure discerned by Buitenwerf divides the book into 6 sections. (Verses 1–92 are left out of account as constituting the end of a different book). The first section is identified with Fragment i. The second consists of Fragment iii and *Sib. Or.* 3:93–161, although the reason for grouping this material together is not appar-

---

[13] Ibid., 124–25.

[14] Ibid., 139–43.

[15] Goodman, "Sibylline Oracles," 631.

[16] Gruen, *Heritage and Hellenism*, 272. The fluidity of the Sibylline collection is also emphasized by D. S. Potter, "Sibyls in the Greek and Roman World," *Journal of Roman Archaeology* 3 (1990) 471–83.

[17] On the nature of pagan Sibylline oracles see H. W. Parke, *Sibyls and Sibylline Prophecy in Classical Antiquity* (ed. B. C. McGing; London: Routledge, 1988) 1–22.

ent. The remaining sections are marked by introductory formulae in which the Sibyl exclaims that God inspires her to prophesy. These formulae are found in 3:162–65; 3:196–98; 3:295–300 and 3:489–91. If these are taken to mark the major sections of the book, the last section (489–829) is disproportionately long. Buitenwerf distinguishes four admonitions within it, in 545–623, 624–731, 732–761 and 762–808. Each of these admonitions is introduced by direct address. Whether these admonitory addresses necessarily indicate new sub-sections might be disputed, but this division of the book is not unreasonable.

Even a cursory reading of Buitenwerf's structure shows that his section 5 (3:295–488) consists of a different kind of material from the other sections. It is essentially a concatenation of very brief pronouncements of doom against a wide range of peoples and places, many of them in Asia. The only reference to Jewish history in this section is in an oracle against Babylon at the beginning. There is also a biblical allusion in the mention of Gog and Magog in verse 319. After this, however, there is no mention of anything Jewish for 170 verses. The only passage in this section that contains any moral admonition is the passionate oracle against Rome in 350–380, and there is no mention of Jews or Judea in that passage. All of this contrasts sharply with the other sections. The first section and part of the second in Buitenwerf's analysis are drawn from the Sibylline fragments, and the attribution of this material to Book Three is uncertain. In any case it is different in kind from the rest of the book. Section 3 (162–195) begins with Solomon and ends with a promise of Jewish rule. Section 4 is largely taken up with praise of the Jews and ends with mention of the restoration under the Persians. Section 6 is dominated by appeals to the Greeks to convert, and predictions of the future exaltation of the Jews. Section 2 (vv. 93–161) is somewhat anomalous, as it contains a lengthy euhemeristic account of Greek mythology, but it also contains a retelling of the Flood (of which only the end survives) and the tower of Babel. Moreover, the following section, which consists of only 33 verses, complements Section 2 by continuing the discourse on world kingdoms. The long Section 5 stands out because of its lack of engagement with Jewish themes, apart from the opening verses, and for the rather disjointed juxtaposition of very brief oracles of destruction.

A few more points should be noted about Section 5. While it exhibits a consistent theme of judgment and destruction, it is episodic rather than continuous. Two-line oracles of destruction against specific places could be added or removed without changing the character of the whole. The oracle against Rome in vv. 350–380 stands out because of its length and coherence, as well as its passion. Most of this section could have been written by a Gentile as easily as by a Jew. Verses 400 to 488 have sometimes been attributed to the Erythrean Sibyl, who is said to have sung of the Trojan war (cf. 3: 414–16) and to have said that Homer would write falsehoods (cf. 3: 419).[18] It should be noted that all the undisputed references to the first century BCE in *Sib. Or.* 3:93–829 fall in Section 5. Likewise, the great bulk of the references to Asian places are found in this section.

There is good reason, then, to doubt whether all of this section comes from the same hand as the rest of the book. The beginning of the section is clearly Jewish, but the typical themes of the rest of the book are displaced here by oracles that are quite similar to pagan Sibylline (and other) oracles. Of course it is possible, and even plausible, that a Jewish sibyllist incorporated some pagan material in his book to help establish Sibylline credentials.[19] We must also, however, reckon with the possibility that some of this material was added secondarily by scribes who thought it was appropriate to a book of Sibylline oracles. These scribes would not have been authors in Buitenwerf's sense. They did not necessarily reconceive the book as a whole, but rather regarded it as an anthology of oracles to which other passages might be added.

The Question of Dating and the Seventh King

The primary argument for a second century date for a core of *Sibylline Oracles* 3 has always rested on three references to the seventh king of Egypt, which are usually thought to require a date in the middle of that century. The reference is obviously to a Ptolemaic king, and, since it does not speak of restoration, it implies tht the line is still extant. Ptolemaic kings were not known usually by numeral in antiquity, and so there is more than one possible identification for

---

[18] Varro in Lactantius, *Div Inst* 1.6; Pausanias 10.2.2. See Collins, *The Sibylline Oracles*, 27.

[19] J. J. Collins, "The Jewish Transformation of Sibylline Oracles," in idem, *Seers, Sibyls and Sages in Hellenistic-Roman Judaism* (Leiden: Brill, 1997) 189.

the seventh king of the line. (Note, however, that in the sixth fragment of Demetrius the Chronographer there is a reference to "Ptolemy
the Fourth" [Clement, *Strom* 1.21.141.1–2]. It is uncertain whether the
reference derives from Demetrius or from Clement). If Alexander
the Great is counted as a king of Egypt, then Ptolemy VI Philometor
was the seventh Ptolemy. His son, Ptolemy Neos Philopator, ruled
briefly with his father and was promptly liquidated after his death.
His rule may have been too brief to be counted. Ptolemy VIII
Euergetes (Physcon) could also arguably be the seventh king, since
he had ruled jointly with his brother Philometor, and briefly alone,
before the accession of Neos Philopator. But there is no reason to
regard the references in the Sibylline Oracles as *ex eventu* prophecy.
The events associated with the reign of the seventh king are clearly
in the future from the perspective of the author. Accordingly, the
seventh king may have been one who was yet to come. The oracles might, for example, have been written during the reign of
Philometor, in hopeful anticipation of a transformation to come in
the reign of his successor, Neos Philopator, or later in his own reign.
But, if the adjective "seventh" is granted numerical significance at
all, these passages could hardly have been composed later than the
reign of Ptolemy Physcon. Once oracles are in circulation they are
copied and reinterpreted even if their literal meaning is no longer
credible.[20] The Sibylline Oracles were copied long after the end of
the Ptolemaic line, despite the obvious non-fulfillment of the oracles.
But we must assume that the oracular predictions were possible in
principle at the time of their composition. Since Philometor was
famously favorable to the Jews, and Physcon was his enemy, a date
during the reign of Philometor seems most likely, although the time
of Physcon is not impossible either.

Erich Gruen, however, has argued that the adjective "seventh"
should not be accorded any numerical significance, and in this he
has been followed (uncritically) by Buitenwerf.[21] Gruen notes that

---

[20] The reinterpretation of the 70 years of Jeremiah's prophecy in Daniel 9 is a
famous example, but there are numerous others in the biblical corpus. See M. Fish-
bane, *Biblical Interpretation in Ancient Israel* (Oxford: Clarendon, 1985) 458–99.

[21] Gruen, *Heritage and Hellenism*, 272–77; similarly his essay, "Jews, Greeks and
Romans in the Third Sibylline Oracle," in M. Goodman, ed., *Jews in a Graeco-
Roman World* (Oxford: Clarendon, 1998) 15–36. See Buitenwerf, *Book III*, 126–130.
Buitenwerf claims the support of Gauger, *Sibyllinische Weissagungen*, 440–51, but while
the latter favors a date around 31 BCE for the redaction of Book Three he allows
that the book may contain oracles from the second century BCE.

"the number seven possessed high symbolic import for the Jews," which indeed it did.[22] He then notes that it recurs in apocalyptic literature and concludes that "the number must be understood as carrying mystical import, an abstract and spiritual sense, not the denotation of royal tenure."[23] Buitenwerf adds that, "the number seven merely indicates that the moment of the turn in history has already been determined. The author has the Sibyl prophesy in a veiled manner that at a certain predetermined moment, God will intervene in history. In other Jewish and Christian prophetic and apocalyptical writings, numbers are used in a similar way."[24]

It is true that the Sibyl prophesies in a veiled manner, as prophets and oracles typically do. If the numeral were part of the royal title, it would have been too specific for her purpose. But numbers in apocalyptic and prophetic writings are not used for "carrying mystical import" in "an abstract and spiritual sense," even though they may seem obscure to people unfamiliar with the genre.

Numbers are used in three quite distinct ways: to calculate the time of a future event, to divide history into periods, and to project a period that is entirely future. The last category, naturally, has no historical coordinates. The thousand-year reign in the Book of Revelation is a case in point. The reference in *Sib. Or.* 3:728 to "seven lengths of annually recurring times" is entirely future, and therefore indefinite.[25] The division of history into periods (four kingdoms, seven weeks of years etc.) is imprecise, but the numbers are not abstract or insignificant. When Daniel speaks of four kingdoms that are to come before divine intervention, he means four, not some indefinite mystical number, and it is not difficult to identify them. Gruen and Buitenwerf cite *1 Enoch* 91:12–17; 93:3–10, that is, the Apocalypse of Weeks, which predicts the turning point of history in the seventh week of years. To be sure, the calculation of world history in terms of weeks of years is not chronologically exact, but the reader would be in little doubt as to the reference of the seventh

---

[22] See A. Yarbro Collins, "Numerical Symbolism in Jewish and Early Christian Apocalyptic Literature," in her *Cosmology and Eschatology in Jewish and Christian Apocalypticism* (JSJSup 50; Leiden: Brill, 1996), 57–89.

[23] Gruen, *Heritage and Hellenism*, 277.

[24] Buitenwerf, *Book III*, 129.

[25] This verse is cited by Gruen, *Heritage and Hellenism*, 277, as a supposedly representative use of the number seven.

week, in which an apostate generation would arise, and at whose
end the turning point would come. In Daniel, the final persecution
is supposed to last for the last half-week of seventy weeks of years
from the time of the profanation of the Temple (cf. Dan 12:7). Since
the time of the profanation was well known, the end of the half-
week pointed to a very specific date. At this point, the division of
history into periods shades over into the first category of numerical
reference, the attempt to predict a future event.

Buitenwerf cites Dan 12:7, 9–13, as supposed examples of indefinite
predictions. Dan 12:7 says that the time until the "end" (of the desecration of the Temple) would be a time, two times and half a time,
or three and a half years, hardly an indefinite period. In Dan
12:12–13, this period is translated into specific numbers of days, first
1,290 days, then, in an evident revision, 1,335.[26] There is nothing
mystical or abstract about these numbers, and they would not have
offered much consolation to the people who were enduring persecution if they were. The specificity of the number was essential to
the prophecy, even though it later required revision and then reinterpretation. Again, the horns of the beast in Daniel 7, the heads of
the dragon in Revelation 12 and the heads and wings of the eagle
in *4 Ezra* 12, all had highly specific referents, even if modern commentators have trouble figuring them out. Where numbers are used
to indicate the time at which something will happen, and there is a
reference to some historical datum (such as the desecration of the
Temple or the number of Roman emperors), then specificity is crucially important. Apocalyptic literature is not vague or mystical just
because a modern interpreter is unfamiliar with it or finds it obscure.[27]

Gruen also has misgivings about the contexts in which the references to the seventh king occur. The first of these references is found
in 3:192–93. At the end of a passage that clearly refers to Rome,
the Sibyl says, "it will cut up everything and fill everything with
evils, with disgraceful love of gain, ill-gotten wealth, in many places,
but especially in Macedonia. It will stir up hatred. Every kind of
deceit will be found among them until the seventh reign, when a

---

[26] For a discussion of these numbers and their function in predicting the "end"
see my commentary, *Daniel* (Hermeneia; Minneapolis: Fortress, 1993) 400–401.
[27] Yarbro Collins, "Numerical Symbolism," 64–69, also refers to "imprecise,
rhetorical calculations," in *4 Ezra* and Revelation, but these are cases where no
specific number is given.

king of Egypt, who will be of the Greeks by race, will rule. And then the people of the great God will again be strong who will be guides in life for all mortals." Many scholars have doubted that an anti-Roman oracle in a Jewish work could date from the second century BCE.[28] However, Rome is not accused here of any offence against Jews or Judea, but rather against Macedonia. Gruen recognizes that the passage refers to the Roman conquest of Macedonia, which was divided after the battle of Pydna in 168 BCE and made a Roman province in 147, all within the reign of Ptolemy VI Philometor.[29] He objects, however, that "no *ex eventu* forecast could have set the fall of Roman power to that period, a time when its might was increasing and its reach extending. Nor can one imagine the Sibyl (or her recorder) making such a pronouncement in the reigns of Philometor or Euergetes themselves when its falsity was patent."[30] But no one has ever suggested that this prophecy was *ex eventu*; it is obviously a future prediction that was never fulfilled. Gruen concludes that the passage "can hardly refer to a present or past scion of the Ptolemaic dynasty." It cannot, of course, refer to a past figure. It is an unrealistic and somewhat utopian prediction of what would happen in the near future. There is no reason why it should not refer to a future point in the reign of the present monarch, or to the reign of his anticipated successor. If this passage were written shortly after the Roman seizure of Macedonia in 147 BCE, it could refer Ptolemy Neos Philopator, son of Philometor, who was heir to the throne and who is sometimes reckoned as Ptolemy VII. The prediction was unrealistic in any case. Roman rule would not end in the reign of any Ptolemaic king, nor would Jews attain world power. But the fact that a prophecy was unrealistic does not mean that it was not specific in its reference.

The second reference to the seventh king is found in *Sib. Or.* 3:318. The context is a prediction of affliction for Egypt:

---

[28] For references, see Collins, *The Sibylline Oracles*, 31. Geffcken, *Die Oracula Sibyllina*, 58, bracketed the reference to the seventh king as a later addition. Nikiprowetzky, *La Troisième Sibylle*, 210–11, argued that the passage required a date in the first century BCE.

[29] Gruen, *Heritage and Hellenism*, 271. Buitenwerf, *Book III*, 188, implausibly suggests that the reference is merely to the fact that Macedonia was the empire preceding that of the Romans.

[30] *Heritage and Hellenism*, 273.

A great affliction will come upon you, Egypt, against your homes . . .
for a sword will pass through your midst
and scattering and death and famine will lay hold of you,
in the seventh generation of kings, and then you will rest.

Predictions of "war, famine and pestilence" are ubiquitous in Greek
and in biblical prophecy. As we have seen already, this entire section of *Sibylline Oracles* 3 (295–488) is dominated by such prophecies
against various places, to a degree that is anomalous in the book.
Gruen jumps to the conclusion that there can be no historical
specificity in any of these oracles, and says that "nothing in the passage gives any reason to evoke the era of Philometor and Euergetes."[31]
But this is obviously not true: "the seventh generation of kings" points
immediately to this era. The reference to a sword passing through
the midst of Egypt has often been interpreted as a reference to the
civil war between Philometor and Euergetes, or to the strife that
continued during the reign of the latter.[32] Gruen dismisses this as
"pure conjecture," but it is a conjecture that fits the context very
well. Here again the prophecy is not *ex eventu*; it is a prediction.
There was ample reason to predict civil strife in Egypt throughout
the reign of Philometor and for some time thereafter. The passage
would have made good sense in the time of Philometor. There is
nothing to suggest that "the seventh generation of kings" was not a
chronological reference.

The third passage concerning the seventh king is found in another
eschatological oracle in *Sib. Or.* 3: 601–623. Again, there is a reference to "war, famine and pestilence," which will come about "when-
ever the young seventh king of Egypt rules his own land, numbered
from the line of the Greeks." A king will come from Asia, who will
"overthrow the kingdom of Egypt" and take away its possessions by
sea. This will be followed by conversion to the true God: "then they
will bend a white knee on the fertile ground to God the great immortal king." After this, "God will give great joy to men" and the earth
will be transformed.

Many scholars have taken this passage as an *ex eventu* prophecy of
the first invasion of Egypt by Antiochus Epiphanes.[33] Such a reading

---

[31] Ibid., 274.
[32] See Collins, *The Sibylline Oracles*, 31.
[33] Ibid., 29–30.

is problematic. While Epiphanes' first campaign in Egypt, in 170 BCE, was successful, it was followed a mere two years later by another invasion which ended in humiliation at the hands of the Romans. It is much more plausible that this passage, like the others that refer to the seventh king, is a real prediction. Invasion from Asia was a recurring nightmare in Egyptian history, dating back to the time of the Hyksos in the second millennium, revived by the invasion of the Persians Cambyses and Artaxerxes Ochus, and projected into the future in Egyptian oracles of the Hellenistic period, such as the Potter's Oracle and the predictions of Nechepso and Petosiris. This passage in *Sibylline Oracles* 3 may be informed by the relatively recent memory of Antiochus' invasion; however, it is not an *ex eventu* prophecy, but part of an eschatological tableau. This tableau is analogous to what is often called the "messianic" or "eschatological woes" in Jewish tradition—the idea that the coming of salvation is preceded by a period of extreme upheavals and distress.[34] The pattern is repeated in *Sib. Or.* 3:635–56, where "king will lay hold of king" and "peoples will ravage peoples" before "God will send a king from the sun who will stop the entire earth from evil war."

Gruen rightly remarks that the model for this tableau "should more properly be sought in something like the thunderings of Isaiah than in the special circumstances of a Ptolemaic reign."[35] But this only means that the prophecy is not *ex eventu*. It does not warrant the conclusion that the reference to "the young seventh king of Egypt" is insignificant. Since the events in question are said to occur while the king is young (or new), the oracle was most probably written before or at the beginning of his reign. Unless we are willing to suppose that no one had any idea how many Ptolemaic kings there had been, such a prophecy would scarcely have been credible after the reign of Philometor. It should be noted that Philometor's son and heir, Ptolemy Philopator, bore the epithet *Neos*, "young."

The three references to the seventh king are not identical. Verse 192 refers to the "seventh reign" of an Egyptian king of Greek descent, v. 318 to "the seventh generation of kings," and v. 608 to "the young seventh king of Egypt" from the dynasty of the Greeks. Buitenwerf argues that the variation suggests that the author did not

---

[34] Compare Dan 7:19–22; 12:1; *4 Ezra* 12:22–30; 13:5–11; 4Q246 ii 2–3 etc.; Mark 13:8 etc.

[35] Gruen, *Heritage and Hellenism*, 276.

refer to a specific Ptolemaic king of Egypt.[36] The argument smacks of desperation. Buitenwerf himself elsewhere grants that "the agreements between the three passages, especially in the use of the number seven, suggest that the author intended to refer to the same period in all three passages."[37] The variation in terminology is simply a matter of poetic style, and in no way lessens the specificity of the references. Neither does the cryptic style of the prophecies, which use a numeral rather than a play on a king's name or some other more specific give-away.[38] This again is simply a matter of oracular style and did not necessarily obscure the reference at all.

The references to the seventh king of the Ptolemaic line are not *ex eventu* prophecies, but their bearing on the date of the composition is nonetheless crucial. These prophecies cannot have been composed at a time when it was clear that more than seven Ptolemies had reigned. The latest Ptolemy who could be regarded as the seventh king of the dynasty was Euergetes II Physcon. But as we have seen, these oracles were most probably composed either before the seventh king came to power or at the very beginning of his reign. A date in the mid-second century remains by far the most likely.

The Role of the Seventh King

The three passages we have considered refer to the reign of the seventh king as a chronological marker. In his time "the people of the great God will again be strong" (192), or the events that lead to the conversion of Egypt will take place (608). Whether this king has an active role in these events depends on whether he should be identified as the "king from the sun" sent by God in v. 652, as I have argued on other occasions.[39] Many recent scholars have argued against the identification, apparently because of resistance to the idea that the exaltation of the Jewish people would be brought about by a Gentile king.[40] Gruen regards this king as a Jewish Messiah, and

---

[36] Buitenwerf, *Book III*, 128–9; 188.
[37] Ibid., 265.
[38] Contra Buitenwerf, *ibid.*, 129.
[39] Collins, *The Sibylline Oracles*, 40–42; "The Sibyl and the Potter," in *Seers, Sibyls and Sages*, 199–210; *Between Athens and Jerusalem*, 92–95.
[40] Barclay, *Jews in the Mediterranean Diaspora*, 223; Gruen, *Heritage and Hellenism*, 277–78; Buitenwerf, *Book III*, 272–75.

cites Isa 41:25 (LXX) which says that God will bring someone *aph' hēliou anatolōn*, from the sunrise. However, he fails to notice that the reference in Isaiah is not to a Jewish Messiah but to the Gentile Cyrus of Persia. There is no other hint of messianic expectation in the Third Sibyl. Passages that speak about the future exaltation of the Jewish people (3:194; 702) do not mention a Jewish king or kingdom. Moreover, messianic expectation is poorly attested, if at all, even in the apocalyptic literature from the land of Israel in the second century BCE.[41]

The phrase "king from the sun" (*ap' ēelioio*) has clear associations with Egyptian royal mythology. The closest parallel is found in the Potter's Oracle, where it refers to the hope for restoration of native Egyptian rule, but the Ptolemies also drew on Pharaonic imagery and claimed association with the sun.[42] Buitenwerf tries to evade those associations by translating "king from the east."[43] This translation is only justified if the phrase is regarded as an abbreviation of *aph' hēliou anatolōn*, from the rising of the sun, the phrase used in Deutero-Isaiah to refer to Cyrus of Persia. There is no parallel for such an abbreviation in any Jewish source. Buitenwerf then identifies this king with the king from Asia in *Sib. Or.* 3:611–14.[44] The latter is viewed by most scholars as a negative, destructive figure.[45] If the book is read in an Egyptian context, the negative associations are obvious. He is said to ravage and despoil Egypt. A king from Syria plays a similar role in the Potter's Oracle, and kings from Asia had negative connotations all the way back to the Hyksos.

---

[41] J. J. Collins, *The Scepter and the Star: The Messiahs of the Dead Sea Scrolls and Other Ancient Literature* (ABRL; New York: Doubleday, 1995), 31–38.

[42] See Collins, *The Sibylline Oracles*, 41–42; "The Sibyl and the Potter," 202–206. Gruen, *Heritage and Hellenism*, 278, n. 134, evidently misunderstands the latter article, which is not an attempt to "get around" the anti-Ptolemaic stance of the Potter's Oracle but is a discussion of the different ways in which the Pharaonic imagery is used in the two texts. The Egyptian associations of the phrase are conceded by Barclay and Gruen. On the Potter's Oracle, see most recently L. Koenen, "Die Apologie des Töpfers an König Amenophis, oder das Töpferorakel," in A. Blasius and B. U. Schipper, ed., *Apokalyptik und Ägypten: eine kritische Analyse der relevanten Texte aus dem griechisch-römischen Ägypten* (OLA 107; Leuven: Peeters, 2002) 139–87.

[43] Buitenwerf, *Book III*, 272–73. He is by no means the first to resort to this evasion. He regards the Egyptian associations as irrelevant because he believes that the book was written in Asia Minor. *Pace* Buitenwerf, I have never regarded this oracle as *ex eventu*.

[44] Buitenwerf, *Book III*, 275.

[45] See Collins, *The Sibylline Oracles*, 39–40. An exception is A. Peretti, *La Sibilla Babilonese nella Propaganda Ellenistica* (Florence: La Nuova Italia Editrice, 1943) 392–93.

Buitenwerf, however, believes that *Sibylline Oracles* 3 originated in
Asia Minor, an issue that we will discuss below. He also regards the
book as a literary unity, and so he views this passage in light of the
enmity between Asia and Rome expressed in 3:350–80.[46] But Rome
plays no part in the long last section of the book, 3:489–829, and
it is difficult to see why an anti-Roman king from Asia should attack
Egypt, in the Ptolemaic era. The invasion of the king from Asia is
better understood as part of the eschatological upheavals that precede
the time of peace that will be ushered in by the king from the sun.

The king from Asia is said to overthrow, or cast down (*rhipsei*)
the kingdom of Egypt during the reign of the young seventh king,
as Antiochus Epiphanes had done early in the reign of Philometor.
His action is disruptive, but he then departs, and does not assume
control of Egypt. The Sibyl does not say whether the seventh
king resumes his rule, and does not explicitly identify him as the "king
from the sun."[47] Yet the seventh king is a king of Egypt, and "king
from the sun" is a pharaonic title.[48] If the two kings are not one
and the same, it is difficult to imagine why the Sibyl should repeatedly use the reign of the seventh Ptolemy as the chronological marker
for a transformation that would be brought about by some other king.

The Provenance of the Third Sibyl

The great majority of scholars have taken the references to the seventh king of Egypt as a clear indication of the Egyptian provenance
of the work. Buitenwerf is exceptional in challenging that consensus,
and may be the first to argue that the entire book was composed
in Asia Minor.[49] He offers primarily two arguments for this conclusion. First is the frequency with which Asia and places in Asia are
mentioned. But the great majority of these places are mentioned in
the section that runs from 295 to 488, which as we have seen is

---

[46] Buitenwerf, *Book III*, 266–67.

[47] It is not unusual for eschatological upheavals to continue after the advent of
the savior figure in apocalyptic literature. In Dan 12:1, even the rise of the archangel
Michael is followed by a period of unprecedented distress. The messiah often comes
under attack (e.g. *4 Ezra* 14:5).

[48] The epithet *neos* is also associated with the god Horus. See R. E. Witt, *Isis in
the Ancient World* (Baltimore: Johns Hopkins, 1997) 210–21.

[49] Buitenwerf, *Book III*, 130–33.

largely anomalous in the book, and much of which is widely and rightly regarded as deriving from different sources than the rest of the book. Of fifteen references to Asia in the book, only three fall outside this section. The disproportional frequency of references to Asia in this part of the book cannot serve as a guide to the provenance of the other sections. Rather, it is the basis for an argument against the compositional unity of the book.

The second argument is that "the Sibyl to whom the book is attributed is designated as the Erythrean Sibyl (III 813–814), the very famous Asian Sibyl."[50] This statement, however, is an oversimplification. The Sibyl in fact claims to have originated in Babylon, and to be "a fire sent to Greece," but that "throughout Greece mortals will say that I am of another country, a shameless one, born of Erythrae." In short, the Sibyl explicitly rejects the designation as the Erythrean Sibyl. Sibyls, including the Erythrean, were well-known throughout the Greek-speaking world. By the fifth century BCE Sibylline oracles were well enough known in Athens to inspire the mockery of Aristophanes.[51] The fact that there was a well-known Sibylline shrine in Asia Minor does not in any way require that the earliest Jewish Sibylline oracles were composed there.

As Buitenwerf is well aware, the obvious objection to Asian provenance is that the future transformation foretold by the Sibyl is dated by reference to a king of Egypt from the line of the Greeks. His response to that objection is weak: "Now between 80 and 40 BCE, Egypt was still an important, widely respected political power. It is, therefore, imaginable that an author who did not live in Egypt might use a reference to an Egyptian king as a chronological means to designate a future period in which certain crucial events would take place."[52] Imaginable, perhaps, but not very likely. Buitenwerf cites no evidence for the supposed respect for Egypt in Asia Minor. Regardless of the Jewish author's attitude to the Ptolemies, the association of the future turning point of history with a Ptolemaic reign suggests very strongly that the core of the book, containing those passages, was written in Ptolemaic Egypt.

---

[50] Ibid., 133.
[51] Aristophanes, *Peace* 1095, 1116; *Knights* 31.
[52] Buitenwerf, *Book III*, 131, cf. 189.

Conclusion

The author of these Sibylline verses was, of course, a Jewish pro-
pagandist, who was interested in the glory of Judaism, not that of
the Ptolemies. The same could be said of the roughly contemporary
Letter of Aristeas, which co-opts Ptolemy Philadelphus to join in the
praise of Judaism.[53] But Jews in the Diaspora were well aware that
their well-being depended on the good graces of their rulers. Even
though the Sibyl is uncompromising in condemning idolatry, and
regards the Egyptians as a "baleful race" (3:348), she consistently
holds out hope for the conversion of the Greeks.[54] This conversion
would come in the reign of the seventh king of Egypt from the
Greek line. The number symbolizes fulfillment, to be sure, but its
chronological value is no less for that. It points to the mid-second
century BCE, a time when Jews prospered in Egypt under the patronage of Ptolemy Philometor. From the perspective of the Egyptian
Jew who adopted the voice of the Sibyl, the triumph of "the people of the great God" would come about in the reign of a Ptolemaic
king, in the context of Ptolemaic rule.

---

[53] See my essay, "Culture and Religion in Hellenistic Judaism," in *The Honeycomb
of the Word. Interpreting the Primary Testament with André Lacocque* (ed. W. D. Edgerton;
Chicago: Exploration Press, 2001), 17–36. Gruen also notes that in the *Letter of
Aristeas* "the emphasis is again and again on Ptolemaic patronage" (*Heritage and
Hellenism*, 214).

[54] Cf. Gruen, *Heritage and Hellenism*, 287: "The Sibyl reaches out to the Hellenic
world, exhorting its people to repentance, urging acknowledgment of the true god
and offering hope of salvation." In contrast, Barclay, *Jews in the Mediterranean Diaspora*,
223, finds only "recurrent criticism of the Greeks and Macedonians."

CHAPTER SIX

SPELLS PLEASING TO GOD:
THE BINDING OF ISAAC IN PHILO THE EPIC POET

The Book of Genesis, chapter 22, recounts the memorable story of Abraham's near-sacrifice of Isaac. This story received numerous embellishments in later Jewish tradition, many of them focusing on the merit of the deed, and shifting emphasis from Abraham to Isaac.[1] The degree to which these traditions influenced the New Testament is a matter of dispute.[2] They are mostly contained in late targumic and midrashic collections, although these may contain exegetical traditions of uncertain age. Only a few texts, however, that address the story of Abraham and Isaac, can be dated securely before the turn of the era. These generally emphasize that Abraham was faithful when he was tested.[3] The Book of Judith indicates that God not only tested Abraham but also Isaac.[4] The Book of Jubilees, written in Hebrew at some time in the second century BCE, claims that the idea of testing Abraham came from Mastema, prince of the fallen angels, just as Satan had proposed the testing of Job.[5] A recently published fragmentary text from Qumran, 4Q225, may be the earliest witness to the view that Isaac was a willing victim and encouraged Abraham in his deed.[6] This view is prominent in later (post-70 CE) literature, such as the *Biblical Antiquities* of Pseudo-Philo (32:2–3)

---

[1] S. Spiegel, *The Last Trial* (New York: Pantheon, 1967); J. L. Kugel, *The Traditions of the Bible* (Cambridge, MA: Harvard, 1998) 302–9.

[2] See C. T. R. Hayward, "The Present State of Research into the Targumic Account of the Sacrifice of Isaac," *JJS* 32(1981) 127–50; B. D. Chilton, "Recent Discussion of the Aqedah," in idem, *Targumic Approaches to the Gospels* (Lanham, MD: University Press of America, 1986) 39–49.

[3] Sir 44:20; 1 Macc 2:52; Jub 17:17–18; 19:8–9. Kugel, *The Traditions of the Bible*, 308.

[4] Judith 8:26–7.

[5] Jub 17:15–18.

[6] G. Vermes, "New Light on the Sacrifice of Isaac from 4Q225," *JJS* 47(1996) 140–46; J. C. VanderKam, "The Aqedah, Jubilees, and PseudoJubilees," in C. A. Evans, ed., *The Quest for Context and Meaning. Studies in Biblical Intertextuality in Honor of James A. Sanders* (Leiden: Brill, 1997) 241–61.

and Targum Neofiti. In the Targum, Isaac asks Abraham to "bind me properly" lest he kick and make the sacrifice unfit. A similar request is restored by the editors in a lacuna in 4Q225, when Isaac speaks to Abraham a second time, after his question about the sacrificial animal.[7] The restoration is plausible, but not certain. It may be that Isaac's willing participation was already implied in the remark in Judith that God tested him as well as Abraham.

Philo's Epic

The concern for Isaac's consent, however, is not attested in the oldest allusions to Genesis 22, in Ben Sira or in Jubilees.[8] Neither is it attested in the passage that is the subject of this essay, a fragment of a Greek epic poem on Jerusalem by one Philo, who is otherwise unknown.[9] Since his work was excerpted by Alexander Polyhistor in the mid first century BCE,[10] he is plausibly dated to the second century. Philo is usually assumed to have written in Alexandria, like his more famous namesake, but some scholars place him in Jerusalem, the city about which he wrote.[11] Decisive evidence of his date and provenance are lacking.[12] Philo's poem is seldom noted in connection with the Aqedah. This may be due in part to the obscurity of

---

[7] כ]פות אותי יפה, bind me well. Unfortunately only the initial כ is actually preserved in the manuscript. For the official publication see J. C. VanderKam and J. T. Milik, "Jubilees: 225. 4QpseudoJubilees^a," in H. Attridge, et al., *Qumran Cave 4. VIII. Parabiblical Texts, Part 1* (DJD 13; Oxford: Clarendon, 1994) 149–52.

[8] Despite some significant modifications, such as the introduction of Mastema, Jubilees stays very close to the biblical text. See VanderKam, "The Aqedah," 244–51.

[9] The fragments are preserved in Eusebius, PE 9.20.1; 9.24.1; 9.37.1–3. Text and translation can be found in C. R. Holladay, *Fragments From Hellenistic Jewish Authors. II. Poets* (Atlanta: Scholars Press, 1989) 205–99; other translations in H. W. Attridge, "Philo the Epic Poet," *OTP* 2. 781–4; N. Walter, "Fragmente jüdisch-hellenistischer Epik: Philon, Theodotos," *JSHRZ* 4,3(1983) 139–53.

[10] J. Strugnell, "General Introduction, with a Note on Alexander Polyhistor," *OTP* 2. 777–9.

[11] So B. Z. Wacholder, *Eupolemus. A Study of Judaeo-Greek Literature* (Cincinnati: Hebrew Union College, 1974) 282–83.

[12] See Y. Gutman, "Philo the Epic Poet," *Scripta Hierosolymitana* 1 (1954) 36–63; H. Lloyd and P. Parsons, *Supplementum Hellenisticum* (Berlin: de Gruyter, 1983) 328–31; G. W. Nickelsburg, "The Bible Rewritten and Expanded," in M. E. Stone, ed., *Jewish Writings of the Second Temple Period* (CRINT 2.2; Philadelphia: Fortress, 1984) 118–21; E. S. Gruen, *Heritage and Hellenism. The Reinvention of Jewish Tradition* (Berkeley: University of California Press, 1998) 125–27; M. Goodman in E. Schürer, *The History of the Jewish People in the Age of Jesus Christ* (Edinburgh: Clark, 1986) 3.559–61.

the poem, which, as we shall see, is often difficult to interpret. But it may also be due to the fact that Philo's construal of the Aqedah is very different from anything that we find in the literature that originated in Hebrew or Aramaic.[13]

Philo's epic appears to have consisted chiefly of a recitation of the biblical history. The title as given by Polyhistor, Περὶ Ἱεροσόλυμα, already indicates an affinity with the literature of the Hellenistic age, which had strong geographical interests and was often concerned with the foundation of cities.[14] Hellenistic epics also show a predilection for obscure and recherché language.[15] In Philo's case this tendency results in some scarcely intelligible passages, since he did not in fact have a great command of the Greek language. The fragments that have survived deal with Abraham, Joseph, and the water supply of Jerusalem. The fragment on Joseph is said to be from the fourteenth book. This should probably be emended to the fourth;[16] even so, the poem must have been lengthy, since it presumably continued down to the Israelite occupation of Jerusalem. The extant fragments about Jerusalem, however, simply praise the loveliness of the city in summer when the streams are flowing. The theme is reminiscent of the biblical psalms: "there is a stream which gladdens the city of God."[17] Joseph is the lord of dreams who sat on the throne of Egypt. The final line is striking: δινεύσας λαθραῖα Χρόνου πλημμυρίδι μοίρης ("spinning secrets of time in a flood of fate"). The

---

[13] Philo the philosopher hews closely to the biblical story, but adds an apologia in response to comparisons between this and other stories of child-sacrifice (*Abr* 167–99). He then adds an allegorical interpretation.

[14] Gutman ("Philo," 60–63) points especially to the analogy of the *Messēniaka* of Rhianus of Crete, who wrote in the second half of the third century BCE. Apollonius of Rhodes, author of the *Argonautica*, also composed a *Ktiseis* a series of poems concerning foundation legends. P. M. Fraser, *Ptolemaic Alexandria* (3 vols; Oxford: Clarendon, 1972) 1:626, comments on the geographical interests of Apollonius as a typically Alexandrian feature. On the Hellenistic epic, see further Fraser, 1:624–49.

[15] See Fraser, *Ptolemaic Alexandria*, 1:633–38 on the scholarly language of Apollonius. The most obscure example of Hellenistic poetry was the Alexandra of Lycophron, which was deliberately difficult to decipher. Philo has often been compared to Lycophron, but Wacholder (*Eupolemus*, 283) is surely right that Philo wished to be understood, since the fragment on Joseph is quite clear.

[16] So already J. Freudenthal, *Alexander Polyhistor und die von ihm erhaltenen Reste judäischer und samaritanischer Geschichtswerke. Hellenistische Studien 1–2* (Breslau: Skutsch, 1874–5) 100.

[17] Ps. 46:4. Note also Ps. 48:2, which claims that Zion is "the joy of all the earth," and cf. Philo's claim that it δείκνυσιν ὑπέρτατα θάμβεα λαῶν ("shows forth the greatest wonders of the peoples").

reference to μοῖρα, "fate," may be included only for its bombastic resonance, but it is typical of the Hellenistic overtones of Philo's poem.

The Fragment on Abraham

The most controversial fragment is that on Abraham. It reads as follows:

"Ἔκλυον ἀρχεγόνοισι τὸ μυρίον ὥς ποτε θεσμοῖς
Ἀβραὰμ κλυτοηχὲς ὑπέρτερον "αμμα τι δεσμῶν
παμφαές, πλήμμυρε μεγαυχήτοισι λογισμοῖς,
θειοφιλῆ θελγήτρα. λιπόντι γὰρ ἀγλαὸν "ερκος
αἰνοφύτων "εκκαυμα βριήπυος αἰετὸς "ισχων
ἀθάνατον ποίησεν ἐὴν φάτιν, ἐξότε κείνου
"εκγονος αἰνογόνοιο πολύμνιον "ελλαχε κῦδος

Then after omission of a few lines:

Ἀρτίχερος θηκτοῖο ξιφηφόρον ἐντύνοντος
λήματι καὶ σφαράγοιο παρακλιδὸν ἀθροισθέντος
ἀλλ᾽ ὁ μὲν ἐν χείρεσσι κερασφόρον ὤπασε κριόν.[18]

Although there have been relatively few discussions of these verses, there has been no lack of diverse interpretations. The range of readings may seen from a comparison of two current English translations, by Carl Holladay and Harold Attridge. Holladay renders as follows:

"They unloosed the loins for our ancestors just as once (they were commanded) by the (divine) ordinances—
O Abraham, (you are) renowned through the preeminent seal of the bonds
Radiant (are you), overflowing with glorious thoughts—
Divinely pleasing gestures. For this one who left the splendid enclosure
Of the awesome race the praiseworthy one with a thundering sound prevented (from carrying out) the immolation,
(And thus) he made his own voice immortal. From then on
The offspring of that awesome child achieved much-hymned renown . . .

---

[18] The text is cited from Holladay, *Fragments*, 2.234, 236. Except that I do not follow his emendation of μυρίον to μηρίον in the first line, and of ὑπέρτερον to ὑπερτέρῳ in the second, and I read "αμμα τι as two words rather than one.

... as the strong-handed one bearing a sharp sword made ready
With firm resolve, and a rustle at one side became stronger—
But he placed in his hand the horned ram."

Attridge's translation is significantly different:

A thousand times have I heard in the ancient laws how once (when
    you achieved something) marvelous
with the bonds' knot, O far-famed Abraham,
resplendently did your god-beloved prayers abound
in wondrous counsels. For when you left the beauteous garden
of dread plants, the praiseworthy thunderer quenched the pyre
and made his promise immortal. From that time forth
the offspring of that awesome born one have won far-hymned praise
    ... as mortal hand readied the sword
with resolve, and crackling (wood) was gathered at the side, he brought
    into his hands a horned ram."

These translations do not exhaust the variety of interpretations of
this passage, but they may serve to highlight the main points of dispute. All commentators accept that the final three verses refer to the
sacrifice of Isaac. Several scholars, however, detect other referents
in the opening verses.

A Reference to Circumcision?

Ben Zion Wacholder claims that "the first book depicted God's
covenant with Abraham (circumcision)."[19] This line of interpretation
originates with a suggestion of Mras, and also underlies Holladay's
translation.[20] The verb ἔκλυον is taken as equivalent of ἐξέλυον,
"they unloosed." Then μυρίον, ten thousand times, is emended to
μηρίον, "thigh," loosely rendered as "loins." In defence of this translation, Holladay points to the LXX use of μηρίον for "loins" (e.g.
Lev 3:4, 10, 15) although he admits that the singular is surprising.
In any case there is no parallel for the phrase "they loosened the
loins" as a way of referring to circumcision. But the emendation and
strained translation are entirely unnecessary. With Attridge and most

---

[19] Wacholder, *Eupolemus*, 283.
[20] Holladay, *Fragments*, 2. 235, 248–9. So also Walter, *Fragmente*, 148. See K. Mras,
Eusebius' Werke. 8. Die Praeparatio Evangelica (GCS 43; 2 vols.; Berlin: Akademie, 1954)
1.506.

older interpreters, ἔκλυον should be taken as a second aorist of
κλύω, to hear. Hence the straightforward translation of Attridge: "A
thousand times have I heard in the ancient laws . . ." The poet is
speaking in the first person. The ancient laws are, of course, simply
the Torah, not specifically the covenant with Abraham.[21]

A Cord of Bonds

Both Holladay and Attridge take the word κλυτοηχὲς as vocative,
and in agreement with Abraham, who is thought to be addressed
in the passage: "O far-famed Abraham." Holladay also takes παμφαές
(radiant) and even πλήμυρρε (overflowing) as vocatives, although the
latter word is not attested as an adjective.[22] Attridge takes παμφαές
as a neuter adjective, used adverbially ("radiantly") and πλήμυρρε as
a verb, with θειοφιλῆ θελγήτρα as the subject. Both of these con-
struals are problematic, however. Holladay leaves line 1, the supposed reference to circumcision, dangling, as he switches from third
person to direct address, and takes πλήμυρρε as an unattested form.
Attridge has to supply a line ("when you achieved something") to
make the transition to direct speech. These problems are resolved if
we take Abraham as the subject of the finite verb πλήμυρρε: "I
heard . . . how once Abraham abounded in glorious thoughts."[23] The
forms κλυτοηχὲς and παμφαές then are not vocatives, but neuter
accusatives, qualifying the noun ἄμμα, which means "cord," or
"something tied."

The syntax of the passage has been obscured by the editors' reading of ἄμμα τι as one word rather than two, and consequently as
a dative, and Mras's consequent emendation of ὑπέρτερον to ὑπερτέρῳ.
If we read ἄμμα as an accusative of respect, however, the syntax
of the passage is cleared up. The words κλυτοηχὲς and παμφαές then
agree with ἄμμα, and θειοφιλῆ θελγήτρα is in apposition to it. (The
plural is due to the plural δεσμῶν, alternatively θελγήτρα may be
read as an independent sentence with the verb implied: the spells
were pleasing to God).[24] The passage should be translated as follows:

---

[21] Pace Holladay, ibid.

[22] Holladay here follows a suggestion of Walter.

[23] One manuscript, N, reads ἐπλήμυρρε, but the augment is often omitted in epic
Greek.

[24] This was suggested to me by Margaret Mitchell.

> Ten thousand times have I heard in the ancient laws how once Abraham
> abounded in glorious reasonings, in respect of the famous, surpassing,
> splendid cord of bonds, spells pleasing to God.

What then is this "cord of bonds" that is the occasion of Abraham's
glory? The perverse determination of some scholars to find a reference to circumcision here is shown by Philippson's emendation of
ἅμματι to αἵματι (blood).[25] Almost as forced is Holladay's suggestion that "bonds" would signify the enduring bond of the covenant
between God and Abraham.[26] The most elaborate interpretation of
the passage has been offered by Gutman, who argues that Philo's
style finds its parallel in the Orphic hymns "in so far as there too
the author's motive is apparent to shroud himself in a cloud of mystical obscurities."[27] He translates:

> A thousand times have I heard how once (the spirit of) Abraham
> abounded in primeval doctrines, the far-echoing lofty and radiant link
> of chains; how (his spirit abounded) with wisdom of great praise, the
> ecstasy beloved of God. For when he left the goodly abode of the
> blessed born, the great-voiced Blessed One prevented the immolation,
> and made immortal His word, from which day much-sung glory fell
> to the lot of the son of the blessed born.[28]

On the basis of this rendering he proceeds to expound Philo's
intention:

> The Law of Israel is in his view one of the principal and basic ele-
> ments in the cosmic process. This Law existed before the creation, but
> when the word came into existence the Law and its commandments
> served as that force of harmony which created order and rule, and
> fused the isolated parts of the cosmos into a process of unity, as they
> could not be fused without it. Men had no conception of the chains
> of this harmony in the cosmos—law and its regulations—till Abraham
> came and revealed them to humanity.[29]

---

[25] L. M. Philippson, *Ezechiel des jüdischen Trauerspieldichters Auszug aus Egypten und
Philo des Älteren Jerusalem* (Berlin: List, 1830) 62.

[26] Holladay, *Fragments*, 251.

[27] Gutman, "Philo," 37.

[28] Ibid., 40. Gutman emends πλήμμυρε to ἐπλήμυρρε and reads ἅμμα τι as two
words. Then the two dative phrases, ἀρχεγόνοισι . . . θεσμοῖς and μεγαυχήτοισι
λογισμοῖς, are in apposition and the two accusative phrases ἅμμα τι δεσμῶν and
θειοφιλῆ θελγήτρα, are also in apposition.

[29] Ibid., 53.

This interpretation depends heavily on three elements, all of them doubtful:

First, it is said that Abraham "abounded in primeval doctrines." Gutman argues that this expression must refer to "codes or doctrines which preceded all things and anticipated all creation, even the creation of the world," and infers the Jewish idea of preexistent wisdom and the preexistent law.[30] However, it is not apparent that ἀρχέγονος necessarily implies existence before creation. In accordance with Philo's generally bombastic style it may simply connote extreme antiquity. Again, θεσμοί are not automatically to be identified as the law of Israel. The parallel with λογισμοῖς suggests traditional wisdom. True, the Jewish law is identified with wisdom in other texts, but there is no clear reference to the Jewish law here, certainly not to the "book of the law of Moses."[31] The point is simply that Abraham is informed by the most ancient wisdom.

Second, the phrase ἅμμα τι δεσμῶν is understood as "link of chains" in the light of Plato's use of δεσμός in the Timaeus, where the heavenly bodies are linked by animate bonds.[32] Philo of Alexandria evidently drew on the Platonic tradition when he said that God was the δεσμός of the universe.[33] However, the cosmic sense of δεσμός depends on its context. In itself the word simply means bond. There is no explicit cosmic reference here.

Third, Gutman translates θεοφιλῆ θέλγητρα as "ecstasy beloved of God." However, θέλγητρα means "charm" or "spell," not an experience such as ecstasy.

A far simpler interpretation is readily available. In Gen 22:9, Abraham binds Isaac before he lays him on the wood. The binding is further highlighted in the Targum. Later tradition refers to the whole incident as the binding of Isaac or *Akedah*. With Attridge, we should recognize here a clear allusion to the binding of Isaac, which is in fact the subject of the entire fragment. It is the binding of Isaac, then, that is designated as θεοφιλῆ θέλγητρα.

---

[30] Ibid., 40–41. Aristobulus, who may have been roughly contemporary with Philo, identifies Torah with Wisdom and says that it existed before heaven and earth (PE 13.12.11). The preexistence of wisdom is found in Prov 8:22 and the identification with the Torah in Sir 24:23.

[31] The phrase of Sir 24:23.

[32] Gutman, "Philo," 44–45. Plato, *Timaeus* 38e.

[33] Philo, *Quis Rerum Divinarum Heres*, 23.

Here again the commentators have been reluctant to take the text at face value. Attridge, who takes the phrase as subject of the verb "abound" translates: "your God-beloved prayers." But as he readily admits, θελγήτρα means charms or spells, and no prayers of Abraham are mentioned in Genesis 22. Holladay, who thinks the phrase refers to circumcision, recognizes the meaning "as a 'charm' in the sense of that which becomes a means of satisfying, or even appeasing God."[34] But he is evidently uncomfortable with the magical overtones of "charms" or "spells" and so he translates "divinely pleasing gestures." Yet spells are often associated with binding, if only in a figurative sense, and this association surely determines Philo's choice of words in this passage.

The Remainder of the Passage

Before we reflect further on what Philo meant by referring to the binding of Isaac as "spells pleasing to God" a few problems in the remainder of the fragment remain to be addressed. The subject of the following sentence is βριήπυος αἰνετός, "the praiseworthy loud-shouting one," presumably God. The adjective βριήπυος is used for Ares in the Iliad, but more generally evokes the motif of Zeus as thunderer. In the context here it represents an interpretation of Gen 22:11, where the angel of the Lord is said to call to Abraham from heaven. He thereby holds back the firewood (ἔκκαυμα ἴσχων), or prevents the burnt offering.[35] Simultaneously, God makes Abraham's fame or reputation (ἐὴν φάτιν) immortal. The personal pronoun usually means "his own," but is frequently used to refer to other persons in post-Homeric epics.[36] Holladay's translation, "he made his own voice immortal" makes little sense. Attridge, "made his promise immortal," sees a reference to Gen 22:16–18, where God promises to make Abraham's offspring as numerous as the sand on the seashore. φάτις can mean a voice from heaven or an oracle, but God did not need to make his voice or oracle immortal; rather the emphasis of the whole fragment is on the fame of Abraham and his son, and how that fame was acquired.

---

[34] Holladay, *Fragments*, 252–3.
[35] Attridge translates "quenched the pyre," but we need not assume that the fire had been lit.
[36] LSJ, 601. Cf. Hesiod, *Works and Days*, 58; Apollonius Rhodios 1.1113.

The prevention of the sacrifice is said to have happened for Abraham "when he had left the splendid enclosure αἰνοφύτων." Attridge translates "the beautiful garden of dread plants" and thinks that the reference is to the wood that Abraham took with him to Mount Moriah. Holladay takes φυτόν in the secondary sense of "offspring" and translates "of the awesome race," a reference to Abraham's departure from Ur of the Chaldees.[37] The latter interpretation seems more satisfactory, since a garden of dread plants is never mentioned in the story of the Akedah, but the reference is obscure in any case.

The first passage cited concludes with the statement that the offspring of that awesome-born one[38] obtained much-hymned renown. Attridge thinks the "awesome-born" one is Isaac, because of the peculiar circumstances of his birth, but allows that a reference to Abraham is also possible. Walter, exploiting the similarity between αἰνογόνοιο and αἰνοφύτων, argues that the reference is to Abraham, as a descendant of the Giants.[39] In Gen 22:17 God promises to bless Abraham's offspring (Israel). Here too the offspring is probably collective and the progenitor Abraham. "Awesome-born" is simply a bombastic epithet, intended to convey a sense of Abraham's heroic stature. But if Isaac is the awesome-born one, the offspring is still Israel.

The supplementary citation about the substitution of the ram raises no problems that are significant for our discussion. It may be useful to recapitulate here our translation of the main fragment: "Ten thousand times have I heard in the ancient laws how once Abraham abounded in glorious reasonings, in respect of the famous, surpassing, splendid cord of bonds, spells pleasing to God. For when he left the splendid enclosure of the awesome race, the praiseworthy thunderer prevented the burnt offering and made his reputation immortal. Thenceforward the offspring of that awesome-born one obtained much-hymned praise."

---

[37] So also Mras and Walter, who further identify the awesome race with the giants of Genesis 6.
[38] Not "awesome child", pace Holladay.
[39] Walter, *Fragmente*, 149.

The Understanding of the Akedah

How then does Philo understand the Akedah? The theme of his poem is the beauty and illustrious history of Jerusalem. He singles out the episode of the Akedah because of its location, on the assumption that Moriah is in fact Mt. Zion. Unlike the biblical account and most Second Temple paraphrases, however, Philo makes no mention of a test. Neither does he mention the faith of Abraham, nor his willingness to sacrifice his only-begotten son, although the intention of sacrifice is clearly implied. Instead, Philo seems to regard the actual binding of Isaac as efficacious. The "cord of bonds" is pleasing to God, and obviates the need for consummation of the sacrifice. In return, God establishes Abraham's reputation and blesses his offspring.

Philo uses the word θελγήτρα, spells, with reference to the binding. Modern translators have avoided the literal meaning of the word, perhaps because of the pejorative view of "magic" in the modern west, but the association of spells with binding is too widespread in antiquity to be coincidental. We must allow, however, that Philo is exploiting this association in an original way. Binding usually figures in curses, as a way of imposing restraints on the victim. The idea of binding as "spells pleasing to God" is a novel adaptation of magic, or quasi-magical, ritual.

Binding Spells

In Jewish magical texts, binding sometimes has cosmic implications. A late mystical text speaks of "the spell and the seal by which one binds the earth and by which one binds the heavens."[40] A magical formula used by Rabbi Joshua bar Peraḥya began "I bind, tie and suppress all demons and harmful spirits that are in the world."[41]

---

[40] See P. Schäfer, "Magic and Religion in Ancient Judaism," in P. Schäfer and H. G. Kippenberg, ed., *Envisioning Magic. A Princeton Seminar and Symposium* (Leiden: Brill, 1997) 42. On magic in ancient Judaism see further P. S. Alexander, "Incantations and Books of Magic," in Schürer, *The History*, 3.342–79 and H. D. Betz, "Jewish Magic in the Greek Magical Papyri," in Schäfer and Kippenberg, ed., *Envisioning Magic*, 45–63..

[41] See Alexander, "Incantations and Books of Magic," 354.

More typically, however, binding was envisioned as a way of restraining human beings.

Binding spells, κατάδεσμοι, are attested in Greek literature from the fifth century BCE. The Fates, or Erinyes, in Aeschylus' *Eumenides* recite a ὕμνος δέσμιος, or "binding song" (*Eum* 306). Plato speaks of peripatetic magicians who perform κατάδεσμοι for a price (*Resp* 2.364b). Most of the spells were purely verbal. Many consist of a list of names. A verb of binding was presumably uttered aloud during the ritual. The binding formula has been described by Christopher Faraone as "a form of performative utterance that is accompanied by a ritually significant act, either the distortion and perforation of a lead tablet or (more rarely) the binding of the hands and legs of a small effigy."[42] These spells provided a means of binding or restraining enemies without killing them. Faraone lists four general categories: commercial curses, curses against athletes or similar kinds of public performers, amatory curses, and judicial curses.[43] In the case of athletes and commercial rivals, the spell is meant to impair their performance. Similarly, judicial spells aimed at restraining the opponent's performance in court.

Most interesting for our purposes are the amatory spells. These fall into two categories. The first, the separation-curse, or *Trennungszauber*, was usually aimed at a rival lover, and sought to inhibit relations between the rival and the beloved. The second category, the aphrodisiac or erotic curse, mentions only the beloved. It sought to afflict the beloved with burnings, itchings or insomnia that could only be relieved by submitting to the suitor.[44] This kind of binding spell is of interest here, as it shows that such spells were not necessarily aimed at enemies, and did not always have hostile intent. Another parallel for a benign use of binding can be found in the *Testament of Job*, a Hellenistic Jewish writing from around the turn of the era.

---

[42] C. A. Faraone, "The Agonistic Context of Early Greek Binding Spells," in C. A. Faraone and D. Obbink, eds., *Magika Hiera. Ancient Greek Magic and Religion* (New York: Oxford, 1991) 3–32 (5).

[43] Ibid., 10. See further J. G. Gager, *Curse Tablets and Binding Spells from the Ancient World* (Oxford: Oxford University Press, 1992), who devotes chapters to competition in theater and circus, amatory issues, legal issues, business, and justice and revenge.

[44] Cf. the "love spell of attraction" in *PGM* IV. 2891–2942. See H. D. Betz, *The Greek Magical Papyri in Translation* (2nd ed.; Chicago: The University of Chicago Press, 1992) 92–94. The spell involves a threat to bind Adonis with steel chains.

There the daughters of Job are give girdles to wear about their breasts, so that it may go well with them all the days of their lives.[45] These are the same girdles that God gave Job when he told him to "gird up your loins like a man."[46] When Job put them on he was healed immediately in body and soul and received the gift of prophecy. For the daughters, the girdles function as phylacteries, and also confer a change of heart and mystical insight into the heavenly world.[47]

The Binding of Isaac

There are then some parallels for binding with positive intent, although we have no close parallel to the binding of Isaac. I would suggest that Philo viewed the binding as a substitute sacrifice. The victim, Isaac, was restrained and thereby dedicated, not to the person performing the ritual (Abraham) as would be the case in an amatory spell, but to God. The actual transfer of the victim to God by sacrifice is rendered unnecessary by the efficacy of the binding.

It may be, of course, that Philo's use of the words θειοφιλῆ θελγήτρα is a mere rhetorical flourish that should not be pressed. Philo uses other terms, such as μοῖρα, fate, with little apparent attention to their nuances. It would be a mistake, however, to dismiss Philo's choice of terms as inconsequential. He was, to be sure, bombastic, but his poem was nonetheless an attempt to reconceive biblical tradition in Hellenistic categories. His understanding of the "cord of bonds" in the binding of Isaac may be quite different from the κατάδεσμοι of the Greeks, but his choice of words suggested at least an analogy. The binding of Isaac was also a performative act, which was efficacious in offering the victim to God as a virtual sacrifice, with far-reaching results. The terminology suggests that Philo understood the efficacy of the binding as a ritual by the analogy of magical spells. I am not aware of any parallel to this peculiar understanding, but it deserves to be noted in the rich history of the interpretation the binding of Isaac.

---

[45] T. Job 46:9.
[46] T. Job 47:5; cf. Job 38:3; 40:7.
[47] See P. W. van der Horst, "Images of Women in the Testament of Job," in M. A. Knibb and P. W. van der Horst, ed., *Studies on the Testament of Job* (SNTSMS 66; Cambridge: Cambridge University Press, 1989) 101–3.

CHAPTER SEVEN

JOSEPH AND ASENETH: JEWISH OR CHRISTIAN?

One of the major shifts in biblical scholarship in recent years has been the transfer of focus away from the original composition of the texts and towards the history of reception and interpretation. James Kugel's books on the "traditions of the Bible" are perhaps the outstanding monument to this scholarly trend.[1] Related to this has been increased interest in the so-called "final form" of the text, and in the importance of diverse textual witnesses in their own right (in the work, for example, of J. A. Sanders).[2] In the context of the Apocrypha and Pseudepigrapha, this trend has led to increased interest in the Christian use and transmission of works hitherto viewed as Jewish.[3] In works such as the *Testaments of the Twelve Patriarchs*[4] or *3 Baruch*,[5] Christian references are no longer seen as intrusive elements to be excised and discarded, but as evidence for intentional editorial activity, and, indeed, for the compositional setting of the work as we have it. In some other cases, such as the story of *Joseph and Aseneth*, the very existence of a Jewish apocryphon is put in question.[6]

---

[1] James L. Kugel, *The Bible as It Was* (Cambridge, MA: Harvard, 1997); *The Traditions of the Bible* (Cambridge: Harvard, 1998).

[2] J. A. Sanders, *Canon and Community* (Philadelphia: Fortress, 1984).

[3] See the issue of the *Journal for the Study of Judaism* devoted to "the Christianization of ancient Jewish writings," edited by J. W. van Henten and B. Schaller, *JSJ* 32/4 (2001), with contributions by R. A. Kraft, M. A. Knibb, D. C. Harlow and C. Böttrich. R. A. Kraft has argued for many years that texts that were transmitted by Christians should be viewed first of all as Christian, and that the burden of proof lies on anyone who would posit a Jewish original. See his essays, "The Pseudepigrapha in Christianity," in John C. Reeves, ed., *Tracing the Threads: Studies in the Vitality of Jewish Pseudepigrapha* (SBLEJL 6; Atlanta: Scholars Press, 1994) 55–86 and "Setting the Stage and Framing Some Central Questions," *JSJ* 32(2001) 371–95. Unfortunately, Kraft has not pursued these questions by actually analyzing specific texts, so his "central questions" remain on a general and hypothetical level.

[4] H. W. Hollander and M. de Jonge, *The Testaments of the Twelve Patriarchs. A Commentary* (SVTP 8; Leiden: Brill, 1985).

[5] D. C. Harlow, *The Greek Apocalypse of Baruch (3 Baruch) in Hellenistic Judaism and Early Christianity* (SVTP 12; Leiden: Brill, 1996).

[6] R. S. Kraemer, *When Aseneth Met Joseph* (New York: Oxford, 1998).

There are, it seems to me, two broad issues at stake in this scholarship.[7] One concerns the nature of Judaism in the Hellenistic and Roman periods. The great bulk of the literature that makes up conventional collections of Jewish Apocrypha and Pseudepigrapha was preserved by Christians rather than by Jews, and very little of it has survived in Hebrew or Aramaic. If this literature was originally authored by Jews, it was disowned and abandoned by rabbinic Judaism (if indeed the rabbis were even aware of its existence). Moreover, the kind of Judaism that can be reconstructed from these texts is very different from that of the rabbis. Much of it has very little interest in halachic issues. There have always been scholars, especially but not exclusively Jewish, who have questioned whether this material was Jewish at all. In some (though not all) cases, the question arises from a clear ideological bias.[8] In any case, the issue concerns the diversity of Judaism in the Second Temple period. The writings of Philo and Josephus provide clear cases of Jewish writings that were of greater interest to Christians in the patristic period than they were to the Rabbis. The recovery of Aramaic and Hebrew fragments of the books of Enoch and Jubilees in the Dead Sea Scrolls have also put the Jewish origin of these books beyond doubt, despite the fact that they were only transmitted by Christians in later centuries. The extent and variety of non-rabbinic, post-biblical Jewish writings is one of the issues at stake.

The other issue concerns the nature of early Christianity, and the degree to which early Christians found their own identity in stories that derived from the Old Testament, without explicit reference to Christ. There is no doubt that Christians copied and read works that were primarily about Old Testament characters. In many cases, they made the relevance of these stories explicit by inserting references to Christ. Consequently, it is often assumed that books that lack such explicit references are not Christian. This assumption is not unreasonable, but the argument is admittedly circular: we lack clear examples of such Christian compositions because we assume that such texts are Jewish. But the opposite position, that books trans-

---

[7] See my reflections in my essay on "The Literature of the Second Temple Period," in the *Oxford Handbook of Jewish Studies* (ed. M. Goodman, Oxford: Oxford University Press, 2002) 53–78, especially 56–58.

[8] E.g. J. Efron's treatment of the Psalms of Solomon in his *Studies on the Hasmonean Period* (Leiden: Brill, 1987) 219–86.

mitted by Christians but lacking explicit Christian references should be treated as Christian compositions, is equally circular. This position is demonstrably unreliable in the cases of Philo and Josephus and of the books of Enoch and Jubilees.

It is often claimed that anything that was transmitted by Christians could have been composed by Christians.[9] But this is evidently not so. The Book of Leviticus has been transmitted faithfully by Christians; yet we can hardly conceive of a Christian composing it. Books are copied and transmitted for various reasons. The people who transmit them are not necessarily interested in the whole works. The original authors, in contrast, must be presumed responsible for all aspects of the writings they composed. It is not enough, then, to ask whether a given writing would have been of interest to Christians. We must ask whether there is anything in it that a Christian author would not be likely to compose. The question of Jewish or Christian authorship of any particular document cannot be decided by general considerations of principle, but requires close analysis of the specific text in question. In short, neither Jewish nor Christian origin can be established by default.[10] Lack of explicit Christian references is not in itself enough to establish that a text is Jewish. But it is equally unsatisfactory merely to assert the possibility that a disputed text *could* have been composed by a Christian. Either position requires supporting evidence. In debates of this sort, conclusive proof is seldom if ever available, but, conversely, assertions of mere possibility (whether of Jewish or of Christian authorship) are never sufficient. What is at issue is the relative degree of probability in any specific case.

The Case of Joseph and Aseneth

The story of *Joseph and Aseneth* provides a good example of an apocryphal work whose provenance is open to question. It is not attested at all before the late fourth century CE, at the earliest, and the oldest textual witness is a sixth century Syriac translation.[11] While many

---

[9] E.g. Kraemer, *When Aseneth Met Joseph*, 247; Kraft, "Setting the Stage," 375.
[10] Pace Kraft, "Setting the Stage," 386.
[11] C. Burchard, "Joseph and Aseneth," *OTP* 2.178–81; Kraemer, *When Aseneth Met Joseph*, 225–6.

aspects of the text are paralleled in Christian writings, there is no explicit Christian reference, although Joseph often appears explicitly as a type of Christ in other writings. The original editor, Battifol, thought the work was Christian.[12] Nearly all recent scholars have regarded it as a product of Hellenistic Judaism between, approximately, 100 BCE and 100 CE.[13] Recently Ross Kraemer has argued strongly that the text is no older than the third or fourth century CE, and that it is at least as likely to be Christian as Jewish. She also has challenged the usual assumption that the book was composed in Egypt, and argued that it could have been written anywhere in the Roman East, with a slight preference for Syria.[14] The difficulty of pinning down the provenance of the work is compounded by its genre. It is a romantic novel, written to entertain and to edify.[15] Insofar as the story is set in Pharaonic Egypt, it seeks to conceal its actual provenance. But even imaginative fictions betray their historical contexts by the interests that they highlight, and by incidental use of local color from their own time and place. If *Joseph and Aseneth* were explicit about its provenance, there would be no debate about it. Our quest, then, is of necessity a matter of inference.

There is, of course, some question as to what we mean by the text. Most scholars in recent years have been persuaded by Burchard's arguments in favor of the longer text.[16] Kraemer prefers the short text edited by Philonenko.[17] This issue requires a more thorough

---

[12] P. Battifol, "Le livre de la prière d'Aseneth," *Studia Patristica* 1/2 (Paris:Leroux, 1889–90) 1–115.

[13] See recently Edith M. Humphrey, *Joseph and Aseneth* (Guides to the Apocrypha and Pseudepigrapha; Sheffield: Sheffield Academic Press, 2000) 28–37; Sabrina Inowlocki, *Des idoles mortes et muettes au dieu vivant: Joseph, Aseneth, et le fils de Pharaon dans un roman du judaisme hellénisé* (Turnhout: Brepols, 2002).

[14] Kraemer, *When Aseneth Met Joseph*, 225–93.

[15] See especially the comments of E. Gruen, *Heritage and Hellenism* (Berkeley: University of California, 1998) 89–99.

[16] Burchard, "Zum Text von 'Joseph und Aseneth'," *JSJ* 1(1970) 3–34. See also Burchard, *Gesammelte Studien zu Joseph und Aseneth* (SVTP 13; Leiden: Brill, 1996). For an overview of the debate see R. Chesnutt, *From Death to Life. Conversion in Joseph and Aseneth* (JSPSup 16; Sheffield: Sheffield Academic Press, 1995) 65–69. Burchard's reconstructed text can be found in A.-M. Denis, *Concordance Grecque des Pseudépigraphes d'Ancien Testament* (Louvain-la-Neuve: Université Catholique de Louvain, 851–9, and in Burchard, *Gesammelte Studien*, 163–209, and is translated, by Burchard, in *OTP* 2.177–247.

[17] M. Philonenko, *Joseph et Aséneth. Introduction, Texte Critique, Traduction et Notes* (SPB 13; Leiden: Brill, 1968). Philonenko's text is translated into English by D. Cook, in H. F. D. Sparks, ed., *The Apocryphal Old Testament* (Oxford: Clarendon, 1984) 465–503.

assessment of the text-critical arguments than I can attempt here (or than Kraemer has offered). It does not seem to me, however, that the issues that I will discuss here stand or fall on the choice of text. It is not the case, for example, that the long form of the text is Christian and the short form Jewish. The main conclusion I would draw from the existence of variant forms of the text is that the text was fluid, and that it is not very likely that any text found in a medieval manuscript was preserved unchanged from the turn of the era. When we speak about the original text, we can only mean the main outline of the text that is common to all variants, not necessarily the exact wording that we have before us in any manuscript.

The Core Issues in the Story

With these considerations in mind, I propose to comment briefly on some disputed issues relating to the provenance of *Joseph and Aseneth*. The first, and in many ways the most basic question, is what is the book about? Joseph and Aseneth contains two distinct though related stories. The first deals with the marriage of Joseph and Aseneth; the second with a conflict involving Pharaoh's son and Joseph's brothers. As far as the first story is concerned, it seems to me that Kraemer is quite right in supposing that it addresses an obvious problem in the biblical text: "how did Joseph, an Israelite, marry an Egyptian woman, who was the daughter of an Egyptian priest, particularly in light of numerous biblical prohibitions against such marriages."[18] The story responds to this problem by explaining how Aseneth abandoned idolatry and converted to the worship of the God of Israel.[19] The subject matter, then, is first, intermarriage, and second, conversion. To be sure, these concerns do not exhaust the story. There are obvious mystical aspects in Aseneth's encounter with the angel, and she is no ordinary convert, but has symbolic significance. But

---

[18] Kraemer, *When Aseneth Met Joseph*, 20.

[19] It should be emphasized that the story is essentially positive: the intention is not to prohibit intermarriage but to show how it can be made possible. It is a fundamental misreading of the story to see it as antagonistic to the Gentile world (as does J. M. G. Barclay, *Jews in the Mediterranean Diaspora* [Edinburgh: Clark, 1996] 204–16). See the perceptive article of G. J. Brooke, "Joseph, Aseneth, and Lévi-Strauss," in G. J. Brooke and J.-D. Kaestli, ed. *Narrativity in Biblical and Related Texts* (Leuven: Peeters/Leuven University Press, 2000) on the manner in which the various oppositions in the text are overcome.

it is important to keep in mind what gives the story its coherence. The problem of intermarriage, and the way that it is treated, is of fundamental importance for establishing the provenance of the story.

It is more difficult to find a generative problem underlying the second story in Joseph and Aseneth. Kraemer suggests that the tale explains how Joseph came to rule Egypt instead of Pharaoh's son, while also providing a novellistic threat to the chastity of the heroine.[20] This is plausible, as far as it goes, but it hardly explains the complexity of the story. Pharaoh's son conspires not only against Joseph but also against Pharaoh. Joseph's brothers are divided. Some side with Pharaoh's son against their own brother. Most noteworthy is the portrayal of Levi, the priest, and Simeon, as formidable warriors, and the attempt of Pharaoh's son to hire them as mercenaries. The story is at pains to show that Levi, especially, is loyal to Pharaoh and wishes no harm to his son. Also Joseph proves his loyalty by giving the crown to Pharaoh's grandson, and being like a father to him. In short, this story is about political relationships and intrigue, military power and reconciliation. These issues do not arise from the biblical text, but must have been matters of concern to the author, and so they too are important for establishing the milieu in which Joseph and Aseneth was written.

The Issue of Intermarriage

The concern with intermarriage as a problem in the first story provides the basic argument for the view that the story is Jewish. The point is not that Christians had no problem with intermarriage, but that this problem was much more central to Judaism than to Christianity. While Kraemer acknowledges that this is the argument that has weighed most heavily with scholars, she devotes only a paragraph to it.[21] (In contrast, she devotes whole chapters to "the Adjuration of Angels" and analogies with Hekalot traditions, which are of dubious relevance). Instead, she attempts to dismiss the issue by asserting that "the very popularity of the text among Christians demonstrates that Christians found the tale quite compelling and presumably had considerable interest in the themes it presented, incuding the mar-

---

[20] Kraemer, *When Aseneth Met Joseph*, 40–41.
[21] Ibid., 247.

riage of an Israelite to a gentile."[22] But even she concedes in a foot-
note that Christians may have been primarily interested in the story
as a metaphor for the conversion of Gentiles to Christianity.[23] As
we have noted already, composition and transmission are quite
different processes. Kraemer's argument is weakened by her failure
to produce evidence of Christian concern with intermarriage, such
as would have generated this story in the first place.

The issue of intermarriage is ubiquitous in ancient Jewish literature.[24] It appears as a concern already in Genesis. The ban on intermarriage with the peoples of the land in Deut 7:1–4 was later
interpreted as applying to all Gentiles. The concern with intermarriage is apparent not only in rigoristic writings from the land of
Israel, such as the book of Jubilees, but also in Jewish literature written in Greek (e.g. Philo, *Spec Leg* 3.29; Josephus, *Ant* 8.191; 12.187).[25]
The comment of Philonenko, "le mariage de Joseph et Aséneth posait
une question à la conscience juive," is indisputably well founded.[26]

The issue of intermarriage is much less prominent in early Christian
writings, but it is present. St. Paul admonishes the Corinthians, "do
not get misyoked with unbelievers, for what have righteousness and
lawlessness in common?" (2 Cor 6:14). The verb "misyoke," *het-
erozygein*, is used in LXX Lev 19:19, where the context concerns
breeding. Philo invokes this verse of Leviticus against adultery and
sexual vice,[27] but also more generally with reference to justice.[28] Paul
discourages dealings with non-Christians, and the admonition certainly applies to intermarriage among other things.[29] He comments
more extensively on the subject of marriage in 1 Corinthians 7.[30]
There, the main thrust of his argument is "that it is well for a man
not to touch a woman" (1 Cor 7:1) but that sexual relations within
marriage are recommended as a safeguard against immorality. The

---

[22] Ibid., 247
[23] Ibid., 275.
[24] See S. J. D. Cohen, *The Beginnings of Jewishness* (Berkeley, CA: University of
California Press, 1999) 241–62.
[25] See further Barclay, *Jews in the Mediterranean Diaspora*, 410–11.
[26] Philonenko, *Joseph et Aséneth*, 101.
[27] Spec. Leg. 3.46.
[28] Spec. Leg. 4.204.
[29] V. P. Furnish, *II Corinthians* (AB 32A; New York: Doubleday, 1984) 361.
[30] See O. L. Yarbrough, *Not Like the Gentiles: Marriage Rules in the Letters of Paul*
(Atlanta: Scholars Press, 1985).

issue of intermarriage is only addressed with respect to existing marriages. There Paul says that the believer should not take the initiative to divorce, but is not bound if the unbelieving partner should separate. Finally, he rules that a widow is free to marry anyone she wishes, but "only in the Lord" (1 Cor 7:39). In 1 Peter 3:1 the existence of marriages between Christians and unbelievers seems to be accepted.

Paul certainly disapproved of new marriages between believers and unbelievers, but it does not appear to have been a major issue for the early Christian communities. The line is drawn between "believers" and "unbelievers." The crucial distinction is between those who accepted Jesus as the Christ or messiah, and those who did not. Tertullian provides one of the most explicit Christian statements on the subject, in his treatise *De Corona*: "Marriage too decks the bridegroom with its crown; and therefore we will not have heathen brides, lest they seduce us even to the idolatry with which among them marriage is initiated. You have the law from the patriarchs indeed; you have the apostle enjoining people to marry in the Lord."[31] Elsewhere, Tertullian specifies that "only in the Lord" means "to a Christian."[32] Condemnations of intermarriage appear occasionally in the Church Fathers and in the canons of Church councils.[33] It should be noted that marriage with Jews was no more acceptable than marriage with Gentiles. The Theodosian Code (435 CE) placed Jewish-Christian marriage on a par with adultery (which was punishable by death).[34]

The theme of intermarriage, then, was not without interest for Christians. Should we infer that a story like *Joseph and Aseneth* could as easily have been written by a Christian as by a Jew? The issue here is one of relative probability. The *possibility* of Christian authorship can not be excluded. The question is whether there is anything

---

[31] Tertullian, *De Corona*, chap. 13, in A. Roberts and J. Donaldson, ed. *The Ante-Nicene Fathers IV* (Grand Rapids: Eerdmans, n.d., original publication, 1885) 101 (henceforth *ANF*).

[32] Tertullian, "To His Wife," Book 2, chapter 2, in ANF 4.45.

[33] For references see Ramsay MacMullen, *Christianizing the Roman Empire (A.D. 100–400)* (New Haven: Yale University Press, 1984) 136, n. 31. These include Cyprian, *Testimonia* 3.62, *De lapsis* 6 and the councils of Elvira, Arles and Hippo. I am indebted to Shaye Cohen for this reference.

[34] *Theodosian Code* 232, 70. M. R. Cohen, *Under Crescent and Cross. The Jews in the Middle Ages* (Princeton: Princeton University Press, 1994) 35, 129.

in this tale of the marriage of an Israelite man and a Gentile woman that makes a Jewish origin more likely?

The first point to consider here is what the conversion of Aseneth entails. Joseph's initial objection even to kissing Aseneth (after he has been assured that she will not molest him!) is formulated in religious rather than ethnic terms: "It is not right for a man who worships God, who with his mouth blesses the living God, and eats the blessed bread of life, and drinks the blessed cup of immortality and is anointed with the blessed unction of incorruption, to kiss a strange woman, who with her mouth blesses dead and dumb idols and eats of their table the bread of anguish, and drinks of their libations the cup of treachery and is anointed with the unction of destruction."[35] He does not say that Hebrews do not marry Egyptian women, or that ethnic intermarriage as such is an abomination to his God. This tendency to emphasize moral and religious claims rather than ethnic particularity is quite compatible with Christian authorship,[36] but it is also quite typical of Hellenistic Judaism.[37]

In Christianity, the line between insider and outsider is typically drawn on grounds of belief or unbelief. Faith as such is not raised as an issue in *Joseph and Aseneth*. The closest we come is when Aseneth first sees Joseph and is overwhelmed by his appearance. Aseneth repents of having spoken evil of him because "I did not know that Joseph is the son of God" (6:6; 6:3 in Burchard's edition).[38] Such recognition scenes are well attested in Jewish literature of the Second Temple period, especially in an eschatological context. In the Similitudes of Enoch, the wicked realize the error of their ways when they see "that Son of Man" in all his glory (1 Enoch 62). In the Wisdom of Solomon 5, the unrighteous are stricken when they see that the righteous are numbered among the sons of God.[39] The analogy with the

---

[35] *Joseph and Aseneth* 8:5. Trans. Cook (above, n. 17) 480.
[36] Compare Tertullian's emphasis on idolatry.
[37] See J. J. Collins, *Between Athens and Jerusalem. Jewish Identity in the Hellenistic Diaspora* (revised ed.; Grand Rapids: Eerdmans, 2000) especially 155–85. Consider, for example, the way in which the Wisdom of Solomon avoids mention of Israel by name, but refers to "a holy people and a blameless race" (Wis 10:15), even in re-telling the story of the Exodus, or the allegorical interpretation of the *kashrut* laws in the Letter of Aristeas.
[38] Pentephres, who does not convert, says that Joseph is "the first-born son of God" in 21:3.
[39] On this theme see especially G. W. E. Nickelsburg, *Resurrection, Immortality, and*

Wisdom of Solomon is especially interesting, since there the right-eous man is also said to be son of God.[40] Whether a Christian author would have portrayed Joseph as "the son of God" is open to question. Joseph is often regarded as a figure of Christ in Christian literature. Aseneth's "faith" that Joseph is the son of God, however, is confined to this one passage, and plays no further role in the story. Neither is there any other indication that Joseph is viewed in this story as a figure of Christ.

Some other factors point more strongly to Jewish authorship of the original story. Although the conversion of Aseneth involves sev-eral ritualistic features (especially in the episode of the honeycomb), there is no clear reference to any known Jewish or Christian ritual of conversion.[41] Circumcision is irrelevant, since Aseneth is a woman. Most significant, however is the absence of baptism. Proselyte bap-tism in Judaism is not attested reliably before the second century CE.[42] If *Joseph and Aseneth* derives from Diaspora Judaism before 100 CE, as most scholars think, then the absence of baptism need not be surprising. In Christianity, however, baptism was the ritual of conversion from the beginning. Its absence in *Joseph and Aseneth* weighs against both Christian authorship and against a date after which the practice of proselyte baptism had become common in Judaism.

While the emphasis in the story is on Aseneth's repudiation of idolatry, a few passages indicate that conversion also had a social and ethnic dimension. The first is the initial description of Aseneth. We are told that "she was quite unlike the daughters of the Egyptians, but in every respect like the daughters of the Hebrews. She was tall as Sarah, and as beautiful as Rebecca, and as fair as Rachel" (1:7–8; 1:5 in Burchard's edition). Kraemer points out that Christian read-ers did not necessarily associate the biblical patriarchs with con-temporary Jews.[43] But the point to note is that Hebrews here are an ethnic group, with distinctive features.[44] No analogous claims could

---

Eternal Life in Intertestamental Judaism (Cambridge, MA: Harvard University Press, 1972) 48–92.

[40] Wis 2:13, 16. The Greek term is *pais*, but the righteous man is said to boast that God is his father.

[41] See the thorough study of this issue by Chesnutt, *From Death to Life*, 118–50.

[42] Ibid., 156–61. See also A. Yarbro Collins, *Cosmology and Eschatology in Jewish and Christian Apocalypticism* (Leiden: Brill, 1996) 224–28.

[43] Kraemer, *When Aseneth Met Joseph*, 247.

[44] The point is rhetorical. The author implies that Hebrew women are excep-

be made about the daughters of the Christians, who were not of one ethnic group. The comment makes much more sense in a Jewish context.

Conversion and marriage necessarily entails transfer from one social group to another. The prayer of Aseneth in chapter 12 claims that her parents repudiate her because of her conversion, but this is not borne out by the story, where her father is delighted at her conversion and marriage. We may suspect that the prayer is a secondary addition. More significant is Aseneth's acceptance by Joseph's family. After the wedding, Aseneth declares to Joseph that "your father Israel is my father" (22:3). This statement, which has no biblical basis, provides a rare acknowledgement of the communal, social, implications of conversion.[45] Aseneth is joined not only to the God of Joseph but also to his blood relatives. The recognition of the family ties entailed by the conversion makes much more sense in a Jewish than in a Christian context.

On the whole, then, the argument that the subject matter of the story points to Jewish authorship remains compelling. The subject of intermarriage was a central Jewish concern and much less important in Christianity. The absence of any reference to baptism, and the (few) expressions of solidarity with the people of Israel also favor Jewish provenance. This is not to say that Christian authorship is completely impossible, but that the balance of probability tilts distinctly towards ancient Judaism.

The Second Story: The Conflict with Pharaoh's Son

The second story in *Joseph and Aseneth* also seems to me to make much better sense in a Jewish context than in a Christian one. While I am not persuaded by Gideon Bohak's thesis that the whole story is an allegory for the founding of the temple at Leontopolis, I find it impossible to read the exploits of Levi in chapters 22–29 without

---

tionally good-looking. To my knowledge, Jews were not distinguished by their appearance in the ancient world.

[45] The ethnic character of the religion to which Aseneth converts is emphasized by Barclay, *Jews in the Mediterranean Diaspora*, 213–4, although even he acknowledges that "this community is not, in the author's view, confined within ethnic boundaries." The ethnic character of Joseph's religion is not emphasized in *Joseph and Aseneth*, but the occasional ethnic references are nonetheless revealing.

being reminded of the careers of Onias and his descendants in Egypt.[46] According to Josephus, Onias took up arms against Ptolemy Physcon, the brother of his patron Philometor, on behalf of the latter's widow, Cleopatra (*Ag Ap* 2.50–52), and later Oniad generals, Chelkias and Ananias, took similar action in support of Cleopatra III in her conflict with her son Ptolemy Lathyrus (*Ant* 13. 284–7). I am not suggesting that *Joseph and Aseneth* should be read as an allegory for either of these incidents, or as alluding to them at all,[47] but that this period provides a context where one might credibly imagine a Jewish priest-soldier intervening in conflicts within the royal family in Egypt. This story would have pointed relevance for Jews in Egypt in the last century of Ptolemaic rule. I am not aware that any other context has been proposed that would make such good sense of the story.[48] Where do we have analogous tales about political intrigue and loyalty to a pagan ruler in early Christianity?

Neither is there anything in this story that can stand as a positive indication of Christian origin. The willingness of Levi and Aseneth to forgive their enemies, and not return evil for evil was obviously congenial to Christians. Such sentiments were alien to the kind of Judaism found in the Dead Sea Scrolls, but were they necessarily alien to Hellenistic Judaism? When the king in the Letter of Aristeas asks his Jewish guests "to whom must one be generous?" he is told that the general opinion is that we should be amicably disposed toward those who are amicably disposed to us, but "my belief is that we must show liberal charity to our opponents so that in this manner we may convert them to what is proper and fitting to them" (*Ep Arist* 227). When Levi restrains Simeon from killing the king's

---

[46] G. Bohak, *Joseph and Aseneth and the Jewish Temple in Heliopolis* (Atlanta: Schlars Press, 1996). On the portrayal of Levi, see especially pp.47–52. See also Collins, *Between Athens and Jerusalem*, 103–110.

[47] Angela Standhartinger seems to think that any attempt to correlate the text with a social historical context must imply a one to one correlation. But her own focus on the *Frauenbild* of the text renders her oblivious to other aspects of its meaning. (A. Standhartinger, *Das Frauenbild im Judentum der hellenistischen zeit: Ein Beitrag anhand von 'Joseph und Aseneth'* [AGJU 26; Leiden: Brill, 1995] 18). Barclay, *Jews in the Mediterranean Diaspora*, 210, n. 44, grants that "the general shape of legends may reveal social and cultural conditions," but refuses to ask what conditions might be revealed by this story.

[48] The conciliatory tone of Joseph and Aseneth seems to me less plausible in the first century CE, the date proposed by D. Sänger, "Erwägungen zur historischen Einordnung und zur Datierung von 'Joseph und Aseneth,' *ZNW* 76 (1985) 86–106.

son, he offers a pragmatic reason: "if he lives, he will be our friend, and his father Pharaoh will be our father" (*Joseph and Aseneth*, 29:4). I see no reason to regard this reasoning as peculiarly Christian.

The Question of Date

What can be said of the date of the composition? This is inevitably bound up with the question of provenance. If the text was written in Egypt, as is usually supposed, then a date before the revolt under Trajan is most likely. Later composition is not impossible, but we lack evidence for ongoing literary activity by Egyptian Jews after the revolt. If the text was not written in Egypt, this argument would lose its force. But it seems to me that Egypt is still the most plausible setting, especially in the case of the second story.[49] While it is possible that this story was composed separately as a supplement to the story of Aseneth's conversion, it is clearly not independent of it. The story of Aseneth's conversion might be older than that of the conflict with Pharaoh's son, but it cannot be later than it. Kraemer's (slight) preference for Syria as the place of origin appeals to the fact that the oldest manuscript witnesses are Syrian (6th or 7th century CE). One might as well have argued, before the discovery of the Dead Sea Scrolls, that the books of Enoch and Jubilees originated in Ethiopia. The "many affinities with Syrian Christian traditions,"[50] especially the Odes of Solomon, are of a general character. It is not apparent that these affinities are closer than those with the works of Philo or with Hellenistic Jewish literature.[51]

Kraemer has argued strenuously for a date no earlier than the third or fourth century. The main argument for this position is the lack of attestation of the text before the fifth century. This point is certainly noteworthy, but it is still an argument from silence, and hardly decisive. The complementary argument, that *Joseph and Aseneth* reflects the religious sensibility of late antiquity, seems to me of mixed value.

The mystical encounter of Aseneth with the angel is an episode in a story of marriage and conversion, not the primary focus of the

---

[49] So also Humphrey, *Joseph and Aseneth*, 30.
[50] Kraemer, *When Aseneth Met Joseph*, 291.
[51] See e.g. the references cited in the notes to Burchard's translation.

narrative. It does not seem to me that any part of the story can reasonably be called "a tale of adjuration of an angel by a woman."[52] An adjuration is an action performed in order to bring about an encounter with a heavenly being. (Kraemer speaks of "those ancient practices and traditions that envision the ability of human beings to adjure [that is, compel] divine beings to appear and to perform the bidding of the adjurer."[53] But there is nothing to indicate that Aseneth performed her actions with a view to calling down an angel or compelling him to appear. She performs rituals of repentance, casting out her idols, putting off her fine clothes and putting on sackcloth and ashes, and fasting. The apparition of the angel is completely unexpected.[54] (We might compare the episode in Daniel chapter 9, where Daniel's prayer of repentance is followed by the apparition of an angel who explains the text of Jeremiah that had been bothering him). Her actions bear some similarity not only to the rituals of adjuration, but more generally to "the phases of ritual elucidated and analyzed by Victor Turner, namely, separation, liminality, transformation, and reintegration."[55] The same can be said, even more obviously, of rituals of conversion.

The affinities with merkavah mysticism and Hellenistic magic as stated by Kraemer seem to me greatly exaggerated. No character in Joseph and Aseneth is going down to the chariot or up to the heavens. The similarities are no more than we might find with visionary texts of the Hellenistic period.[56] No confidence can be placed in Kraemer's explanation of the bees in terms of Neoplatonism.[57] The episode of the bees is the most obscure part of the entire book, and has given rise to a bewildering range of explanations. For Bohak, the bees symbolize priests;[58] for Kraemer, they are souls. But it is not apparent from the story that they are either. The bees of Paradise,

---

[52] Kraemer, *When Aseneth Met Joseph*, 90

[53] Ibid.

[54] So also R. D. Chesnutt, review of Kraemer, *When Aseneth Met Joseph*, in *JBL* 119(2000) 761.

[55] Kraemer, *When Aseneth Met Joseph*, 95. See further R. C. Douglas, "Liminality and Conversion in Joseph and Aseneth," *JSP* 3(1988) 31–42.

[56] Note the interesting treatment of the visionary material in Joseph and Aseneth in E. M. Humphrey, *The Ladies and the Cities: Transformation and Apocalyptic Identity in Joseph and Aseneth, 4 Ezra, the Apocalypse and The Shepherd of Hermas* (JSPSup 17; Sheffield: Sheffield Academic Press, 1995).

[57] Kraemer, *When Aseneth Met Joseph*, 167–72.

[58] Bohak, *Joseph and Aseneth*, 1–18.

we are told, make the honey that is the food of immortality. Subsequently, they die and rise again, and go off to Aseneth's tower. Souls do not die, in the Platonic tradition. I suspect that Philonenko was on the right track in looking to the Egyptian symbolism of the bees,[59] but they are not only associated with the goddess Neith. They are ubiquitous in ancient Egypt, and especially associated with royalty.[60] Their symbolism in *Joseph and Aseneth*, however, is obscure, and all interpretations hitherto proposed are controversial.[61]

The strongest case for late antique sensibility adduced by Kraemer, in my judgment, is the similarity between Joseph and depictions of Helios.[62] Solar imagery was not a novelty of late antiquity, as can be seen from its widespread use in Philo, but the best parallels we have to the figure of Joseph riding on his chariot are in mosaics of the third century CE or thereabouts. But this passage in chapter 5 is not what we might call a structural pillar of the story. It is more in the character of an embellishment. It is clear from the differences between the extant texts of Joseph and Aseneth that the story could be embellished to varying degrees, while the storyline remained intact. If the story was originally composed in the Hellenistic period, as I continue to believe, there was ample time for embellishment before the extant forms of the text were produced. In fact, none of the examples that Kraemer has adduced as evidence of late antique sensibility in Joseph and Aseneth, pertain to the core of what the story is about. Moreover, many scholars have noted the resemblance to the Christian Eucharist in the passages that refer to eating the bread of life and drinking the cup of immortality.[63] The current consensus is that these passages symbolize the Jewish way of life.[64] But one could grant that there are late antique elements in this story without thereby being forced to suppose that the whole story was composed in the third or fourth century CE.

[59] Philonenko, *Joseph et Aséneth*, 65.
[60] J. Leclant, "Biene," in W. Helck and O. Eberhard, ed., *Lexikon der Ägyptologie* (Wiesbaden: Harrassowitz, 1975) I.786–90.
[61] E. M. Humphrey, "On Bees and Best Guesses: The Problem of Sitz im Leben from Internal Evidence, as Illustrated by *Joseph and Aseneth*," *Currents in Research: Biblical Studies* 7(1999) 223–36.
[62] Kraemer, *When Aseneth Met Joseph*, 156–63.
[63] G. D. Kilpatrick, "The Last Supper," *ET* 64(1952/53) 4–8; J. Jeremias, "The Last Supper," *ET* 64(1952/53) 91–92.
[64] Chesnutt, *From Death to Life*, 128–37.

Conclusion

Joseph and Aseneth is an imaginative fiction. Whatever we conclude about its provenance is a matter of inference, not of certainty. Nonetheless, some inferences can claim more probability than others. In this case, the balance of probability still favors the consensus view that the story originated in Hellenistic Judaism.

The arguments for Jewish authorship concern first of all the basic subject matter of the story. While a story of intermarriage of an Israelite and an Egyptian was not without interest for Christians, it was of far more central importance in a Jewish context. The likelihood of Jewish authorship is confirmed by the laudatory reference to Hebrew women in chapter 1, and by Aseneth's embrace of Joseph's father and brothers after her wedding. The fact that the conversion does not involve baptism weighs heavily against Christian composition, and against a late date for the story. Unlike so many pseudepigraphic writings about biblical figures, this story has no unequivocally Christian elements.

The lack of clear Christian elements seems to me to argue against any claim of extensive Christian redaction, let alone Christian authorship in *Joseph and Aseneth*. The Christian copyists already found much that was congenial to their interests in the tale. The story of Aseneth's transformation was highly suggestive for the transformation of converts to Christianity. But the fact that Christians found material congenial did not mean that they composed it. Christianity was built on Jewish foundations, not only in its messianic expectation but also in its appropriation of Greek philosophy and culture. The Hellenization of Christianity followed the trail of the Hellenization of Judaism in such authors as Philo. *Joseph and Aseneth* belongs to this world of Hellenized Judaism, which was, on the whole, repudiated by the rabbis, and owed its preservation to Christianity.

CHAPTER EIGHT

LIFE AFTER DEATH IN PSEUDO-PHOCYLIDES

The subject of life after death is introduced parenthetically in the Sayings of Pseudo-Phocylides (97–115), in the context of an exhortation on moderation and equanimity. As is typical of aphoristic collections, sayings are juxtaposed because of thematic association rather than strict consequential logic. Advice on moderation in grief is followed by admonitions against disturbing graves or dissolving the human frame.[1] This, in turn, leads to the reflections on life after death. The passage, beginning at vs. 103, reads as follows:

καὶ τάχα δ' ἐκ γαίης ἐλπίζομεν ἐς φάος ἐλθεῖν
λείψαν' ἀποιχομένων. Ὀπίσω δὲ θεοὶ τελέθονται
ψυχαὶ γὰρ μίμνουσιν ἀκήριοι ἐν φθιμένοισιν
πνεῦμα γὰρ ἐστι θεοῦ χρῆσις θνητοῖσι καὶ εἰκών
σῶμα γὰρ ἐκ γαίης ἔχομεν κἄπειτα πρὸς αὖ γῆν
λυόμενοι κόνις ἐσμέν. ἀὴρ δ' ἀνὰ πνεῦμα δέδεκται...
πάντες ἴσον νέκυες, ψυχῶν δὲ θεὸς βασιλεύει
κοινὰ μέλαθρα δόμων αἰώνια καὶ πατρὶς Ἅιδης
ξυνὸς χῶρος ἅπασι πένησί τε καὶ βασιλεῦσιν
οὐ πολὺν ἄνθρωποι ζῶμεν χρόνον ἀλλ' ἐπίκαιρον
ψυχὴ δ' ἀθάνατος καὶ ἀγήρως ζῆ διὰ παντός

The passage is translated as follows by van der Horst (with my own variations in parentheses):

> For (and) in fact[2] we hope that the remains of the departed will soon (perhaps) come to the light again out of the earth. And afterwards they become gods.
> For the souls remain unharmed in the deceased (among the dead).
> For the spirit is a loan from God to mortals, and his image.
> For we have a body out of earth, and when afterwards we are resolved again into earth we are but dust; but the air has received our spirit. . . .
> All alike are corpses, but God rules over the souls

---

[1] W. T. Wilson, *The Mysteries of Righteousness. The Literary Composition and Genre of the Sentences of Pseudo-Phocylides* (TSAJ 40; Tübingen: Mohr-Siebeck, 1994) claims that vss. 9–131 are structured according to the four cardinal virtues, and relates vss. 55–96 to moderation, but 97–121 to courage. Vss. 97–98, however, are clearly concerned with moderation.

[2] There is no Greek counterpart for "in fact."

> Hades is our common eternal home and fatherland,
> a common place for all, poor and kings.
> We humans live not a long time but for a season.
> But our soul is immortal and lives ageless forever.[3]

This short passage appears to contain a bewildering range of different ideas about the afterlife. The hope that the remains will come to light out of the earth follows on an admonition against dissolving the human frame, and so would seem to imply a physical resurrection. In contrast, several statements affirm the immortality of the soul. But here again there is a complication. According to vs. 105, "souls remain unharmed among the dead," but the air (ἀήρ) receives the spirit (πνεῦμα). Most scholars assume that the soul and the spirit are one and the same, but some have argued that they should be distinguished. Finally, the statement that Hades is our common eternal home echoes an older eschatology, whereby the shade descends to Hades and there is neither physical resurrection nor ascent of the spirit to the heavens.

Scholarly assessments of this confusing passage are of two kinds. On the one hand, H. C. Cavallin refers to "the unharmonized juxtaposition of contradictory ideas about afterlife."[4] Van der Horst cites with approval a dictum of Arthur Darby Nock about "the widespread tendency of language about the afterlife to admit of inconsistencies."[5] Johannes Thomas suggests that the author is stringing together whatever ideas are brought to mind by the theme of death.[6] Pascale Derron claims that Pseudo-Phocylides assembles ideas of afterlife that were current in his time, and declines to make a synthesis.[7] Such eclectic juxtaposition of ideas is typical of aphoristic wisdom, and Pseudo-Phocylides was no philosopher. On the other hand, Felix Christ and Ulrich Fischer have tried to find a coherent doctrine of life after death in Pseudo Phocylides.[8] Christ, who refers

---

[3] Trans. P. W. van der Horst, *The Sentences of Pseudo-Phocylides* (SVTP 4; Leiden: Brill, 1978).

[4] H. C. Cavallin, *Life After Death. Paul's Argument for the Resurrection of the Dead in 1 Cor 15. Part I. An Enquiry into the Jewish Background* (Lund: Gleerup, 1974) 153.

[5] A. D. Nock, *Essays on Religion and the Ancient World* (Oxford: Oxford University Press, 1972) I.507, n. 19. Cf. Van der Horst, *The Sentences*, 188–9.

[6] J. Thomas, *Der jüdische Phokylides* (NTOA 23; Fribourg: Universitätsverlag/Göttingen: Vandenhoeck & Ruprecht, 1992) 206.

[7] P. Derron, *Pseudo-Phocylide. Sentences* (Paris: Les Belles Lettres, 1986) 25.

[8] F. Christ, "Das Leben nach dem Tode bei Pseudo-Phokylides," *Theologische*

to the passage as "ein typisch synkretistisches Amalgam,"[9] argues for
a tripartite anthropology, involving body, soul (ψυχή) and πνεῦμα,
each of which is assigned a different place after death, until they
are brought together in the resurrection. Fischer also affirms a tri-
partite anthropology, but he denies that Pseudo Phocylides envisions
resurrection of the body. Consequently, he denies that all three elements are combined again at the resurrection.[10]

The disagreements between these scholars involve two main issues.
First, does Ps. Phocylides envision physical resurrection? And if so,
how is this idea related to the belief in immortality of the soul?
Second, does Pseudo-Phocylides assume a bi-partite (body-soul) or a
tri-partite (body-soul-spirit) anthropology? A third question is raised
indirectly: how does Pseudo-Phocylides relate to the spectrum of
Jewish ideas about the afterlife in the centuries around the turn of
the era?

Physical Resurrection?

An apparent belief in physical resurrection is expressed in verses
103–104: "we hope that the remains of the departed will perhaps
come to the light again out of the earth." This is characterized by
van der Horst as "a very literalistic doctrine of the resurrection,"
which was "typically Jewish and very un-Greek."[11] There were in
fact many stories in the Greek world of individuals who had returned
from the dead, but most educated Greeks would have found the resurrection of the physical body incomprehensible or ridiculous.[12] It is
not quite accurate, however, to say that such an idea was typically
Jewish.[13] Jewish texts from the second century BCE to first century
CE exhibit a wide range of conceptions of life after death, and only

---

Zeitschrift 31(1975) 140–7; U. Fischer, *Eschatologie und Jenseitserwartung im Hellenistischen
Diasporajudentum* (BZNW 44; Berlin: de Gruyter, 1978) 125–43.
    [9] Christ, *Das Leben nach dem Tode*, 147.
    [10] Fischer, *Eschatologie*, 140.
    [11] Van der Horst, *The Sentences*, 185.
    [12] D. B. Martin, *The Corinthian Body* (New Haven: Yale University Press, 1995)
114. Martin insists, correctly, that the usual contrast between Jewish and Greek
views on this subject is oversimplified and ultimately misleading (p. 110).
    [13] The classic contrast of Jewish and Greek eschatology is that of O. Cullmann,
"Immortality of the Soul or Resurrection of the Dead," in K. Stendahl, ed., *Immortality
and Resurrection* (New York: Harper, 1965) 9–35.

rarely affirm resurrection of the physical body.[14] Interestingly enough, some of the earliest texts that emphasize the physical character of the resurrection, such as 2 Maccabees 7 and Sib Or 4:181–2, were written in Greek, by authors who came from the Diaspora.[15] Nonetheless, belief in physical resurrection was atypical of Diaspora Judaism, and it is quite alien to the philosophically sophisticated works of Philo or the Wisdom of Solomon. 4 Maccabees, which deals with the same story of martyrdom as 2 Maccabees 7, eliminates the references to physical resurrection. Jewish epitaphs from the Greek-speaking Diaspora down to the end of the first century only rarely express any hope for an afterlife, and then speak of the flight of the soul to the holy ones[16] or of astral immortality.[17] Since the *Sentences* are steeped in Greek moral philosophy, it is rather surprising to encounter a literalistic belief in physical resurrection here.

The reference to "the remains of the departed," in vss. 103–4, follows an admonition against dissolving the human frame (ἁρμονίην ἀναλυέμεν).[18] Fischer points out that these verses (102 and 103) are linked only by καὶ, not by any words indicating a causal connection (such as γάρ). Instead, vss. 103–4 are linked to vs. 105 ("For the souls remain unharmed among the dead"). Fischer infers that the souls are the "remains," and so that Pseudo-Phocylides does not affirm bodily resurrection, but only immortality of the soul. But, as van der Horst has pointed out, "there are no parallels for λείψαν'

[14] This is recognized by van der Horst, *The Sentences*, 185. On the range of Jewish conceptions see G. W. E. Nickelsburg, *Resurrection, Immortality and Eternal Life in Intertestamental Judaism* (Harvard Theological Studies 26; Cambridge, MA: Harvard University Press, 1972); Cavallin, *Life After Death*; J. J. Collins. "The Afterlife in Apocalyptic Literature," in A. J. Avery-Peck and J. Neusner, ed., *Judaism in Late Antiquity. Part 4. Death, Life-After-Death, Resurrection and The World-to-Come in the Judaisms of Antiquity* (Leiden: Brill, 2000) 119–39.

[15] 2 Maccabees describes events in Jerusalem, but it is an abridgement of the work of one Jason of Cyrene, and the Greek style betrays a better Hellenistic education than is likely to have been available in Jerusalem. Sib Or 4 is usually thought to have been composed in Syria or Asia Minor.

[16] W. Horbury and D. Noy, *Jewish Inscriptions of Graeco-Roman Egypt* (Cambridge: Cambridge University Press, 1992) 69 (inscription no. 33 = CIJ 1510).

[17] CIJ 788. P. W. van der Horst, *Ancient Jewish Epitaphs* (Kampen: Kok Pharos, 1991) 123–3.

[18] Christ, "Das Leben nach dem Tode," 141, suggests that this is a polemical reference to the practice of gathering bones into ossuaries for secondary burial. Van der Horst, *The Sentences*, 184, insists that "there is not the slightest hint of the use of ossilegia in this text," and supports the view that it refers to the dissection of cadavers, which was practiced in Alexandria. It is difficult to see, however, how

ἀποιχομένων in the sense of souls, whereas its use for the bodily remains of the dead is common."[19] Λείψανα can be used for remains other than physical; for example, the remains of good people are their deeds.[20] But Fischer's solution would require that the word be used here in a way that is without parallel. The reference to physical resurrection cannot be denied.

But Pseudo-Phocylides is not necessarily so committed to belief in physical resurrection as the usual translations would suggest. The Greek reads:

καὶ τάχα δ᾽ ἐκ γαίης ἐλπίζομεν ἐς φάος ἐλθεῖν
λείψαν᾽ ἀποιχόμενων. Ὀπίσω δὲ θεοὶ τελέθονται

Van der Horst notes that τάχα can mean either "soon" or "perhaps, probably," and declares that "in view of v. 104b the first meaning is here the most feasible."[21] He translates "soon," and in this he is in agreement with all recent commentators. But Pseudo-Phocylides was no apocalyptic visionary, and there is no other hint in the poem of imminent eschatology. I would suggest that "perhaps" is the more appropriate translation here.[22] This is the only time in this passage where he speaks of hope.[23] In contrast, he categorically affirms the immortality of the soul twice (105, 115). Of that he has no doubt. The resurrection of the physical body is acknowledged as a possibility to be hoped for. Presumably, the author was aware that some Jews held this belief, and he affirms it tentatively. The subject is raised here by the admonition against "dissolving the human frame" but the admonition is not made contingent on the belief. Rather, the hope of resurrection is introduced as a supplementary supporting consideration. The tone is speculative rather than certain.

Vs. 104b, "and afterwards they become gods" does not in any way require that the resurrection take place soon. While earlier

the admonition would not apply to the practice of secondary burial, which most certainly involved the dissolution of the human frame.

[19] Van der Horst, *Essays on the Jewish World of Early Christianity* (NTOA 14; Fribourg: Universitätsverlag/Göttingen: Vandenhoeck & Ruprecht, 1990) 36

[20] H. G. Liddell and R. Scott, *A Greek-English Lexicon*, revised and augmented by H. S. Jones with the assistance of R. McKenzie (Oxford: Clarendon, 1940) 1037.

[21] Van der Horst, *The Sentences*, 185.

[22] This was already suggested by L. Schmidt, in a review of J. Bernays, *Ueber das phokylideische Gedicht*, in Jahrbücher für classische Philologie 3 (1857) 510–19.

[23] Van der Horst adds "in fact" without any basis in the Greek.

scholars found this statement shocking in a Jewish text, it is now widely recognized that it is simply a variant of a common Jewish belief, that the righteous are elevated to heaven after death to shine like stars or become companions of the angels (who are often called אלהים, gods, in contemporary Hebrew texts, such as the Dead Sea Scrolls).[24] The point at issue here is how this belief can accommodate a hope for physical resurrection. Normally, the soul or spirit was thought to ascend to heaven, and while this might still have bodily form, it was what St. Paul would call a "spiritual body" (σῶμα πνευματικόν). In the words of Plutarch, "we must not violate nature by sending the bodies of good men with their souls to heaven."[25] Even St. Paul was emphatic that "flesh and blood cannot inherit the kingdom of God" (1 Cor 15:50). It must first be transformed into a different kind of body. Pseudo-Phocylides does not discuss the transformation, but he allows space for it by claiming that physical resurrection and apotheosis are sequential stages in the afterlife. This attempt to accommodate different eschatological conceptions as stages in a process is typical of the apocalyptic literature of the late first century CE. So, for example, 4 Ezra affirms both a messianic reign on earth and a new creation, by having the messiah reign for 400 years and then die, to make way for a return to primeval silence and a new creation (4 Ezra 7:28–31). In the New Testament, Revelation similarly provides for a reign on earth for 1,000 years, followed by a new heaven and a new earth. The account of the resurrection in 2 Baruch is especially relevant to Pseudo-Phocylides:

> For the earth will certainly then restore the dead it now receives so as to preserve them: it will make no change in their form, but as it has received them, so it will restore them, and as I delivered them to it, so also will it raise them. For those who are then alive must be shown that the dead have come to life again, and that those who had departed have returned. And when they have recognized those they know now, then the judgement will begin . . ." (2 Bar 50:2–4).[26]

---

[24] J. J. Collins, "Powers in Heaven. God, Gods and Angels in the Dead Sea Scrolls, in J. J. Collins and R. A. Kugler, *Religion in the Dead Sea Scrolls* (Grand Rapids: Eerdmans, 2000) 1–28. For the belief that the righteous would be raised up to heaven after death see Dan 12:2; 1 Enoch 104:2–6.

[25] Plutarch, *Romulus*, 28.8. See Martin, *The Corinthian Body*, 113.

[26] Trans. R. H. Charles, revised by L. H. Brockington, in H. F. D. Sparks, *The Apocryphal Old Testament* (Oxford: Clarendon, 1984) 869.

Then, after the judgement, the appearance of both righteous and wicked will change: the righteous "will be transformed so that they look like angels" (51:5), while the wicked become decaying shadows of their former selves. 2 Baruch, then, provides both for physical resurrection and for transformation to an angelic state. These were originally two quite distinct conceptions of the afterlife, but in the later apocalypses different traditions are combined. Pseudo-Phocylides is engaging in a similar synthesis of distinct traditions.

Soul and Spirit

The form of afterlife that is most emphatically affirmed by Pseudo-Phocylides is the immortality of the soul, which is asserted in vss. 105 and 115. The first of these statements is somewhat puzzling: ψυχαὶ γὰρ μίμνουσιν ἀκήριοι ἐν φθιμένοισιν. Van der Horst translates: "for the souls remain unharmed in the deceased." The initial impression here is that the soul remains alive in the dead body. But then in vs. 108 we are told that the air receives the spirit. Vss. 111–113 suggest that the soul lives on in Hades. In light of the latter point, the phrase ἐν φθιμένοισιν in vs. 105 is better translated as "among the dead" (i.e. in Hades). Most commentators assume that the soul (ψυχή) and the spirit (πνεῦμα) are one and the same, and consequently find a contradiction between vss. 105 and 108.[27] Christ and Fischer, however, argue that Pseudo-Phocylides is making a three-fold distinction between body, soul and spirit.[28] So vs. 105 begins ψυχαὶ γὰρ, vs. 106 πνεῦμα γάρ, and vs. 108 σῶμα γάρ. In this reading, each element goes to a different place at death: the body returns to dust, the soul goes to Hades, and the spirit goes up to the air.

Pseudo-Phocylides' understanding of the make-up of the human being draws on the opening chapters of Genesis. The statement that the body is from earth and returns to dust (vss. 107–8) echoes Gen 3:19. The reference to the image of God in vs. 106 alludes to Gen 1:27. The mention of the spirit, πνεῦμα, derives from Gen 2:7b, which reads in the LXX:

---

[27] E.g. van der Horst, *The Sentences*, 189.
[28] Christ, *Das Leben nach dem Tode*, 144; Fischer, *Eschatologie*, 140.

Ἐνεφύσησεν εἰς τὸ πρόσωπον αὐτοῦ πνοὴν ζωῆς, καὶ ἐγένετο ὁ ἄνθρωπος εἰς ψυχὴν ζῶσαν.

As Philo explains: that which he breathed in was nothing else than divine spirit (οὐδὲν ἦν ἕτερον ἤ πνεῦμα θεῖον).[29] Philo also links the in-breathing of the spirit to the imprint of the image of God: "Moses likened the fashion of the reasonable soul to no created thing, but averred it to be a genuine coinage of that dread Spirit, the Divine and Invisible One, signed and impressed by the seal of God, the stamp of which is the Eternal Word. His words are 'God in-breathed into his face a breath of Life;' so that it cannot but be that he that receives is made in the likeness of Him Who sends forth the breath. Accordingly we also read that man has been made after the image of God."[30] More precisely, Philo held that the human being "was made a likeness and imitation of the Logos when the divine breath was breathed into his face."[31] He is very specific that "it is in respect of the Mind, the sovereign element of the soul, that the word 'image' is used."[32] The image then is not the human being as a whole, but is imprinted on the mind by the divine spirit.

Both the formulation of Gen 2:7b and the various statements of Philo on the image of God invite a distinction between ψυχή and πνεῦμα. This distinction has been discussed extensively in the context of 1 Corinthians 15, where St. Paul draws a contrast between the σῶμα ψυχικόν that is buried and the σῶμα πνευματικόν that is raised. In his Harvard dissertation, Birger Pearson argued that the distinction was derived from Hellenistic-Jewish exegesis of Genesis.

At least some Hellenistic philosophers distinguished between the soul and the mind (νοῦς), with the latter being the higher element. So, for example, Plutarch wrote that "every soul partakes of mind; none is completely irrational or deprived of mind,"[33] but souls are also mixed to varying degrees with the flesh and passions. Pearson

---

[29] *De Opif.* 135.
[30] *Plant* 18–19.
[31] *De Opif.* 139. Compare also *Det* 83. See G. Sterling, "Wisdom among the Perfect: Creation Traditions in Alexandrian Judaism and Corinthian Christianity," *Novum Testamentum* 37(1995) 355–84 (especially 357–67) and, in general, J. Jervell, *Imago Dei. Gen. I 26f. im Spätjudentum, in der Gnosis und in den paulinischen Briefen* (Göttingen: Vandenhoeck & Ruprecht, 1960).
[32] *De Opif.* 69; Cf. *Spec. Leg.* I 81 and many other passages.
[33] Plutarch, *de genio Socratis*, 591 D-F.

contends that the Hellenistic Jewish authors substituted πνεῦμα for νοῦς as the divine element (or alternated between the two terms and related this to Gen 1:27, where humanity is created in the image of God.[34] Philo does not in fact draw a clear distinction between ψυχή and πνεῦμα, and sometimes uses them interchangeably.[35] He distinguishes between the mind, as the dominant part of the soul, and the soul as a whole,[36] but can also refer to the soul as a divine fragment from the upper air (ἡ δέ ψυχή αἰθέρος ἐστίν, ἀπόσπασμα θεῖον).[37] It does not appear that a distinction between soul and spirit was a standard part of Hellenistic Jewish exegetical tradition.[38] Nonetheless, the occasional distinction between ψυχή and πνεῦμα in the exegesis of Genesis is illuminating for the case of Pseudo-Phocylides.[39] If ψυχή and πνεῦμα are one and the same, then vs. 108 is contradictory to the statements about the souls in vss. 105 and 111. While it is possible that Pseudo-Phocylides is merely stringing together traditional sentiments, without regard for consistency, an interpretation that does not posit incoherence must be preferred.

If ψυχή and πνεῦμα are distinguished here, the implication is that the element by which human beings share in the image of God is withdrawn at death. According to vss. 107–108, the body becomes dust and the air receives the spirit. Thus far Pseudo-Phocylides reflects a quite traditional anthropology. We may compare the account of death in Qoheleth: "the dust returns to the earth as it was, and the spirit returns to God who gave it" (Qoh 12:7).

But what then of the soul? Two things are said about it. First, it "is immortal and lives ageless forever" (115). Second, the place where

---

[34] Pearson, *The Pneumatikos-Psychikos Terminology*, 11–12. It should be noted that non-Jewish authors could also refer to the higher part of the self as πνεῦμα. See Martin, *The Corinthian Body*, 275, n. 64.

[35] R. A. Horsley, "Pneumatikos vs. Psychikos: distinctions of Spiritual Status among the Corinthians," *HTR* 69(1976) 271–2. See also D. Winston, *Logos and Mystical Philosophy in Philo of Alexandria* (Cincinnati: Hebrew Union College, 1985) 27–42 on Philo's concept of the ψυχή.

[36] Her 55: "We use 'soul' in two senses, both for the whole soul and also for its dominant part, which properly speaking is the soul's soul."

[37] Leg. All. 3.161.

[38] Josephus, in his paraphrase of Gen 2:7 says that God injected a spirit into Adam, and a soul (*Ant* 1.34), but even here it is possible that he is using a hendiadys, and that the two are regarded as the same.

[39] Pseudo-Phocylides has not been part of the discussion of the *psychikos-pneumatikos* distinction.

it lives on is the Netherworld, or Hades. According to vs. 108 it remains "unharmed among the dead" (ἐν φθιμένοισιν). The statement that "God rules over the souls" (111) conjures up a picture of a god of the Netherworld, such as Pluto or Osiris, except that for the Jewish author this God is also the God of the living. Vs. 112 continues: "Hades is our common home." The idea that the soul lives on in Hades is found already in Homer. In the words of Albrecht Dihle: "The soul goes to the underworld and may sometimes show itself to a living person in a dream prior to burial of the corpse, taking on the appearance of the living man for this purpose. In the underworld it leads a shadowy existence which has little to do with the self of man . . . Nothing is expected of the shadowy existence of the ψυχή in the underworld."[40] This concept was essentially similar to the Hebrew נפש which also lived on in Sheol as a shade. The Platonic idea of the immortal soul was quite different from this, and implied a much fuller life after death, since the soul was now the seat of the personality. While the older ideas of the afterlife were repudiated by philosophers, they lived on in popular religion into the Hellenistic age.[41] Consider, for example, an epitaph from the "land of Onias" at Leontopolis: "'How old were you when you slipped down into the shadowy region of Lethe?' At twenty years old I went to the mournful place of the dead . . . 'Childless I went to the house of Hades.' May the earth, the guardian of the dead, be light upon you."[42]

Precisely how Pseudo-Phocylides understood the immortal soul is unclear. It seems to be immortal by its nature: immortality is not a reward for righteousness.[43] Nothing is said of a judgement after death; the reference to Hades as a "our common home" suggests that there is no separation of righteous and wicked, at least initially. If the spirit is withdrawn, the life of the soul must be diminished, but Pseudo-Phocylides appears to view it positively. The fact that the

---

[40] A. Dihle, "ψυχή in the Greek World," *TDNT* 9(1974) 609.

[41] See the classic study of E. Rohde, *Psyche. The Cult of Souls and Belief in Immortality among the Greeks* (New York: Harcourt, Brace & Co., 1925) 524–7.

[42] W. Horbury and D. Noy, *Jewish Inscriptions of Graeco-Roman Egypt* (Cambridge: Cambridge University Press, 1992) 90 (no. 38 = *CIJ* no. 1530).

[43] Pearson, *The Pneumatikos-Psychikos Terminology*, 21, asserts that "no Jew, not even Philo, could go so far as to assert with Plato that the soul was immortal by its very nature and therefore incapable of mortality." This does not hold true for Pseudo-Phocylides.

soul remains unharmed means that it is available for resurrection. Again, we are given no indication as to whether everyone is to be raised.[44] We should hardly expect that everyone would "become gods." If the resurrection is selective, this might explain the rather tentative formulation of Pseudo-Phocylides: "we hope that the remains of the departed will perhaps come to the light again." The resurrection would presumably require that the spirit be again united with the soul and the bodily remains.[45]

Conclusion

Pseudo-Phocylides was not a philosopher, but a purveyor of conventional ideas. There is no doubt that he relied on traditional formulations, and these stand in some tension with each other. Much remains unclear in his exposition of the afterlife. Nonetheless, the judgement that the passage consists of "the unharmonized juxtaposition of contradictory ideas" is hardly justified. If the reading proposed here is correct, Pseudo-Phocylides combined different ideas of the afterlife, but strung them together in a way that achieved a measure of coherence. After death, the physical body returns to the earth, the soul goes to Hades, and the spirit returns to the air, to God. The immediate expectation after death, then, conforms to the popular conception of Hades, which is copiously attested in epitaphs, Gentile and Jewish, throughout the Hellenistic period. Since the soul remains unharmed, however, Pseudo-Phocylides can affirm the widespread belief in the immortality of the soul, even though that belief, in its philosophical formulations, envisioned something rather different from a shadowy afterlife in Hades. Hades, however, was not the end. Pseudo-Phocylides affirmed the hope that bodily remains would again come to light out of the earth. This hope was grounded in Jewish rather than Greek traditions, but was by no means commonplace in Judaism. It is expressed tentatively here, as a hope rather than as a firm belief. Unlike the immortality of the soul, it was not guaranteed for everyone. The ultimate hope was to "become

---

[44] Note that Dan 12:2, the classic biblical attestation of resurrection, does not imply that everyone will be raised. See J. J. Collins, *Daniel* (Hermeneia; Minneapolis: Fortress, 1993) 392.

[45] Contra Fischer, *Eschatologie*, 140.

gods," by exaltation to the heavens or the stars, as envisioned in Jewish apocalypses from early second century BCE on.

These ideas about the afterlife seem to be cobbled together from popular beliefs and traditions. Pseudo-Phocylides lacks the philosophical sophistication of Philo, or even of the Wisdom of Solomon, and the visionary certainty of the apocalypses. The poem has usually been assumed to have been composed in Alexandria, but the evidence of this assumption is very slight. Vs. 39: "strangers should be held in equal honor with citizens" certainly has resonance in an Alexandrian context in the first century CE.[46] The other main argument for Alexandrian provenance, the supposed reference to the dissection of corpses in vs. 102, must be considered doubtful, as the reference may be to the Jewish practice of secondary burial. There is nothing at all to tie Pseudo-Phocylides to any specific location outside of Egypt.[47] The closest parallel to his view of the afterlife is perhaps the passage cited above from 2 Baruch, but Pseudo-Phocylides adds to this a Hellenistic veneer, by speaking of Hades and of the immortality of the soul. The *Sentences* certainly come from a Greek-speaking environment. Egypt remains the most likely candidate. But at least on the matter of the afterlife, it attests to a form of Jewish belief that is rather different from that of Philo or the Wisdom of Solomon, and may be more reflective of popular ideas about death and the hereafter. Whatever its provenance, this poem is an intriguing witness to the variety of Judaism in the Hellenistic period.

Postscript

Pieter van der Horst has written a rejoinder to this essay, defending the interpretation that he put forward in his commentary.[48] I had not argued that van der Horst's interpretation was impossible. The passage is far too enigmatic to permit certainty. I had long accepted van der Horst's reading until it was challenged in a class I co-taught with Christopher Faraone at the University of Chicago,

---

[46] Compare Philo, *De Vita Mosis* 1.35 argues that strangers should be regarded as settlers and friends, who are near to being citizens. Wis 19:13–13 complains that the Egyptians practiced the most bitter hatred of strangers.

[47] *Pace* J. Barclay, *Jews in the Mediterranean Diaspora* (Edinburgh: Clark, 1996) 336.

[48] P. W. van der Horst, "Pseudo-Phocylides on the Afterlife: A Rejoinder to John J. Collins," *JSJ* 35(2004) 70–75.

and I was forced to re-examine it. It seems to me, however, some
of our differences are due to unduly rigid presuppositions on his part
about Jewish eschatology in this period. In the end, his interpretation requires us to assume that Pseudo-Phocylides was incoherent in
this passage, and while this is possible, it is not a conclusion that
should be readily accepted.

The more significant objections raised by van der Horst concern
the translation of lines 103 and 104 and the relation between soul
and spirit in 105–15.[49]

The first issue is a matter of nuance. We agree that Pseudo-
Phocylides endorses the belief in bodily resurrection, but on my reading he does so tentatively. Van der Horst introduces the confident
expression "in fact." In my essay I said that there was no Greek
counterpart for this expression. Van der Horst provides a helpful
explanation of the reasoning behind his translation. "For in fact," it
appears, is all a translation of one Greek word, καὶ. "For" is a reasonable rendering, as it makes explicit the connection with the fore-
going warning against disintegrating the human frame. The more
loaded expression, "in fact," is justified on the grounds that the con-
junction is often used before intensive adverbs. But is it so used here?
The answer depends on whether we translate τάχα as "soon" or
"perhaps."[50] Van der Horst argues that "the whole poem speaks a
strong and self-assured language, with never a trace of hesitancy, so
that a lame 'perhaps,' especially in such a vital matter as the nature
of life after death, would be wholly inappropriate."[51] It seems to me,
however, that dogmatism about what is "wholly inappropriate" is
itself "wholly inappropriate" here. This is the only passage in the
poem that speaks of matters beyond this life. The assumption that
the author must have been self-assured about them is entirely gratuitous. *Pace* van der Horst, a tentative stance on bodily resurrection
is in no way ruled out be 104b, "and thereafter they become gods."

---

[49] On the "un-Greek" nature of bodily resurrection, which he raises as an issue
on p. 73, we do not disagree at all. I merely acknowledged the point made
by Dale Martin that there are many Greek stories of (non-eschatological) bodily
resurrection.
[50] Van der Horst again uses circular reasoning in this case: the reading of καὶ
as intensive "makes it all the more probable that 'soon' and not 'perhaps' is meant
here" (p. 72).
[51] "Pseudo-Phocylides on the Afterlife," 73.

Any scenario of life after death should be tentative, and Pseudo-Phocylides was sophisticated enough to realize that.

The most important issue raised in the rejoinder, and also in my essay, is the relation between "soul" and "spirit." Again, any solution requires us to infer some things that are not explicit in the text, and must accordingly be tentative. The crux here concerns the relation between vs. 105, which says that "the souls remain unharmed ἐν φθιμένοισιν" and vs. 108, which says that "the air has received our spirit." I have suggested that ἐν φθιμένοισιν be translated "among the dead" (i.e. in Hades) rather than "in the deceased" (so van der Horst in his commentary, apparently meaning "in the dead bodies").[52] Van der Horst appears to accept this understanding of the verse, at least for the sake of the argument, but he objects to the distinction between soul and spirit. "Why would God rule over the souls of humans elsewhere (in Hades, says Collins) while the spirits of these same humans are with him in heaven (taken back again into the air)? That does not make sense. Only if one assumes that souls and spirits are identical can this anomaly be avoided."[53] But in fact the assumption that souls and spirits are identical only creates difficulties. For it to work at all van der Horst has to assume that Pseudo-Phocylides identified Hades with the air above, like the Stoic Cornutus. This may be possible, but Pseudo-Phocylides gives no other hint of it. His explicit references to Hades in vss. 110 and 112 are quite traditional, and it seems much more natural to assume that he located it, like the Hebrew Sheol, in the netherworld. But of course Pseudo-Phocylides does not actually say that the souls go to Hades; he says that they remain ἐν φθιμένοισιν, among the dead, or those who have perished. That would be a very odd way to designate those who were with God in heaven, as van der Horst's reading would require.[54] It makes much better sense to accept that the poet was distinguishing three elements of the human being, the body (vs. 103), the soul, which remains among the dead (vs. 105) and the spirit, which returns to God, to the air above. This reading also has the advantage of

---

[52] Van der Horst does not clarify what he means by "in the deceased" either in the commentary or in the article.

[53] "Pseudo-Phocylides on the Afterlife," 74.

[54] The difficulty would only be increased if the phrase were translated "in the deceased."

allowing Pseudo-Phocylides a measure of coherence, rather than the mere juxtaposition of contradictory ideas.

Finally, a brief comment is in order on the question whether the reference to dissolving the human frame may refer to the practice of collecting bones in ossuaries. The use of ossuaries was common in Palestine in this period, but was not, as far as we know, common in Alexandria. I do not see any basis for van der Horst's apparent assumption that an Alexandrian Jew would not have known about a practice that was common in Palestine, or have been concerned about it. Moreover, as I stated above, the evidence for Alexandrian provenance is extremely slight. Van der Horst wrote in his commentary (p. 82): "That Alexandria is to be preferred as the city where the poem probably originated is actually based on only a single line (v. 102), where it is said that it is not right to dissect a human body." He now argues that the reference in vs. 102 must be to dissection for anatomical research because of the presumed Alexandrian provenance of Pseudo-Phocylides. This reasoning is blatantly circular. A reference to dissection is possible, but a reference to the practice of secondary burial cannot be excluded.

CHAPTER NINE

THE REINTERPRETATION OF APOCALYPTIC
TRADITIONS IN THE WISDOM OF SOLOMON

The Wisdom of Solomon, written in Greek in Alexandria around the middle of the first century CE,[1] is in many ways a different kind of book from the older Hebrew wisdom writings of Proverbs, Qoheleth and Ben Sira. Some of the differences concern literary form. Proverbial sayings have very little role,[2] and the structure of the book is not nearly as loose as that of Proverbs or Ben Sira. The author uses the techniques of Greek philosophy to present a coherent argument about the value and expediency of wisdom. The book has been described as a *logos protreptikos*,[3] or didactic exhortation, or, alternatively, as an *encomium* that describes and commends wisdom.[4] The hortatory aspects of the book are most clearly in evidence in the opening section, 1:1–6:21. This section begins and ends with an exhortation to justice, but much of it is taken up with a contrast between the righteous and the wicked. The wicked explain their reasoning in a long speech in 2:1–24; but then articulate their dismay in another speech in 5:1–23, when the judgment is revealed.[5] The designation *encomium* is suggested primarily by the middle section of the book (6:22–9:18) which purports to tell "what wisdom is and how she came to be." The final section of the book, chapters 10–19, elaborates the theme

---

[1] See D. Winston, *The Wisdom of Solomon* (AB 43; New York: Doubleday, 1979) 20–25. I demur only at Winston's statement that "the apocalyptic vision in which the author describes the annihilation of the wicked with such ferocious passion (5:16–23) could only be called forth by a desperate historical situation in which the future of the Jewish community of Alexandria (and for a while even that of Palestine) was dangerously threatened..."

[2] The closest approximations to proverbial wisdom are found in Wis 3:10–4:20.

[3] J. M. Reese, *Hellenistic Influence on the Book of Wisdom and its Consequences* (Analecta Biblica 41; Rome: Pontifical Biblical Institute, 1971) 119–21; Winston, *The Wisdom of Solomon*, 18.

[4] P. Bizzetti, *Il Libro della Sapienza* (Brescia: Paideia, 1984) 157. See the review of Bizzetti by Winston in *CBQ* 48(1986), 525–7.

[5] On the structure of this section of the book see M. Kolarcik, *The Ambiguity of Death in the Book of Wisdom 1–6* (Analecta Biblica 127; Rome: Pontifical Biblical Institute, 1991) 29–62.

by citing well-known examples from biblical history, especially from
the Exodus story. The whole book amounts to a sustained argument
advocating the importance of wisdom.[6]

But the differences between the Wisdom of Solomon and the older
wisdom books are not all matters of literary form. There are also
considerable differences in worldview. In large part these are attrib-
utable to the influence of Greek philosophy on the later book. Wisdom
is portrayed in terms often used for the Stoic Logos, as a spirit that
holds all things together and orders all things well.[7] The philosophical context of the book, is now recognized as Middle Platonism,
which combines elements of Stoicism with the Platonic idea of a
transcendent deity.[8] Wisdom here is not itself the deity, but is "a
breath of the power of God, and a pure emanation of the glory of
the Almighty . . . a reflection of eternal light, a spotless mirror of the
working of God" (7:25–26). Wisdom mediates between God and the
cosmos and between God and humanity: "in every generation she
passes into holy souls and makes them friends of God and prophets"
(7:27). The workings of wisdom in history are expounded in chapters 10–19, where the success of the heroes of biblical history is
attributed to the guidance of wisdom, beginning with Adam, whom
she delivered from his transgression. All of this has precedents in the
older wisdom books. Proverbs affirmed that Wisdom played a role
in creation, and Ben Sira had taken the revolutionary step of using
examples from Israelite history to illustrate the workings of wisdom.

There was, however, a further respect in which the Wisdom of
Solomon differed from Proverbs, Qoheleth and Ben Sira. The older
Hebrew wisdom had stubbornly denied that there was any judgment
or reward after death. "Who knows," asks Qoheleth, "whether the
human spirit goes upward and the spirit of animals goes downward

---

[6] For a recent defence of the unity of the book see G. Scarpat, *Libro della Sapienza*
(3 vols.; Brescia: Paideia, 1986–99) 3.299–304.

[7] Wis 8:1. See H. Hübner, "Die Sapientia Salomonis und die antike Philosophie,"
in idem, ed., *Die Weisheit Salomos im Horizont Biblischer Theologie* (Neukirchen-Vluyn:
Neukirchener Verlag, 1993) 55–81; H. Engel, "'Was Weisheit ist und wie sie entstand, will ich verkunden.' Weish 7,22–8,1 innerhalb des egkōmion tēs sophias
(6,22–11,1) als Stärkung der Plausibilität des Judentums angesichts hellenistischer
Philosophie und Religiosität," in G. Hentschel and E. Zenger, eds., *Lehrerin der
Gerechtigkeit* (Leipzig: Benno, 1991) 67–102; C. Larcher, *Le Livre de la Sagesse ou la
Sagesse de Salomon* (Paris: Gabalda, 1984) 479–518. On the cosmology of the book
see further Scarpat, *Libro della Sapienza*, 2.45–50.

[8] Winston, *The Wisdom of Solomon*, 33.

to the earth?"[9] Ben Sira asserts emphatically: "Whether life is for ten years or a hundred or a thousand, there are no questions asked in Hades."[10] In contrast, the belief in immortality is central to the Wisdom of Solomon. The way in which this belief is formulated is colored by Greek, Platonic, philosophy. But the author of Wisdom was also heir to Jewish traditions about eternal life and a judgment after death, that had emerged in the apocalyptic writings of the last two centuries before the common era, in the books of Enoch and Daniel, and in the Dead Sea Scrolls.[11] These traditions had already made an impact on Hebrew wisdom literature, as we now know from the fragmentary wisdom texts found at Qumran, especially 4QInstruction.[12] In the Wisdom of Solomon, apocalyptic influence is most readily to be seen in three areas: 1. The judgment scenes in chapters 1–5; 2. The motif of the divine warrior in 5:17–23; and 3. The transformation of the cosmos in the account of the Exodus in chapters 16–19.

The Judgment Scenes in Wisdom 1–5

As several scholars have noted, the judgment scene in Wisdom 5 is modeled on the beginning of the servant song in Isa 52:13–53:12.[13]

---

[9] Qoh 3:21.

[10] Sir 41:4. See further J. J. Collins, "The Root of Immortality. Death in the Context of Jewish Wisdom," in idem, *Seers, Sibyls and Sages in Hellenistic-Roman Judaism* (Leiden: Brill, 1997) 351–67.

[11] J.J. Collins, *The Apocalyptic Imagination* (2nd ed.; Grand Rapids, MI: Eerdmans, 1998) 1–115; 145–76; *Apocalypticism in the Dead Sea Scrolls* (London: Routledge, 1997). The relevance of this literature for the study of *Wisdom* was noted already by P. Grelot, "L'Eschatologie de la Sagesse et les Apocalypses Juives," in A. Barucq, ed., *A la Rencontre de Dieu: Memorial Albert Gelin* (Le Puy: Mappus, 1961) 165–78. See now also S. Burkes, "Wisdom and Apocalypticism in the Wisdom of Solomon," *Harvard Theological Review* 95 (2002) 21–44.

[12] For the texts see J. Strugnell, D. Harrington and T. Elgvin, *Qumran Cave 4. XXIV. Sapiential Texts, Part 2* (DJD XXXIV; Oxford: Clarendon, 1999). For the relation to apocalyptic literature see Collins, *Apocalypticism in the Dead Sea Scrolls*, 32–42; *Jewish Wisdom in the Hellenistic Age* (Louisville, KY: Westminster, 1997) 112–31; A. Lange, *Weisheit und Prädestination: Weisheitliche Urordnung und Prädestination in der Textfunden von Qumran* (Leiden: Brill, 1995), T. Elgvin, "Wisdom with and without Apocalyptic", *Sapiential, Liturgical and Poetical Texts from Qumran. Proceedings of the IOQS Conference, Oslo, August 1998* (D. Falk, F. García Martínez, E. Schuller, eds.; Leiden: Brill, 2000) 15–38.

[13] G. W. E. Nickelsburg, *Resurrection, Immortality and Eternal Life in Intertestamental Judaism* (Cambridge, MA: Harvard, 1972), 68–92; L. Ruppert, "Gerechte und Frevler

In Isa 52:13–15, we are told that the servant shall be lifted up, and that he shall startle nations and kings shall shut their mouths because of him. In the opening verses of chapter 53 anonymous speakers, presumably the kings of the earth, express their amazement that one so despised should be exalted. The transformation of the despised servant became a paradigm of the transformation of the righteous in apocalyptic literature. It is reflected in Dan 11–12, where the martyrs of the Maccabean era are called *maskilim*, an allusion to the servant song, which begins *hinneh yaskil ʿabdi* ("behold my servant shall prosper").[14] Where the servant made many righteous, the *maskilim* make many understand (Dan 11:33). In the end, they are lifted up to shine like the stars in heaven. A closer parallel to the Wisdom of Solomon is found in the Similitudes of Enoch (*1 Enoch* 37–71), which was also probably composed in the first century CE. *1 Enoch* 62 describes the dismay that will come upon the kings of the earth when they see the Son of Man sitting on his throne of glory. The Son of Man in the Similitudes was never a lowly figure, but he is hidden for a time, and the powerful do not believe in him until they see him in glory. They recognize that if this figure is glorified, their self-understanding was ill-founded. Wisdom 5 does not demonstrably depend on either Daniel or the Similitudes, but it makes a similar use of Isaiah 52–53: The righteous at first seem to be of no account, but eventually they are revealed in glory. Moreover, this chapter resolves the conflict between the unjust and the righteous that was described in Wisdom chapter 2. This passage (2:12–20) brings to mind the suffering of the servant of the Lord in Isaiah 53. (The righteous man is called *pais theou*, which may mean servant as well as child of God.) This figure is representative of those who are exalted, to the amazement of their enemies, in Wisdom chapter 5.

The exaltation of the righteous man in Wisdom 5 is expressed in language familiar from the Hebrew and Aramaic apocalyptic literature: "How has he been reckoned among the sons of God, and his lot is among the holy ones" (5:5). The sons of God and the holy ones are the angels. Compare the claim of the hymnist in the Hodayot

---

(Gottlose) in Sap 1,1–6,21: Zum Neuverständnis und zur Aktualisierung alttestamentlicher Traditionen in der Sapientia Salomonis," in Hübner, ed., *Die Weisheit Salomos*, 22–32.

[14] See J. J. Collins, *Daniel* (Hermeneia; Minneapolis: Fortress, 1993), 385.

from Qumran: "You have purified the corrupt spirit from great sin so that he can take his place with the host of the holy ones and can enter into communion with the sons of heaven" (1QH 11:21–22) or again: "For your glory you have purified man from sin . . . to become united with the sons of your truth in the lot of your holy ones" (1QH 19:10–11). The Epistle of Enoch promises the righteous that "you will have great joy as the angels in heaven . . . for you will be companions to the host of heaven" (*1 Enoch* 104:2–6). The Epistle also develops the theme of the mistaken understanding of the wicked:

> But when you die, the sinners say about you, As we die, the right-eous have died, and of what use to them were their deeds? Behold, like us they have died in sadness and in darkness, and what advan-tage do they have over us? From now on we are equal . . . I say to you, you sinners, You are content to eat and drink, and strip men naked and steal and sin and acquire possessions and see good days. But you saw the righteous, how their end was peace, for no wrong was found in them until the day of their death.

This passage is very close to the false reasoning of the wicked in Wisdom 2, where they pursue a life of self-indulgence and exploita-tion in the belief that "we were born by mere chance, and here-after we shall be as though we had never been" (2:2). This reasoning is declared to be false, because "they did not know the mysteries of God" (2:22), or realize that when the righteous seemed to die they were really in peace.

In light of these parallels, Lothar Ruppert has argued that Wis 2:12–20 and 5:1–7 are a distinct source, which he calls a "diptych," originally composed in Hebrew or Aramaic in the land of Israel, but brought to Egypt and translated into Greek before it was incorpo-rated into the Wisdom of Solomon.[15] He supposes that this docu-ment served as propaganda for a hasidic-apocalyptic group, that was critical of the Hellenistic leanings of the proto-Sadducees. I doubt that such a document can be reconstructed from the Wisdom of Solomon. The passages in question are very well embedded in their contexts. It is likely that the author had an apocalyptic source, quite possibly composed originally in Hebrew or Aramaic, but he must have adapted it for his purposes, and not simply inserted it. Moreover,

---

[15] L. Ruppert, *Der leidende Gerechte* (Würzburg: Katholisches Bibelwerk, 1972), 70–105; "Gerechte und Frevler," 15–19.

the idea of immortality, as we find it in Wisdom of Solomon, does
not take the form of resurrection, even the resurrection of the spirit
that is envisioned in the early Enoch literature,[16] and this argues
against the simple incorporation of a Semitic apocalyptic source.
Also, the apocalyptic overtones of the opening chapters of Wisdom
of Solomon are not confined to Ruppert's alleged diptych. Already
in chapter 1 we find that Death is personified in a manner that
recalls the figure of Mot in Ugaritic myth, which in turn is reflected
in biblical passages such as Isa 25:7, where God is said to swallow
up death forever. The startling statement that "God did not make
death" (Wis 1:13) may perhaps be illuminated by the mythological
pre-history of death. The adversaries of Baal in the Ugaritic myth,
Death and Sea, are uncreated, and in much of the Hebrew Bible
God's work in creation consists of mastering primeval adversaries
and confining them.[17] The notion of a "kingdom of Hades" (1:14)
recalls the kingdom of Belial in the Dead Sea Scrolls.[18] There are
also apocalyptic overtones to the concept of "the mysteries of God."
The word *raz*, mystery, figures prominently in Daniel and again in
the Dead Sea Scrolls, where we read in several texts of the *raz nihyeh*
"the mystery that is to be."[19] In the Wisdom of Solomon, the chief
mystery of God is immortality. The fact that the apocalyptic motifs
in Wisdom 1–5 are not confined to the supposed diptych argues that
the author was conversant with a range of apocalyptic sources, but
adapted them freely for his purpose.

   Ruppert contends that despite the use of Greek philosophical terminology in the Wisdom of Solomon, the thought of the book is
still determined by biblical and Jewish traditions. This, however, is
only half the story. What we now have in Wisdom 1–5 is not an
apocalypse, but a wisdom text that attempts to make a philosophically coherent argument. The philosophical sources of the book must
be acknowledged just as fully as the Jewish, apocalyptic sources.

---

[16] See my essay, "The Afterlife in Apocalyptic Literature," in A. J. Avery-Peck
and J. Neusner, ed., *Judaism in Late Antiquity. Part Four. Death, Life-After-Death, Resurrection
and the World to Come in the Judaisms of Antiquity* (Leiden: Brill, 2000) 119–39.
[17] J. D. Levenson, *Creation and the Persistence of Evil* (SanFrancisco: HarperSanFrancisco,
1988) 14–50.
[18] 1QM 14:9; 1QS 1:23–24; 2:19.
[19] 1QS 11:3; 4Q Instruction (4Q415–18) passim. See Collins, *Apocalypticism in the
Dead Sea Scrolls*, 40; *Jewish Wisdom in the Hellenistic Age*, 121–3.

We have noted that the plot against the righteous man in the Wisdom 2 calls to mind the servant poem of Isa 53, but it also has a notable parallel in a Greek philosophical discourse, the test case of the truly just man offered by Glaucon in the second book of Plato's *Republic*.[20] Glaucon argues that we must imagine the just and the unjust in their pure states: the just must not only be the best of men, but must be thought to be the worst. Moreover, "the just man who is thought unjust will be scourged, racked, bound—he will have his eyes burnt out; and at last, after suffering every kind of evil, he will be impaled" (*Republic* 361). Socrates' rejoinder to Glaucon occupies most of the *Republic*, but significantly for our purpose, it culminates in Book 10 with a discourse on "the greatest prizes and rewards which await virtue." "Are you not aware," asks Socrates, "that the soul of man is immortal and imperishable?" (*Republic* 10.608). Socrates proceeds to argue for the immortality of the soul on the grounds that no evil corrupts or destroys the soul. In light of immortality, the advantages of the wicked are inconsequential. Socrates argues that justice attains rewards in this life, but "all these are as nothing, either in number or greatness in comparison with those other recompenses which await both the just and the unjust after death" (614). Plato brings the *Republic* to a close by narrating the myth of Er, the Pamphylian, who died on the battle-field but returned to life after twelve days and told of the judgment of the dead and the process of reincarnation.

The immortality of the soul is also crucially important in the Wisdom of Solomon. In 8:19–20 Solomon boasts that "a good soul fell to my lot, or rather being good I entered an undefiled body." The language recalls the myth of Er, where Lachesis, daughter of Necessity initiates a new cycle of mortality by proclaiming: "Let him to whom falls the first lot first select a life to which he shall cleave of necessity" (*Republic* 617E). The Wisdom of Solomon does not envision reincarnation, and never addresses the question of the pre-existence of the soul. Wis 8:20, "being good I entered an undefiled body," would seem to identify the person primarily with the soul. Similarly in 9:15 we read that "a perishable body weighs down the soul," an idea that is paralleled in both Plato and Philo.[21] There

---

[20] Collins, *Jewish Wisdom*, 195.
[21] Winston, *The Wisdom of Solomon*, 207.

is never any reference to bodily resurrection, or indeed to resurrection of any sort. Yet, the hope of the righteous is full of immortality (3:4) and they only seem to die; they are said to "live forever" and their reward is with the Lord (5:15). It seems clear then that the immortality envisioned by the Wisdom of Solomon is immortality of the soul.

In the *Republic*, Socrates tries to persuade Glaucon of the immortality of the soul by rational argument. In the Wisdom of Solomon, immortality is classified among the mysteries of God. Despite the apocalyptic overtones of the word mystery, however, the book gives no account of angelic revelation such as we find in *Enoch* or Daniel. The understanding of revelation in the Wisdom of Solomon is most clearly stated in the introduction to Solomon's prayer in 8:21: "But I perceived that I would not possess wisdom unless God gave her to me—and it was a mark of insight to know whose gift she was." This is not Platonic reasoning, but neither is it apocalyptic revelation. Wisdom helps the natural reasoning faculty; it does not simply supersede it from above.

The Wisdom of Solomon does not fully share Plato's understanding of immortality, even apart from the issue of reincarnation. According to Plato, all souls are immortal, and they cannot be dissolved by evil or wickedness. In the Jewish book too, God made all things, and presumably all souls, for immortality. But the wicked invited Death, and experience it. Righteousness is immortal, but unrighteousness apparently is not. Pseudo-Solomon is at pains to make clear that the souls of the righteous are in the hand of God and that they live forever. But he says little of the fate of the wicked. In the judgment scene in chapter 5 they lament that their wealth has vanished like a shadow, and "we also as soon as we were born, ceased to be, and we had no sign of virtue to show but were consumed in our wickedness" (5:13). The hope of the ungodly is like thistledown, or smoke in the wind. All of this would seem to suggest that the wicked simply cease to exist; *contra* Plato, their souls are dissolved by their wickedness. In fact, the correspondence of punishment to sin is a recurring theme in the Wisdom of Solomon, especially in chapters 11–19. It is entirely appropriate, then, that as the wicked believed that they would be dissolved, so they are.

But if the wicked simply cease to exist, how are we to account for the judgment scene in chapter 5, where they are clearly present after death to witness the exaltation of the righteous? I suggest that this apocalyptic judgment scene plays a role similar to that of the Myth of Er in Plato's *Republic*—it is a fable or myth, introduced to facilitate the discussion.[22] We usually assume that judgment scenes in apocalyptic texts should be taken more literally. That assumption is open to question. It is characteristic of apocalyptic texts that they juxtapose slightly different visions of the end-time. (For example, there are four such visions in Daniel 7–12.) In the terminology of Ian Ramsey, they are not "picture models," that aspire to exact correspondence with reality, but "disclosure" or "analogue" models that try to convey a "structure, or web of relationship."[23] They are ventures in imagination that try to give concrete expression to matters that are beyond human experience. In this respect, the status of the judgment scene in the Wisdom of Solomon may not be so different from that of similar scenes in Daniel or Enoch. The difference is that in the apocalypses these visionary scenes are the only means of expressing transcendent realities. The Wisdom of Solomon, however, also employs philosophical language which attempts to express these realities in a more precise and accurate way, and which provides some criteria against which the visionary language can be measured.

The personification of Death, and the kingdom of Hades, also appear somewhat less full-bodied in the Wisdom of Solomon than they do in prophetic and apocalyptic texts. Wisdom only hints that there is a negative power that is somehow independent of God. We are not told where Death comes from. The devil also makes a brief and enigmatic appearance in explaining the origin of evil in 2:24: "By the devil's envy death entered into the world." But there is no real place for a devil in the worldview of the Wisdom of Solomon, and even death is an anomaly. God, we are told, created all things *eis to einai*, that they may exist, and the forces of the cosmos tend to the preservation of life. There is no kingdom of Hades upon earth. The personification of Death and the mention of the devil are also figurative language, ways of expressing the negative forces, which the author wants to disassociate from God and wisdom. Whatever its

---

[22] Cf. Plato, *Laws* 4.713: "May I still make use of fable to some extent, in the hope that I may be better able to answer your question?"

[23] I. T. Ramsey, *Models and Mystery* (Oxford: Oxford University Press, 1964) 1–21; compare B. E. Meland, *Fallible Forms and Symbols* (Philadelphia: Fortress, 1976) 26, 130; M. Black, *Models and Metaphors. Studies in Language and Philosophy* (Ithaca, NY: Cornell, 1962) 219–43.

mythological overtones, Death is spiritualized here. It is a state
brought about by the words and deed of the ungodly. It is only
experienced by those who are of the portion (*meris*) of Death, not
by the righteous, who only seem to die. Ultimately, it is a state of
non-being. Death is not quite de-mythologized here, since it is in
fact personified. But it does not enjoy the vivid mythological life that
it did in Ugaritic myth, or that Belial enjoys in the Dead Sea Scrolls.

The Divine Warrior

We find another venture in mythological language with apocalyptic
overtones in Wis 5:17–23. This passage describes a theophany of
God as Divine Warrior, a constellation of motifs that can be traced
back to the storm-theophany of Baal in Canaanite texts of the second millennium.[24] This imagery had been claimed for the God of
Israel from an early point in such texts as Deuteronomy 33 and
Judges 5. It had also informed the celebration of the Exodus in the
Psalms, which sometimes suggest a divine attack on the sea. (Ps
77:16–20: "the waters saw you, they were afraid, the very deep trembled . . . your arrows flashed on every side . . . the earth trembled and
shook"). The immediate source of this imagery in Wisdom 5 is found
in Isa 59:15–20. There the Lord saw that there was no justice and
set out to redress the situation. "He put on righteousness like a
breastplate, and a helmet of salvation on his head; he put on garments of vengeance for clothing and wrapped himself in fury as in
a mantle." We are assured that his adversaries will be forced to pay
according to their deeds. Paul Hanson has made a persuasive case
that this text reflects dissensions in the Jewish community in the early
post-exilic period.[25] The oracles of Isaiah 56–66 reflect the views of
a party that felt itself increasingly disenfranchised and called on God
to come to their aid: "O that you would rend the heaven and come
down" (Isa 64:1). Hanson categorizes this material as proto-apoca-
lyptic, and indeed this imagery also figures prominently in later apocalyptic texts from the Hellenistic and Roman era (e.g. the opening
chapter of *1 Enoch*).

---

[24] See especially F. M. Cross, *Canaanite Myth and Hebrew Epic* (Cambridge, MA:
Harvard, 1973) 145–94.
[25] P. D. Hanson, *The Dawn of Apocalyptic* (Philadelphia: Fortress, 1975) 113–34.

The imagery of Isaiah 59 is reproduced with minor modifications in Wisdom 5: "he will put on righteousness as a breastplate, and wear impartial justice as a helmet; he will take holiness as an invincible shield, and sharpen stern wrath for a sword." Our question here is whether the understanding of this material is altered by its new context in the Wisdom of Solomon. The primary difference would seem to lie in the involvement of creation. Wis 5:16 says that God will arm all creation to repel his enemies, and 5:20 affirms that creation will join him in his fight. To some degree, the involvement of creation is already implied in the traditional imagery of the Divine Warrior. In Judges 5 we are told that the stars fought from heaven against Sisera. In Psalm 77 the clouds poured down water and lightning illuminated the world when God led Israel through the sea. All of this, however, is understood as a miraculous departure from the normal workings of nature. The future intervention of the Divine Warrior, as envisioned in Isaiah 59, is similarly a departure from the working of nature, the action of a deity who intervenes in this world to reverse its course. In the Wisdom of Solomon, in contrast, creation itself is programmed to ensure the implementation of justice.

The Transformation of the Cosmos

The role of creation in implementing the judgment of God is illustrated in the account of the Exodus in Wisdom 16–19.[26] The story of the exodus is taken to show that "creation, serving you who made it, exerts itself to punish the unrighteous, and in kindness relaxes on behalf of those who trust in you" (16:24). Pseudo-Solomon draws here on Stoic cosmology, in which the elements admit of different degrees of tension or relaxation.[27] Nothing new is created, but elements are modified or interchanged. Again in the last chapter of the book we are told that "the whole creation in its nature was fashioned

---

[26] See the essays of A. Passaro, "L'Argomento Cosmologico di Sap 19.18 e la Concezione della Creazione nel Libro della Sapienza," in F. Armetta and M. Naro, ed., *In Charitate Pax. Studi in onore del cardinale Salvatore De Giorgi* (Palermo: Pontificia Facoltà di Sicilia "San Giovanni Evangelista," 1999) 47–61 and "Escatologia, profezia e apocalittica. Indagine su Sap 19," in S. Manfredi and A. Passaro, ed., *Abscondita in Lucem. Scritti in onore di mons. Benedetto Rocco* (Caltanisetta: Salvatore Sciascia, 1998) 103–117.

[27] Winston, *The Wisdom of Solomon*, 300.

anew," in accordance with God's commands, so that his children would not be harmed (19:6).[28] This is not the new heaven and new earth of apocalyptic visions, however. "For the elements changed places with one another as on a harp the notes vary the nature of the rhythm, while each note remains the same" (19:18).[29] The cosmos is a closed system, although it admits of infinite variation. Philo also uses the idea of tension and slackening to explain changes in nature. The bow that God sets in the clouds after the flood indicates that "in the laxness and force of earthly things there will not take place a dissolution by their being completely loosened to the point of incongruity nor will there be force up to the point of causing a break" (*QG* 2.63). God also provided the manna by changing around the elements (*Mos* 2.266–7).[30]

We might infer from these statements about the role of nature in the Wisdom of Solomon, that justice must ultimately prevail in the cosmos.[31] Just as the Exodus ends with a reshuffling of the elements so that the Israelites are sustained and their enemies are undone, so, we might think, must it also be at the end of history. In Wis 18:15 we are told that, on the eve of the Exodus, "your almighty word leaped from heaven, from the royal throne, into the midst of the land that was doomed, a stern warrior carrying the sharp sword of your authentic command, and stood and filled all things with death" (by killing the first-born of the Egyptians). This image brings to mind the vision of John of Patmos in Revelation 19:

> Then I saw the heaven opened, and there was a white horse! Its rider is called Faithful and True, and in righteousness he judges and makes war . . . He is clothed in a robe dipped in blood, and his name is called the Word of God . . . From his mouth comes a sharp sword with which to strike down the nations . . .

The contexts of the two scenes, however, are very different. The militant intervention of the Word in the Wisdom of Solomon rep-

---

[28] On the exegetical aspect of this passage, and the implied understanding of Genesis 1 and Exodus 14, see P. Enns, *Exodus Retold. Ancient Exegesis of the Departure from Egypt in Wis 10:15–21 and 19:1–9* (HSM 57; Atlanta: Scholars Press, 1997) 112–18.
[29] On the analogy of the harp, see Scarpat, *Libro della Sapienza*, 3.304–8.
[30] Winston, *The Wisdom of Solomon*, 330–1.
[31] See e.g. P. Beauchamp, "Le salut corporel des justes et la conclusion du livre de la Sagesse," *Biblica* 46 (1964) 491–526.

resents an incident in history. In Revelation it signals the end of history, and the coming of the final judgment.

It is not apparent, however, that the Wisdom of Solomon actually envisions an end of history. The judgment scene in chapter five can be understood as the judgment of the dead. It does not require that history, and this world as we know it, have passed away. Neither does Philo seem to have envisioned an end of this world. The world is not indestructible, for Philo, since it "has become what it is, and its becoming is the beginning of its destruction," but he allows that it may be made immortal by the providence of God (*Decal.* 58). Elsewhere he refers to the view of some philosophers that "though by nature destructible it will never be destroyed, being held together by a bond of superior strength, namely the will of its Maker" (*Her.* 246). This would seem to conform to the view of Plato in the *Timaeus* (41A), that "all that is bound may be undone, but only an evil being would wish to undo that which is harmonious and happy."[32] In such a view of the world there is ultimately little place for apocalyptic eschatology such as we find in Revelation or 4 Ezra.

Philo, however, makes a place for traditional Jewish eschatology. In his treatise *De praemiis et poenis*, Philo first discourses on the penalties that await those "who have been seduced by the polytheistic creeds which finally lead to atheism and have forgotten the teaching of their race and of their fathers in which they were trained from their earliest years" (162). The discussion is part of an exposition of the laws of Moses, and so the reference is clearly to the Jewish people. If these people repent, says Philo, following Lev 26:40, they will find favor with God. "Even though they dwell in the uttermost parts of the earth, in slavery to those who led them away captive, one signal, as it were, one day will bring liberty to all. This conversion in a body to virtue will strike awe into their masters, who will set them free, ashamed to rule over men better than themselves" (164). They will then be gathered to their appointed place, while the curses will be turned against their enemies. "There will come forth a man," says Philo, citing Balaam's Oracle, "and leading his host to war he will subdue great and populous nations" (95). Harry Wolfson concluded from these passages that "the solution found by Philo for

---

[32] Plato is speaking of the creation of the lesser gods, who are not indestructible but are promised immortality.

the Jewish problem of his time was the revival of the old prophetic promises of the ultimate disappearance of the Diaspora."[33] But even Wolfson also noted that "the depiction of the messianic age in Philo is quite evidently colored with Stoic phraseology." Philo repeatedly formulates his antitheses in terms of the virtuous and the wicked, rather than of ethnic particularism. His God is one "to whom all must belong who follow truth unfeigned instead of mythical figments" (*Praem.*, 162). Those who are killed in the messianic war are "some fanatics whose lust for war defies restraint or remonstrance" (94) and those who receive the eschatological blessings are "those who follow God and always and everywhere cleave to his commandments" (98). Yet this treatise is remarkable for its lack of allegorical interpretation. Philo, like the author of Wisdom, had a stubborn streak of ethnic particularism that was not entirely dissolved by his universalizing philosophy.[34] His main emphasis is certainly on the conversion of humanity to virtue, which he identifies with the stipulations of Mosaic law, but he at least affirms the ingathering of the exiles and the messianic age, even if they are far from the center of his thought. In contrast, the Wisdom of Solomon makes no mention of a return of the exiles or a messianic age. It may be that the author affirmed them, insofar as they were found in the Torah, but he makes no mention of them in his book. The cosmos is programmed to deal with unrighteousness when it arises, but the only definitive resolution of the problem is found in the respective fates of righteous and wicked after death.

The worldview of the Wisdom of Solomon, and of Philo, is ultimately very different from that of the apocalypses emanating from the land of Israel. In the apocalypses, history has a pattern, but wisdom and justice are absent for long stretches. This idea is beautifully expressed in the Similitudes of Enoch, in 1 *Enoch* 42:

> Wisdom found no place where she could dwell, and her dwelling was in heaven. Wisdom went out in order to dwell among the sons of men, but did not find a dwelling; wisdom returned to her place and took her seat in the midst of the angels. And iniquity came out from her chambers; those whom she did not seek she found, and dwelt among them, like rain in the desert, and like dew on parched ground.

---

[33] H. A. Wolfson, *Philo* (Cambridge, MA: Harvard, 1948), 2.407.
[34] See my essay, "Natural Theology and Biblical Tradition. The Case of Hellenistic Judaism," *CBQ* 60 (1998) 1–15.

Such a retreat on the part of Wisdom would be unthinkable in the Wisdom of Solomon. In the apocalypses, the collaboration of nature in punishing the wicked is deferred until the eschatological period. In the Wisdom of Solomon, it is an ongoing feature of cosmos and history. Even in the height of his sharp polemic against the perversity of Canaanites and Egyptians, the Alexandrian author maintains his faith that the cosmos is in harmony with its maker.

Epilogue

The apocalyptic motifs in the Wisdom of Solomon do not ultimately shape the worldview of the text. They are reinterpreted through the lens of Hellenistic philosophy. They do, however, contribute to the Hellenistic fusion of Greek and Oriental thought that characterizes Hellenistic Jewish literature.[35] They also raise some interesting questions about the relation of the Wisdom of Solomon, and the Greco-Jewish literature more generally, to the literary traditions of the land of Israel.

The first question concerns the range of traditions that were available to a Jewish writer in Alexandria around the turn of the era. While the primary Jewish source on which the author of Wisdom drew was obviously the Bible, chapters 1–5 at least show familiarity with apocalyptic traditions that are not attested in the Septuagint, but only in such books as 1 Enoch and the Dead Sea Scrolls. Some such literature must have been translated into Greek, and circulated in Alexandria.

A second question concerns the development of the Jewish wisdom tradition. The Wisdom of Solomon is related to the older wisdom literature in various ways. The portrayal of the figure of Wisdom is obviously related to Proverbs 8 and Sirach 24 as well as to Stoic philosophy. Wisdom departs from the tradition of Proverbs and Sirach, however, precisely in the affirmation of immortality, which is one of the areas where it is influenced, in part, by apocalyptic traditions. We now have a corpus of Hebrew wisdom literature in the Dead Sea Scrolls, which combines the pragmatic, ethical concerns

---

[35] J. J. Collins, "Cosmos and Salvation: Jewish Wisdom and Apocalypticism in the Hellenistic Age," in idem, *Seers, Sibyls and Sages in Hellenistic-Roman Judaism* (Leiden: Brill, 1997) 317–338.

of Proverbs and Ben Sira with a belief in the judgment of the dead, and a worldview that is shaped by "the mystery that is made to be" (*raz nihyeh*), just as the worldview of the Wisdom of Solomon is shaped by "the mysteries of God" (Wis 2:22).[36] The question arises whether there may have been more continuity in the Jewish wisdom traditions of the Hellenistic age than had been previously thought. There is now evidence for a kind of eschatologized wisdom, that is, wisdom literature that incorporates beliefs about eschatology, that is distinct from the apocalyptic literature, although it was probably influenced by it. The links between the eschatologized wisdom of the Dead Sea Scrolls and the Hellenistic wisdom of the Wisdom of Solomon offer a fascinating area for future research. This topic, however, will have to be the subject of another essay.[37]

---

[36] See above, note 12.
[37] See my essay, "The Mysteries of God," in this volume.

CHAPTER TEN

THE MYSTERIES OF GOD:
CREATION AND ESCHATOLOGY IN 4QINSTRUCTION AND *THE WISDOM OF SOLOMON*

The Wisdom of Solomon is in many ways a different kind of book from the wisdom books of the Hebrew Bible or the teachings of Ben Sira. Unlike these older books, it was composed in Greek, and shows considerable acquaintance with Greek philosophy. It also departs rather sharply from the Hebrew wisdom tradition in its appraisal of life and death.[1] Qoheleth had famously questioned whether the spirit of humans goes upward while the spirit of animals goes downward to the earth, since all alike die.[2] Ben Sira, in the early second century BCE, still clung to the view that whether life is for ten or a hundred or a thousand years, there is no inquiry about it in Hades.[3] In *the Wisdom of Solomon*, those who think that humanity is doomed to Hades or Sheol are regarded as fools:

> Thus they reasoned, but they were led astray,
> for their wickedness blinded them
> and they did not know the mysteries of God (μυστήρια θεοῦ)
> nor hoped for the wages of holiness,
> nor discerned the prize for blameless souls;
> for God created man for incorruption
> and made him the image of his own eternity.[4]
> By the envy of the devil death entered the world,
> and those who are of his lot experience it. (Wis 2, 21–24).

The novelty of the worldview of *the Wisdom of Solomon* is commonly attributed to the influence of two factors: Hellenistic, Platonic,

---

[1] See my essay, 'The Root of Immortality. Death in the Context of Jewish Wisdom," in *Seers, Sibyls, and Sages in Hellenistic-Roman Judaism* (Leiden: Brill, 1997) 351–67.

[2] Qoh 3:19–21. On Qoheleth's treatment of death see S. L. Burkes, *Death in Qoheleth and Egyptian Biographies of the Late Period* (Atlanta: Society of Biblical Literature, 1999) 35–80.

[3] Sir 41:4.

[4] Or: his own proper being (reading *idiotētos* instead of *aidiotētos*). See G. Scarpat, *Libro della Sapienza* (Brescia: Paideia, 1989) 1.198–9.

philosophy, and Jewish apocalyptic traditions.[5] It is widely agreed
that the author drew on an apocalyptic source in chapters 2 and 5.[6]
The reference to mysteries becomes intelligible in this context.
Traditional Hebrew wisdom teachers, such as Qoheleth and Ben
Sira, relied on an empirical epistemology, and were wary of claims
of revelation. In contrast, the apocalyptic literature claimed to dis-
close mysteries that were beyond the reach of normal human com-
prehension. Daniel succeeds where the Babylonian wise men fail
because "there is a God in heaven who reveals mysteries" (Aramaic
raz).[7] In the Epistle of Enoch, the term mystery is used for the information that Enoch has learned from the tablets of heaven, and which
is largely concerned with the fate of the righteous after death
(1 Enoch 103:1).[8]

---

[5] The philosophical background is demonstrated throughout the commentary of
D. Winston, *The Wisdom of Solomon* (Anchor Bible 43; New York, Doubleday, 1979).
For the apocalyptic background see P. Grelot, "L'Eschatologie de la Sagesse et les
Apocalypses Juives," in A. Barucq, ed., *A la Rencontre de Dieu: Memorial Albert Gelin*
(LePuy, Mappus, 1961) 165–78. On the combination of the two, see J. J. Collins,
Jewish Wisdom in the Hellenistic Age (Louisville, Westminster John Knox, 1997) 183–7;
idem, "Apocalyptic Eschatology in Philosophical Dress in the Wisdom of Solomon,"
in J. L. Kugel, ed., *Shem in the Tents of Japhet. Essays on the Encounter of Judaism and
Hellenism* (Leiden, Brill, 2002) 93–107.
[6] See especially L. Ruppert, *Der leidende Gerechte* (Würzburg, Katholisches Bibelwerk, 1972) 70–105; idem, "Gerechte und Frevler (Gottlose) in Sap 1,1–6,21," in
H. Hübner, ed., *Die Weisheit Salomos in Horizont Biblischer Theologie* (Neukirchen-Vluyn:
Neukirchener Verlag, 1993) 1–54. Ruppert argues that Wis 2:12–20 and 5:1–7 constitute a distinct source, which he calls a diptych, originally composed in Hebrew
or Aramaic but translated into Greek before it was incorporated into the Wisdom
of Solomon. It is unlikely that such a source can be isolated in Wisdom of Solomon.
The material appears to be fully re-worked and integrated into its present context.
Note also the parallels between Wisdom and the Books of Enoch highlighted by
G. W. E. Nickelsburg, *Resurrection, Immortality and Eternal Life in Intertestamental Judaism*
(Cambridge, MA: Harvard University Press, 1972) 76–8, 128–30; idem, *1 Enoch 1.
A Commentary on the Book of 1 Enoch. Chapters 1–36; 81–108* (Hermeneia; Minneapolis,
Fortress, 2001) 78–9.
[7] The only attestation of the word *raz*, mystery, in the Hebrew Bible is in the
Aramaic part of the Book of Daniel, where it occurs 9 times. See further R. E.
Brown, *The Semitic Background of the Term 'Mystery' in the New Testament* (Philadelphia,
Fortress, 1968) who also surveys the use of "mystery" in the Dead Sea Scrolls that
were available at that time.
[8] The Aramaic of this passage is not extant. The word *raz* is used at 1 Enoch
106:19: "For I know the mysteries of the Lord that the holy ones have revealed
and shown to me, and that I have read on the tablets of heaven" (4Q204 5 ii 26).

The רז נהיה

The publication of the wisdom texts from Qumran, however, shows that *the Wisdom of Solomon* was not the first Jewish wisdom text to entertain the concept of "mystery". In 4QInstruction, the expression רז נהיה appears more than 20 times.[9] The phrase also occurs in some other texts from Qumran: twice in the Book of Mysteries (1Q27 1 i 3,4 = 4Q300 3 4) and in 1QS 11:3–4. The word נהיה is a niphal participle of the verb to be. The exact connotation of this phrase is a matter of debate.[10] In biblical Hebrew, the niphal of the verb to be has the connotation "to be done". It is used of the utterance of a word: כי מאתי נהיה הדבר הזה (1 Kgs 12:24; cf. 2 Chron 11:4), or of an event that has (or has not) taken place: כמוהו לא נהיה מן העלם (Joel 2:2). In the Dead Sea Scrolls, it is often taken to refer to the future: the mystery that is to be, or that is to come. This understanding of the phrase was first suggested by the context in 1Q27 (the Book of Mysteries):

> And they do not know the רז נהיה nor understand ancient matters (קדמוניות). And they do not know what is going to happen to them, and they will not save themselves by the רז נהיה.[11]

The editor, J.T. Milik, rendered the phrase as "le mystère future".[12] The text goes on to speak of signs of what will happen. On Milik's interpretation, the future mystery complements the "ancient matters."

---

[9] A closer parallel to the phrase in Wisdom of Solomon is found in the Instruction on the Two Spirits (1QS 3:23), which refers to רזי אל, the mysteries of God. The ability of the Angel of Darkness to corrupt even the righteous is ascribed to "the mysteries of God." Later in the Instruction, in 1QS 4:18, we are told that "God, in the mysteries of his knowledge and in the wisdom of his glory, has determined an end to the existence of injustice".

[10] A. Lange, *Weisheit und Prädestination. Weisheitliche Urordnung und Prädestination in den Textfunden von Qumran* (Leiden: Brill, 1995) 57–60; D. J. Harrington, "The Rāz Nihyeh in a Qumran Wisdom Text (1Q26, 4Q415–418, 4Q423)", in *RevQ* 17 (1996) 549–53 (Milik Festschrift); T. Elgvin, *An Analysis of 4QInstruction*, Diss. Hebrew University, 1998, 75–83; idem, "The Mystery to Come: Early Essene Theology of Revelation," in F. H. Cryer, T. L. Thompson, ed., *Qumran between the Old and New Testaments* (Sheffield: Sheffield Academic Press, 1998) 113–50; M. J. Goff, *The Worldly and Heavenly Wisdom of 4QInstruction* (Leiden: Brill, 2003) 30–79.

[11] The rebuke of the wicked for not knowing the mysteries is a striking parallel to Wis 2:21–24.

[12] J. T. Milik, "Livre des Mystères," in D. Barthélemy and J. T. Milik, *Qumran Cave 1* (DJD1; Oxford: Clarendon, 1955) 103–4.

A future sense is supported by Sir 42:19 and 48:25, where the plural נהיות is translated into Greek as τὰ ἐσόμενα.

The verb "to be" is also used in the niphal in the Instruction on the Two Spirits (1QS 3:15: from the God of knowledge comes כול הויה ונהייה). This is commonly translated as "all that is and shall be," again on the assumption that the terms are complementary rather than synonymous. Again, in CD 2:9–10 לכל הוי עולמים ונהיות עד the נהיות עד is parallel to הוי עולמים—whatever has happened for-ever. Complementary parallelism gives excellent sense, but synony-mous parallelism can not be ruled out. In 1QS 11:3–4 we read "from the source of his knowledge he has disclosed his light, and my eyes have observed his wonders, and the light of my heart the רז נהיה". Some scholars have given the phrase a more abstract trans-lation, such as "the mystery of existence"[13] but נהיה is a verbal form, not an abstract noun.[14] Ultimately, the meaning of the phrase must be determined from the contexts in which it is used in 4QInstruction.

Many of those contexts are fragmentary, and the reference to the mystery is allusive in any case.[15] Typically, the addressee is told that his ear has been uncovered with respect to the mystery, or is told to gaze on it, or to seek it, or not be distracted from it. It is by the mystery that God has established the foundation of truth (4Q417 1 i 8–9). The mystery involves "all the paths of truth" and enables one to know what is good and bad (4Q416 2 iii 14–15; cf. 4Q418 9 15). It concerns "the birth times of salvation, and who is to inherit glory and iniquity" (4Q417 2 i 10–11),[16] and enables the one who

---

[13] R. Eisenman and M. Wise, *The Dead Sea Scrolls Uncovered* (Rockport: Element, 1992) 241–55, and F. García Martínez and E. J. Tigchelaar, *The Dead Sea Scrolls Study Edition* (Leiden, Brill, 1998) 845–77, translate "the mystery of existence"; M. Wise, M. Abegg and E. Cook, *The Dead Sea Scrolls. A New Translation* (San Francisco:, HarperSanFrancisco, 1996) 378–90: "the secret of the way things are".

[14] Lange, *Weisheit und Prädestination*, 57, captures the temporal dimension with "Geheimnis des Werdens." A. Rofé, "Revealed Wisdom: From the Bible to Qumran," in J.J. Collins, G. E. Sterling and R. A. Clements, eds., *Sapiential Perspectives: Wisdom Literature in Light of the Dead Sea Scrolls* (Leiden: Brill, 2004) 1–11, construes the word נהיה as a perfect rather than as a participle, and translates "the mystery of what happened, or what happens".

[15] For a concise summary see D. J. Harrington, "Mystery," in L. H. Schiffman and J. C. VanderKam, ed., *The Encyclopedia of the Dead Sea Scrolls* (New York: Oxford University Press, 2000) 588–91.

[16] On the concept of the "birth times" see M. Morgenstern, "The Meaning of בית מולדים in the Qumran Wisdom Texts," in *JJS* 51 (2000) 141–44, who argues that the term refers to horoscopes at the time of birth. But see also the qualification

seeks it out to know his inheritance (4Q418 9 9). By contemplating
the mystery, one can know the תולדות, which is variously understood
as the generations or the nature and characteristics of humanity
(אדם), the judgment of human beings (אנוש) and the weight (evalua-
tion?) of the periods.[17] It is clear from this contextual usage that the
רז נהיה includes knowledge of eschatological reward and punishment,
but it also includes the origin of the human and even the cosmic
condition (תולדות). Harrington aptly notes that the range of material embraced by the mystery is similar to that covered in the Instruction
on the Two Spirits: origin, ways in the world, and eschatological
outcome.[18] Lange describes it as "eine Welt- und Schöpfungsordnung"
which combines primeval, historical, eschatological and ethical elements.[19] Elgvin defines it as "a comprehensive word for God's mys-
terious plan for creation and history . . . 'salvation history' in a wider
meaning".[20] This mystery provides a context for human action. By
understanding it, one can walk in righteousness (4Q416 2 iii 9–10)
and discern between good and evil (4Q417 1 i 6–8).[21]

   There are some clear points of analogy between the רז נהיה in
the text from Qumran and the mysteries of God in *the Wisdom of
Solomon*. In both texts, understanding the mystery is the key to right
behavior. This is so primarily because it discloses the ultimate outcome of righteous or wicked behavior—the reward of piety and the
prize of blameless souls, in the idiom of Wisdom, or "who is to
inherit glory and iniquity" in the phrase of 4Q Instruction. But this
outcome is not arbitrary. It is grounded in the way in which God
created humanity in the first case.

---

of this view by E. J. C. Tigchelaar, *To Increase Learning for the Understanding Ones* (Leiden:
Brill, 2002) 238. In this case, knowledge of the birth times of salvation enables one
to know who is to be saved or damned. Strugnell and Harrington read עמל, toil,
instead of עול, iniquity (DJD 34.173). See Tigchelaar, *To Increase Learning*, 56.
   [17] 4Q418 77. J. Strugnell and D. Harrington, in *Qumran Cave 4. XXIV. Sapiential
Texts, Part 2. 4QInstruction (Mûsār lĕMēvîn): 4Q415ff.* (DJD 34; Oxford: Clarendon,
1999) 298. Compare the use of תולדות in the Instruction on the Two Spirits, 1QS
3:13.
   [18] Harrington, "Mystery," 590.
   [19] Lange, *Weisheit und Prädestination*, 60.
   [20] Elgvin, *An Analysis of 4QInstruction*, 80.
   [21] Formerly 4Q417 2, and cited in this way by Harrington, "Mystery," 590.

The Hope of the Righteous in Wisdom

It is generally recognized that *the Wisdom of Solomon* understands the afterlife in terms of the immortality of the soul.[22] The noun "immortality" (*athanasia*) occurs 5 times in the book (3:4; 4:1; 8:13.17; 15:3) and the adjective "immortal" (*athanatos*) once (in 1:15, à propos of righteousness). In 4:1 and 8:13, immortality is associated with memory, and refers to an undying reputation. In 3:4, we are told that the hope of the righteous is full of immortality. In 8:17, there is immortality in kinship with wisdom, and in 15:3 righteousness and the knowledge of God are the root of immortality. A related term, "incorruption" (*aphtharsia*) appears 3 times (2:23; 6:18 and 6:19), and the adjective *aphthartos* twice (12:1 and 18:4). This term was associated with Epicurean philosophy.[23] The Epicureans explained the eternal life of the gods by saying that they consisted of incorruptible matter. According to Wisdom, humanity was created "for incorruptibility" (2:23). Incorruptibility is assured by keeping the laws of wisdom, and it causes one to be near to God (6:18–19). God's *pneuma* is imperishable (12:1), as is the light of the law (18:4). According to Philo, "incorruption is akin to eternality,"[24] and equally there seems to be no practical difference between immortality and incorruptibility in Wisdom. At no point does Wisdom speak of resurrection of the body, or even of resurrection of the spirit, in such a way as to imply that life is interrupted at death.[25] The righteous only seem to die

---

[22] See the discussion by Winston, *The Wisdom of Solomon*, 25–32, who notes that Wisdom modifies Platonic doctrine on this subject in significant ways. See also the discussion by C. Larcher, *Études sur le Livre de la Sagesse* (Paris: Gabalda, 1969) 236–327, who acknowledges the influence of Greek concepts but places greater weight on biblical influences. On the terminology see also J. M. Reese, *Hellenistic Influence on the Book of Wisdom and its Consequences* (Analecta Biblica 41; Rome: Pontifical Biblical Institute, 1970) 64–65.

[23] Winston, *The Wisdom of Solomon*, 121.

[24] *De Abr* 55.

[25] Several authors have tried to find an implicit doctrine of bodily resurrection in Wisdom. See especially P. Beauchamp, "Le salut corporel des justes et la conclusion du livre de la Sagesse," in *Bib* 45 (1964) 491–526; E. Puech, *La Croyance des Esséniens en la Vie Future: Immortalité, Résurrection, Vie Éternelle?* (Paris: Gabalda, 1993) 92–98; idem, "Il Libro della Sapienza e i Manoscritti del Mar Morto: Un Primo Approccio," in G. Bellia and A. Passaro, eds., *Il Libro della Sapienza. Tradizione, Redazione, Teologia* (Rome: Città Nuova, 2004) 131–55. Beauchamp points to the transformation of nature at the end of the book; Puech to the judgement scene in chapter 5. Grelot, "L'Eschatologie de la Sagesse," 176–7, acknowledges that Wisdom does not speak of corporeal resurrection, but notes, correctly, that resurrection of the spirit is more typical of the apocalypses.

(3:2), but are at peace. For Wisdom, as for Philo, the death that matters is the death of the soul, or spiritual death.[26] God did not make this death (1:13), and the righteous do not experience it. The wicked experience death, because they are worthy to be of its lot (1:16). Wisdom does not refer to any punishment of the wicked after death; it appears that they simply cease to exist. They lament that just as their wealth vanished like a shadow, "so we also, as soon as we were born, ceased to be, and we had no sign of virtue to show, but were consumed in our wickedness" (5:13). Their hope is like thistledown or smoke, dispersed in the wind.[27]

Chrysostome Larcher raised the question whether bodily resurrection is not implied in Wis 3:7–8: "in the time of their visitation they will shine forth, and will run like sparks through the stubble," a passage that has often been understood in terms of astral immortality.[28] There is an obvious, parallel to Dan 12:3, where the maśkîlîm shine like the brightness of the sky, and are like the stars forever.[29] But the idea of astral immortality was widespread in the Hellenistic world, as a form of immortality of the soul.[30] Throughout the Greco-Roman world, the soul was thought to consist of some kind of substance, be it air, fire, or *pneuma*.[31] For the Stoics, all existence was physical. Even those who rejected the Stoic view, like Cicero, still considered the soul fiery or airy.[32] Philo says that the rational soul is "of the upper air (αἰθέρος)" a divine particle, the pneuma breathed in by God.[33] It was precisely because the soul consisted of heavenly, fiery matter that it could ascend to the stars after death. In *the Wisdom of Solomon*, wisdom is conceived as a fine substance spread

---

[26] M. Kolarcik, *The Ambiguity of Death in the Book of Wisdom 1–6* (Analecta Biblica 127; Rome: Pontifical Biblical Institute, 1991) 180, and especially K. M. Hogan, "The Exegetical Background of the 'Ambiguity of Death' in the Wisdom of Solomon," in *JSJ* 30 (1999) 1–24.

[27] Compare the fate of the Gentiles in 2 Bar 82:3–7.

[28] C. Larcher, *Le Livre de la Sagesse ou la Sagesse de Salomon* (Paris: Gabalda, 1983) 1.285. The astral interpretation was argued most famously by A. Dupont-Sommer, "De l'immortalité astrale dans la Sagesse de Salomon," in *Revue des Etudes Grecques* 62 (1949) 80–87, but he emended the text, to read "in the galaxy" rather than in the stubble.

[29] Compare also 1 Enoch 38:4; 39:7; 104:2; 4 Ezra 7:97; 2 Bar 51:10. etc. Winston, *The Wisdom of Solomon*, 128.

[30] See A. Scott, *Origen and the Life of the Stars* (Oxford: Clarendon, 1991).

[31] See D. B. Martin, *The Corinthian Body* (New Haven: Yale, 1995) 108–20.

[32] *Tusculan Disputations* 1.17.41; 1.19.43; Martin, *The Corinthian Body*, 115.

[33] Philo, *Leg. Alleg.* 3.161.

throughout creation,[34] and it is not unlikely that the author conceived of the soul as a substance that could shine forth.

Maurice Gilbert argues that the image of sparks in the stubble describes the destruction of the wicked in several prophetic texts.[35] Of the texts he cites, the closest parallel is provided by Zech 12:6, where the Hebrew כלפיד בעמיר is rendered in the LXX as ὡς λαμπάδα πυρὸς ἐν καλάμῃ.[36] Gilbert, with all due tentativeness, suggests that the image in Wisdom refers to an apocalyptic destruction of the wicked on earth, after the righteous have been glorified. He acknowledges, however, that this reading poses difficulties. There is no clear parallel for an eschatological battle after the resurrection of the just, in any Jewish writing of this period. The analogy with sparks is obviously figurative, and such language should not be pressed. Wisdom may borrow imagery from prophetic texts without necessarily using it in the same way. The suggestion that this imagery conveys a belief in resurrection in Wis 3:7–8 raises more problems than it solves. Again, the judgment scene in chapter 5, which portrays a post-mortem confrontation between the righteous and the wicked, is figurative speech to dramatize the contrast between the two ways of life, in the manner of Platonic myth.[37] The hope of the righteous in Wisdom is not resurrection, but immortality.

The objection is often raised that immortality in Wisdom does not derive from the inherent nature of the soul, as it does in Plato, but is a gift of God, and contingent on righteousness.[38] It is certainly true that Wisdom modifies Greek philosophy in light of Jewish belief

---

[34] Wis 7:22–8:1. On this passage see Larcher, *Le Livre de la Sagesse*, 1.479–518; H. Hübner, "Die Sapientia Salomonis und die antike Philosophie," in H. Hübner, ed., *Die Weisheit Salomos im Horizont Biblischer Theologie* (Neukirchen-Vluyn: Neukirchener Verlag, 1993) 55–81; H. Engel, "Was Weisheit ist, und wie sie entstand, 'will ich verkünden': Weish 7,22–8,1 innerhalb des *egkōmion tēs sophias* (6,22–11,1) als Stärkung der Plausibilität des Judentums angesichts hellenistischer Philosophie und Religiosität," in G. Hentschel and E. Zenger, ed., *Lehrerin der Gerechtigkeit* (Leipzig: Benno, 1991) 67–102.

[35] M. Gilbert, "Sagesse 3,7–9; 5,15–23 et l'apocalyptique," in García Martínez, ed., *Wisdom and Apocalyptic*, 307–22.

[36] The same image, of a torch of fire in straw, is used in 1QM 11:10. I owe this reference to Jean Duhaime.

[37] On the interpretation of the judgement scene in the philosophical context of the book see Collins, "Apocalyptic Eschatology in Philosophical Dress," 100–101.

[38] So e.g. M. J. Lagrange, "Le livre de la Sagesse. Sa doctrine des fins dernières," in *Revue Biblique* 16 (1907) 94; Puech, *La Croyance des Esséniens*, 93: "un don gratuit de Dieu comme récompense d'une bonne conduite".

at certain crucial points, as Philo also does.[39] There is no mention of metempsychosis, but it should be noted that this is also true of Cicero's *Tusculan Disputations* and *Dream of Scipio*, despite their Platonic inspiration.[40] There is a hint of the Platonic doctrine of the pre-existence of the soul in Wis 8:19–20: "I was indeed a child well-endowed, having had a noble soul fall to my lot, or rather being noble I entered an undefiled body." Such an idea was not inconceivable in a Jewish context. Philo held that souls were pre-existent, and that "some, such as have earthward tendencies and material tastes, descend to be fast bound in mortal bodies".[41] The vacillation between two formulations in Wisdom, however, shows that pre-existence was not important for the author's anthropology. The idea that immortality was contingent on righteousness was distinctively Jewish. Immortality was not strictly a reward for righteousness, however. It was the original design of the creator for all humanity.

Hope for the Afterlife in 4QInstruction

4QInstruction also entertains the hope for immortality. This includes the traditional hope for immortality by remembrance. 4Q416 2 iii 6–8 tells the addressee: "Let not thy spirit be corrupted by it (money?). And then thou shalt sleep in faithfulness, and at thy death thy memory will flow[er forev]er, and אהריתך will inherit joy". Strugnell and Harrington translate אהריתך as "your posterity",[42] but the word could be taken as "your hereafter." Other passages are less ambiguous. Some people, we are told, are to inherit glory, while others inherit toil (4Q417 2 i 11). 4Q418 126 ii 7–8 promises "to raise up the head of the poor . . . in glory everlasting and peace eternal."

As in *the Wisdom of Solomon*, the hope for the afterlife is formulated in terms of immortality rather than of resurrection: everlasting glory and peace (compare Wis 3:1–3). There is no clear reference to bodily resurrection in 4QInstruction. Torleif Elgvin, in his dissertation, claimed to find such a reference in 4Q418 69 ii 7:

---

[39] See Winston, *The Wisdom of Solomon*, 25–32. Also Reese, *Hellenistic Influence*, 32–89.

[40] See Winston, *The Wisdom of Solomon*, 28–29; J. Dillon, *The Middle Platonists*, (London: Duckworth, 1977) 96–102.

[41] *De Somn* 1.138; cf. *De Plant* 11–14.

[42] Strugnell and Harrington, in DJD 34.112.

דורשי אמת יעורו למשפטי[ן]: "the seekers of truth will wake up to the judgments [of God]".[43] The final *yod* is only a trace, and Strugnell and Harrington read a *kaph*.[44] They translate "those who investigate the truth shall rouse themselves to judge y[ou.]" Puech accepts the same material reading, but still takes the passage to refer to resurrection: "les chercheurs fidèles seront réveillés pour votre jugement."[45] The crucial questions here concern the identity of "those who investigate the truth", and the meaning of the verb יעורו (to wake or arouse). Elgvin and Puech take the investigators to be righteous human beings; Strugnell and Harrington take them to be angelic judges. The immediate context reads as follows, in the translation of Strugnell and Harrington:

4. And now, O you foolish-minded ones, what is good to a man who has not
5. [been created? And what] is tranquillity to a man who has not come into activity? And what is judgement to a man who has not been established? And what lament shall the dead make over their own death?
6. You were fashioned [by the power of G]od, but to the everlasting pit shall your return be. For it shall awaken [to condemn] you[r] sin, [and the creatures of]
7. its dark places [ ] shall cry out against your pleading, and all those who will endure forever, those who investigate the truth, shall rouse themselves to judge y[ou. And then]
8. will all the foolish-minded be destroyed. And the children of iniquity shall not be found any more, [and a]ll those who hold fast to wickedness shall wither [away. And then,]
9. at the passing of judgement upon you, the foundations of the firmament will cry out.[46]

The context, then, is an admonition to the wicked, which is followed after this passage by an exhortation to "the truly chosen ones". It should be noted that the pit is said to awaken, using the verb (קיץ) that is used in the context of resurrection in Daniel 12. The awakening of the pit, however, is not a matter of resurrection, but of arousal. The verb עור lends itself to a similar interpretation. (Compare

---

[43] Elgvin, *An Analysis*, 113–7.
[44] So also E. J. Tigchelaar, *To Increase Learning for the Understanding Ones* (Leiden: Brill, 2001) 210. This reading is now accepted also by Elgvin (oral communication).
[45] Puech, "Il Libro della Sapienza."
[46] DJD 34, p. 283.

Isa 51:9, where the arm of the Lord is addressed: עורי עורי (עורי עורי). Puech cites 1QH 14:32 as an alleged use of the verb עור with reference to resurrection.[47] The passage reads: "then the sword of God will hasten in the era of judgment, and all the sons of his truth will arise to destroy [the sons of] wickedness." Here again it is by no means certain that the reference is to resurrection. It may rather be a matter of arousal for battle. Those who seek, or investigate, the truth are indentified as "those who will endure forever" בול נהיה עולם. Puech translates this phrase as "tous les destinés-à-l'éternité." But as we have seen, the niphal of the verb to be does not have an exclusively future sense. The phrase might be better translated simply as "those who endure forever", with reference to angelic beings rather than to resurrected humans. (The beings in question may be compared the "angels of destruction" who administer the punishment of the damned in CD 2:6 and 1QS 3:12.)[48] In all, then, it seems very doubtful that this passage can be taken as evidence for the idea of resurrection in 4QInstruction.

Of course the alternative to resurrection in the Hebrew wisdom text is not the Platonic idea of the immortality of the soul. The exhortation to the righteous that follows this passage in 4Q418 69 asks:

> As for the Sons of Heaven, whose lot is eternal life, will they truly say, 'we are weary of doing the works of Truth, and [we] have grown weary of them at all times'? Will [they] not walk in light everlasting . . . glory and abundance of splendor . . . in the council of the divine ones?[49]

It is disputed whether the primary reference of this passage is to angels (as maintained by the editors) or the human righteous.[50] In fact, the passage clearly supposes that the human righteous share the lot of the angels, and may hope for eternal life in the council

---

[47] The verse in question is numbered 14:29 in F. García Martínez and E. J. Tigchelaar, *The Dead Sea Scrolls Study Edition* (Leiden: Brill, 1997) 1. 176–7.

[48] C. H. T. Fletcher-Louis, *All the Glory of Adam. Liturgical Anthropology in the Dead Sea Scrolls* (Leiden: Brill, 2002) 118 argues that the verb דרש is not used with angels as subjects in 4QInstruction or in the Scrolls in general, whereas it is commonly used of human beings. But neither are the human righteous ever said to rise to judge the wicked. The language of the passage is exceptional in any case.

[49] On the angelic life, compare also 4Q418 55 (DJD 34, pp. 265–6).

[50] Fletcher-Louis, *All the Glory of Adam*, 119–20.

of the divine ones. The idea that the righteous humans could be
elevated to share the life of the angelic host is well attested in the
last centuries before the common era. In the early apocalypses of
Daniel and Enoch, this is the fate of the righteous after death. In
the Hodayot from Qumran, the angelic state can be anticipated even
in this life.[51] It does not seem to me that 4QInstruction envisions
present exaltation to the degree that we find it in the Hodayot.[52]
There is, nonetheless, a close association between the earthly righteous and the angelic host. If we assume, with the editors, that the
primary reference in 4Q418 69 is to the angels, it is nonetheless
clear that the person of understanding should aspire to a similar life.
4Q418 81 3–5 has been plausibly restored to read "among all the
[God]ly [Ones] has he cast thy lot".[53] The motif of fellowship with
the angels as the eschatological reward of the righteous is also picked
up in *the Wisdom of Solomon*. In the judgment scene, in Wis 5:5, the
oppressors ask in astonishment when they see the righteous transformed: "Why have they been numbered among the children of
God? And why is their lot among the holy ones?"

The association with the holy ones is a point of continuity between
the wisdom texts and the early apocalypses of Daniel and Enoch.
In Dan 12:3, the resurrected משכילים shine like the stars. In 1 Enoch
104 the righteous are assured that they will "shine like the lights of
heaven", "have great joy like the angels of heaven" and "become
associates of the host of heaven." The wisdom texts differ from the
apocalypses, however, insofar as they do not use the language of resurrection, but rather suggest that the life of the spirit is continuous.
The language of 4QInstruction, with the motifs of light and everlasting glory, has a noteworthy parallel in the Instruction on the
Two Spirits, where the visitation of the Sons of Light is described
as "healing, plentiful peace in a long life, fruitful offspring with all
everlasting blessings, and eternal joy in life without end, a crown of
glory and a garment of majesty in unending light".[54] Eternal life in

---

[51] See the classic study of H.-W. Kuhn, *Enderwartung und gegenwärtiges Heil* (Göttingen:
Vandenhoeck & Ruprecht, 1966); Nickelsburg, *Resurrection*, 146–56; J. J. Collins,
Apocalypticism in the Dead Sea Scrolls (London: Routledge, 1997) 119–23.
[52] See further my comments in "The Eschatologizing of Wisdom in the Dead
Sea Scrolls," in Collins, Sterling and Clements, eds., *Sapiential Perspectives*, 49–65.
[53] DJD 34, pp. 300, 302.
[54] 1QS 4:6–8. There are numerous parallels between the Instruction on the Two

such formulations, is not necessarily incorporeal. The "garment of majesty" may denote what St. Paul would call "a spiritual body" (1 Cor 15:44). As we have already seen, the immortal soul was commonly thought to consist of a heavenly substance (such as *aither* or *pneuma*) in Hellenistic-Roman thought. In Jewish sources, the idea seems to be a transformed or glorified *nephesh*, which was not quite pure spirit in the Platonic sense. But there is no indication, either in 4QInstruction or in the Instruction on the Two Spirits, that eternal life involves a resurrected body of flesh and blood. As St. Paul would say, "flesh and blood cannot inherit the kingdom of God, nor does the perishable inherit the imperishable".[55] Neither does it seem to involve a resurrection, in the sense that life is suspended for a time between death and glorification. While the texts are not as clear on the matter as we might wish, the view seems to be that the spirit simply lives on when the body dies. A similar view of the afterlife may be found in Jubilees 23:31, which says of the just that "their bones will rest in the earth, and their spirits will have much joy."

The idea of eternal life, as we find it in 4QInstruction or in the Instruction on the Two Spirits, does not appear to be influenced by Hellenistic philosophy. One possible source of such a hope in the biblical tradition lies in the cultic experience of the presence of God, as we find it expressed in the Psalms. In Ps 73:23–26, the psalmist says: "Nevertheless I am continually with you; you hold my right hand. You guide me with your counsel, and afterward you will receive me (תקחני) with honor ... My flesh and my heart may fail, but god is the strength of my heart and my portion forever." Similarly in Psalm 49:16 we read that "God will ransom my soul from the power of Sheol, for he will take me."[56] Whether these psalms actually reflect a hope for eternal life on the part of the psalmist is disputed.[57] On the positive side, the use of the verb "to take" or "to receive" (לקח) recalls the assumption of Enoch (Gen 5:24). On the

---

Spirits and 4QInstruction. See Lange, *Weisheit und Prädestination*, 126–30; Tigchelaar, *To Increase Learning*, 194–207.

[55] 1 Cor 15:50.

[56] Compare also Ps 16:9–10.

[57] For the positive view: M. Dahood, *Psalms III* (Anchor Bible 17A; New York: Doubleday, 1970) XLI–LII; Puech, *La Croyance*, 46–59. For the negative: B. Vawter, "Intimations of Immortality and the Old Testament," in *JBL* 91 (1972) 158–71 (reprinted in idem, *The Path of Wisdom* [Wilmington, DE: Glazier, 1986] 140–60).

negative side is the predominant rejection of any such hope in
the psalms. Even Psalm 49 affirms that the wise die together with the
fool and the dolt (vs. 11) and twice declares that "humankind shall
not live in glory" (vss. 13,21, English 12,20). In any case, this hope
arises out of the sense that the presence of God is an experience
that transcends time: "For a day in your courts is better than a thousand elsewhere" (Ps 84:10). The fellowship with the angels in the
sectarian scrolls is also rooted in the context of worship, as can be
seen, for example in the Songs of the Sabbath Sacrifice.[58] I am not
persuaded that the few references to priestly matters in 4QInstruction
require that that text originated in the milieu of the temple, as Armin
Lange has argued,[59] but it could be influenced by cultic traditions
nonetheless. An alternative, or rather complementary, source for a
hope for eternal life is found within the wisdom tradition itself.
According to Prov 12:28: "in the paths of righteousness there is life,
in walking its path there is no death." Wisdom claims that "who-
ever finds me finds life . . . all who hate me love death" (Prov 8:35–36).[60]
Here again there is debate as to whether such statements can be
taken literally,[61] but in any case they provide a biblical basis for the
hope that the life nourished by wisdom will not be cut off by death.
Both the cultic and the sapiential traditions, then, provide a basis
for a hope of immortality that does not use the more mythological
language of resurrection.

---

[58] The cultic context of fellowship with the angels is emphasized by Fletcher-
Louis, *All the Glory of Adam*, especially pp. 56–87. He speaks, however, of "angelo-
morphism" rather than fellowship, stressing the angelic nature of the human
participants. Fletcher-Louis argues that the Songs of Sabbath Sacrifice refer primarily to "angelomorphic" humans rather than to angels. While much of his thesis is speculative, the connection between the angels and the cult is clear.

[59] A. Lange, "In Diskussion mit dem Tempel. Zur Auseinandersetzung zwischen
Kohelet und weisheitlichen Kreisen am Jerusalemer Tempel," in A. Schoors, ed.,
Qohelet in the Context of Wisdom (BETL 136; Leuven: Peeters, 1998) 113–59. See espe-
cially 4Q418 81 and 4Q423 5. See the critique of Lange's position by T. Elgvin,
"Priestly Sages? The Milieus of Origin of 4QMysteries and 4QInstruction," in
Collins, Sterling and Clements, eds., *Sapiential Perspectives*, 67–87.

[60] See the classic article of G. Von Rad, *Life and Death in the OT*, in G. Kittel,
ed., *Theological Dictionary of the New Testament* vol. 2 (Grand Rapids: Eerdmans, 1964)
843–9.

[61] Puech, *La Croyance*, 59–65.

Similarities in Eschatological Hope

There are, then, significant similarities between the eschatology of *the Wisdom of Solomon* and that of the older Hebrew 4QInstruction. Both speak of immortality or eternal life rather than resurrection.[62] Neither envisions a resurrection of the body of flesh and blood. Both speak of fellowship with the angels as the reward of the righteous, although this language is only used sparingly and figuratively in *the Wisdom of Solomon*. The Hellenistic book is also informed by Greek philosophical ideas of immortality, which modify the nature of the hope, even though it also adapts and modifies the philosophical doctrines in light of Jewish tradition. Nonetheless, it would seem that the author of Wisdom was familiar with traditions that were broadly similar to what we find in 4QInstruction. The biggest discrepancy in the eschatology is perhaps the fact that Wisdom does not envision the punishment of the damned after death, but only their disappearance.

Creation and Immortality

Both the Greek and the Hebrew wisdom texts seek to ground their view of humanity in their understanding of creation. According to Wis 2:23 God created the human being (ἄνθρωπος/Adam) for incorruption (ἐπ᾽ ἀφθαρσίᾳ) and made him "the image of his own eternity." Immortality, then, is entailed by the creation of human beings in the image of God (Gen 1:27). Death, presumably the death of the soul, is not made by God, but enters the world through the envy of the devil (apparently a reference to the story of the Fall, although it has also been related to the story of Cain and Abel).[63]

---

[62] M. Delcor, "L'Immortalité de l'âme dans le livre de la Sagesse et dans les documents de Qumrân," *Nouvelle Revue Théologique* 77 (1955) 614–30, noted the affinity between Wisdom and the sectarian scrolls in this respect, but concluded that the milieu of Wisdom was not philosophical. The conclusion does not follow. Continuity with Hebraic wisdom does not mean that Wisdom has not reconceived its subject in philosophical categories.

[63] For references, see Winston, *The Wisdom of Solomon*, 121. If the reference is to Genesis 3, this is one of the earliest texts to identify the serpent as the devil. On the interpretation of Gen 1–3 in Wisdom see further M. Gilbert, "La relecture de Gn 1–3 dans le Livre de la Sagesse," in L. Derousseaux, ed., *La création dans l'Orient Ancien* (LD 127; Paris: Cerf, 1987) 323–44.

The association of immortality with creation in the image of God is widespread in Hellenistic Judaism.[64] Philo explains that the likeness is not a matter of bodily form: "No, it is in respect of the mind, the sovereign element of the soul, that the word 'image' is used".[65] He also distinguishes between the man made in the image of God in Gen 1:27 and the man fashioned from clay in Gen 2:7. The latter "is an object of sense-perception, partaking already of such or such quality, consisting of body and soul, man or woman, by nature mortal; while he that was after the image was an idea or type or seal, an object of thought, incorporeal, neither male nor female by nature incorruptible (ἄφθαρτος)."[66] It should be borne in mind that Philo is primarily interested in the allegorical meaning of Genesis as an account of universal psychological phenomena. The contrast is between two types or kinds of human being, rather than between two men. Philo also recognizes that the types can be mixed in individual cases:

> [The first man's] father was no mortal but the eternal God, whose image he was in a sense, in virtue of the ruling mind within the soul. Yet though he should have kept that image undefiled and followed as far as he could in the steps of his parent's virtues, when the opposites were set before him to choose or avoid, good and evil, honorable and base, true and false, he was quick to choose the false, the base and the evil and spurn the good and honorable and true, with the natural consequence that he exchanged immortality for mortality, forfeited his blessedness and happiness, and found an easy passage to a life of toil and misery.[67]

Philo's interpretation of Genesis is complex, and draws on various exegetical traditions that are sometimes in tension with each other.[68] Our concern here is not with Philo, however, but the light his discussions of Genesis may shed on *the Wisdom of Solomon*. While Wisdom never expounds a doctrine of double creation, such as we find in Philo,[69] there is some evidence that it associates the immortality of

---

[64] In addition to the references in Philo and Wisdom of Solomon, note Pseudo-Phocylides 106, and my essay, "Life after Death in Pseudo-Phocylides."

[65] *De Opificio Mundi* 69.

[66] *De Opificio Mundi* 134.

[67] *Virt* 204–5.

[68] For a nuanced exposition, see T. H. Tobin, S. J., *The Creation of Man: Philo and the History of Interpretation* (CBQMS 14; Washington, D. C.: Catholic Biblical Association, 1983).

[69] Tobin, *The Creation of Man*, 102–34.

the soul with Gen 1:27 and the mortality of the body with Gen 2:7. In Wis 7:1, Solomon acknowledges that "I also am mortal, like everyone else, a descendant of the first-formed child of earth". We may compare Philo's description of the "molded man" of Gen 2:7 as "by nature mortal".[70] The earth symbolizes the material aspect of human existence, which, we are told in 9:15, "weighs down the soul." In contrast, the image of God is made for incorruptibility. Humanity became corrupted through "the envy of the devil." Adam, however, did not automatically suffer the full consequences of the Fall. According to Wis 10:1–2, Wisdom "delivered him from his transgression, and gave him strength to rule all things". Both immortality and spiritual death remain as possibilities for all human beings.

The creation of humanity in the image of God also plays a part in the understanding of the human condition in 4QInstruction. In a controversial passage in 4Q417 1 i 14–18 we are told that God gave the vision of Hagu, or book of rememberance, as an inheritance "to אנוש, with a spiritual people, for his fashioning is (or: He fashioned him)[71] according to the pattern of the holy ones" (כתבנית קדושים יצרו). In contrast, the Hagu was not given to the "the spirit of flesh" because it failed to distinguish between good and evil.[72] The allusions to Genesis are transparent.[73] אנוש is not the patriarch Enosh,[74] but the original human creature, as also in 1QS 3:17–18:

והואה ברא אנוש לממשלת תבל.

The pattern of the holy ones is a paraphrase of "in the image of God" בצלם אלוהים, in Gen 1:27.[75] The term אלוהים is often used in

---

[70] *De Opificio Mundi* 134; Hogan, The 'Ambiguity of Death,'" 16.

[71] Either translation is possible, and the sense is essentially the same in either case.

[72] Strugnell and Harrington in DJD 34, pp. 151, 155. On the Vision of Hagu, see Elgvin, *An Analysis of 4QInstruction*, 92–94 and most recently C. Werman, "What is the Book of Hagu?" in Collins, Sterling and Clements, ed., *Sapiential Perspectives*, 125–40.

[73] For full exposition of this passage, see my essay, "In the Likeness of the Holy Ones: The Creation of Humankind in a Wisdom Text from Qumran," in D. W. Parry and E. Ulrich, ed., *The Provo International Conference on the Dead Sea Scrolls*, (Leiden: Brill, 1999) 609–18; also Goff, *The Worldly and Heavenly Wisdom*, 92–115.

[74] So Lange, *Weisheit und Prädestination*, 87; J. Frey, "The Notion of 'Flesh' in 4QInstruction and the Background of Pauline Usage," in D. K. Falk, F. García Martínez and E. M. Schuller, ed., *Sapiential, Liturgical and Poetical Texts from Qumran* (Leiden: Brill, 2000) 218. Strugnell and Harrington leave the reference open (DJD 34, p. 164).

[75] The allusion is recognized by Strugnell and Harrington, in DJD 34, p. 165

the DSS as a plural for angels or heavenly beings, and is taken as
the plural "holy ones" here. Elgvin has drawn attention to an apt
parallel in 1 Enoch 69:11: "For men were created no differently
from the angels, that they might remain righteous and pure, and
death, which destroys everything, would not have touched them".[76]

The "people of spirit" who are fashioned in the likeness of the
angels are contrasted with "the spirit of flesh" who fail to distinguish
between good and evil. The latter phrase, "good and evil" brings to
mind the second creation story in Genesis 2. This surely suggests
that the two accounts of creation, Gen 1:27 and Gen 2:7, are being
read as contrasting paradigms of humanity, just as they are in Philo,
even if the conceptual framework in Philo is quite different. On this
reading, 4QInstruction bears some resemblance to the more developed dualism of the Instruction on the Two Spirits, which says that
when God created אנוש to rule the world (cf. Gen 1:28), he placed
within him two spirits, so that they would know good and evil (1QS
4:26). While the formulation is significantly different, both texts would
then see the distinction between two types of humanity as having its
origin in creation.[77]

Against this interpretation, Torleif Elgvin has argued that the use
of יצר, fashion, in connection with "the pattern of the holy ones"
shows that the two creation stories are being conflated, since this is
the verb used in Gen 2:7.[78] On this reading, "4QInstruction sees
only one Adam in the biblical text. Before he sinned, he shared
angelic glory and wisdom; after his fall he shared the conditions of
רוח בשר".[79]

Elgvin agrees that "Adam of the Urzeit is a type of the enlightened community of the Endzeit".[80] This interpretation might shed

---

and Elgvin, *An Analysis of 4Qinstruction*," 90. The hesitation of Fletcher-Louis, *All the Glory of Adam*, 115–6, is surprising, in view of his own statement that "there can be no doubt that our passage is oriented to creation as it is originally intended" .

[76] Elgvin, *An Analysis of 4QInstruction*, 90.

[77] Compare also the later rabbinic doctrine of two yēṣērs, or inclinations. Midrash Rabbah 14,3; G. F. Moore, *Judaism in the First Centuries of the Christian Era* (New York: Schocken, 1975) 1. 474–96; E. E. Urbach, *The Sages: Their Concepts and Beliefs* (Jerusalem: Magnes, 1975) 1.471–83; G. H. Cohen Stuart, *The Struggle in Man between Good and Evil: An Inquiry into the Origin of the Rabbinic Concept of Yeser haraʿ* (Kampen: Kok, 1984) 5.

[78] Elgvin, *An Analysis of 4QInstruction*, 91.

[79] Ibid.

[80] Ibid.

some light on the formulation of 4Q417 1 i 19: וֹעוד לוֹא נתן הגוי
לרוח בשׂר: but no more has Hagu been given to the spirit of flesh.[81]
This would mean that the Vision of Hagu was initially given to
Adam, but withdrawn when he failed to distinguish between good
and evil. In this case, however, we might wonder why Adam failed
to distinguish between good and evil in the first case, since he had
been endowed with the vision of Hagu as his inheritance.

It is not clear to me, however, that 4QInstruction envisions a Fall,
or a sin of Adam, at all. We find further echoes of Genesis 2–3 in
the very fragmentary text 4Q423, which appears to take the garden
as a metaphor for life, which may be either delightful or full of
thorns depending on whether the gardener is faithful or not.[82] Even
there, however, there is no clear reference to a primeval sin. Rather,
Genesis is treated as a paradigmatic story that outlines two perma-
nent possibilities in life. While much is unclear in 4QInstruction,
because of the fragmentary state of the text, the contrast between
the people of spirit, who are formed in the image of the holy ones,
and the spirit of flesh, appears to be primordial. The fact that the
verb "to fashion" is imported into the paraphrase of Genesis 1 does
not necessarily mean that the two accounts are being fused into a
single creation.

The context of the passage about the כתבנית קדושים in 4Q417 1 i
concerns eschatological retribution. The addressee is told to medi-
tate on the רז נהיה "and then you shall know truth and iniquity,
wisdom [and foolish]ness you shall [recognize] every ac[t] in all
their ways, together with their visitation (פקודהם) in all periods everlasting, and the eternal visitation. Then you shall discern between
the [goo]d and [evil according to their deeds]". The visitations are
already inscribed. The Vision of Hagu and book of remembrance
contain the destiny of those who keep God's word, but also, presumably, the inscribed visitation of the sons of Sheth. So, while
4QInstruction does not say directly that immortality results from
being in the image of God or the likeness of the Holy Ones, it
clearly implies that there are contrasting destinies for the "people of

---

[81] Harrington and Strugnell translate "no more" (DJD 34, p. 155). Elgvin translates "not before" (*An Analysis*, 85), but this would be problematic on his own interpretation, since the Hagu had been given to Adam.
[82] This passage is edited by Elgvin in DJD 34, pp. 505–39. See also his comments in *An Analysis of 4QInstruction*, 71–75.

spirit" and the "spirit of flesh". 4QInstruction closely resembles the Instruction on the Two Spirits at this point. Also, immortality is explicitly associated with the angelic state in 1 Enoch. The watchers are told that they had been "spiritual, holy, living an eternal life" before they had relations with human women (1 Enoch 15:3). According to 1 Enoch 69:11, death would not have touched humanity if they had not been corrupted by the Watchers, for they were created no different from the angels.

Similarities and Differences

The Wisdom of Solomon shares with 4QInstruction the view that it was the intention of the creator that humanity should be immortal. This view was grounded in the understanding of Gen 1:27, which says that Adam was created in the image of God. The two texts understand the meaning of the image somewhat differently. The Qumran text relates it to the angels, while Wisdom speaks more abstractly of the eternity of God (or his proper being, if we read *idiotētos* rather than *aidiotētos* in 2:23). In both cases, however, it entails immortality. Both texts draw a contrast, however indirectly, between the image of God, of Gen 1:27, and the creature born from the earth or the spirit of flesh, which is related to the story of Genesis 2. 4QInstruction relates this distinction to two kinds of people and two kinds of behavior. *The Wisdom of Solomon*, in contrast, draws the distinction between two aspects of the same human being. Solomon is mortal, as a descendant of Adam, with respect to his fleshly body, but he too is created for incorruption. There is a fundamental difference between the two books in their understanding of the flesh. The Hebrew book does not associate the flesh as such with corruption and mortality, in the manner of the Alexandrian authors. Flesh represents the weakness of unaided human nature, and sometimes it is regarded as sinful.[83] Those who share in the spirit of flesh, however, are no less immortal than the people of spirit. In contrast to Wisdom, where the wicked simply cease to exist, the wicked in 4QInstruction survive for punishment in the hereafter.

---

[83] Jörg Frey, "The Notion of 'Flesh' in 4QInstruction and the Background of Pauline Usage," in D. Falk et al., eds., *Sapiential, Liturgical and Poetical Texts from Qumran* (Leiden: Brill, 2000) 197–226.

Conclusion

The editors of 4QInstruction described it as a "missing link" in the development of the Jewish wisdom literature, between the 'secular' or common wisdom of Proverbs and the Torah-centered wisdom of Ben Sira.[84] I would suggest that it might better be described as a missing link between the older Hebrew wisdom and the Hellenistic Wisdom of Solomon. Some of the shifts in worldview that distinguish the Hellenistic book from Proverbs and Ben Sira are anticipated in 4QInstruction. These include the notion of a mystery, which concerns the comprehensive plan of God for humanity, and which involves an immortal destiny, grounded in creation in the divine image.

I do not wish to argue that the author of Wisdom was familiar with 4QInstruction, despite some intriguing parallels. For example, Wisdom repeatedly uses the word ἐπισκοπή, visitation,[85] which is used in the LXX to translate the Hebrew פְּקֻדָּה. This Hebrew term occurs with disproportional frequency in 4QInstruction.[86] It seems to me that the relation between the two books is of a more general sort. On one level, it involves exegetical traditions. Both books understand the opening chapters of Genesis typologically, and distinguish between the creation in the image of God in Genesis 1 and the creation of the fallible being in Genesis 2, although they understand these stories in somewhat different ways. On another level it involves the influence of common traditions. These may well include some apocalyptic texts, such as the Epistle of Enoch, but they also include the traditional wisdom literature, such as Proverbs, which spoke of life as a transcendent fruit of wisdom, without appeal to the language of resurrection. In the case of the Wisdom of Solomon, these common sources were filtered through a lens of Greek philosophy, of which there is no trace in the wisdom text from Qumran.

Perhaps the most important common element shared by 4QInstruction and *the Wisdom of Solomon*, however, was the concept of mystery. Both texts share the belief that right action follows from right understanding. This belief was integral to the Hebrew wisdom

---

[84] Strugnell and Harrington, DJD 34, p. 36.
[85] Wis 2:20; 3:7. 13; 4:15; 14:11; 19:15. See Scarpat, *Libro della Sapienza*, 1.195–6.
[86] Strugnell and Harrington in DJD 34, 28. See Tigchelaar, *To Increase Learning*, 240–42. The term occurs 16 times in 4QInstruction and 6 or 7 times in the Instruction on the Two Spirits.

tradition, just as it was to Greek philosophy. But both these texts also shared the view that right knowledge was not available to everyone. According to the Hebrew text, it was a mystery that was only revealed to the elect, and apparently documented in the Vision of Hagu. The Hellenistic wisdom book does not use the language of revelation, but implies that the mystery is availabe to those who reason rightly. In both cases, however, right understanding involves a grasp of spiritual truths, of things unseen, and the true destiny of human beings concerns their fate after death, not their prosperity in this world.

CHAPTER ELEVEN

ANTI-SEMITISM IN ANTIQUITY?
THE CASE OF ALEXANDRIA

I

The Riots in Alexandria

In 38 CE, an incident occurred occurred in Alexandria that is often described as the first pogrom.[1] When Agrippa, the grandson of King Herod who had just been given the rank of king by Caligula,[2] stopped in Alexandria on his way back from Rome, an Alexandrian mob staged a mime in the gymnasium mocking him, and proceeded to call for the installation of images in the synagogues. The demand was accepted and implemented by the governor Flaccus. A few days later, Flaccus issued a proclamation in which the Jews were declared to be foreigners and aliens. Then, according to Philo, who is our only source for these events, he permitted the mob "to pillage the Jews as at the sacking of a city."[3] Whereas Jews had previously occupied two of the city's five districts, and some also lived in the others, they were now herded into a very small part of one. Their houses and places of business were ransacked. Those who ventured outside this ghetto were attacked, beaten and murdered. Some were burnt to death in the middle of the city. Others were dragged and trampled. Relatives who tried to intervene were arrested and tortured, and in some cases crucified. Then Flaccus arrested 39 members of the Jewish gerousia, and had them flogged in the theatre, so that some of them died. To add insult to injury, they were beaten

---

[1] The details are supplied by Philo in his treatise *In Flaccum*. See now Pieter W. van der Horst, *Philo's Flaccus. The First Pogrom. Introduction, Translation and Commentary* (Leiden: Brill, 2003).

[2] On Agrippa, see Emil Schürer, *The History of the Jewish People in the Time of Jesus Christ* (revised and edited by Geza Vermes and Fergus Millar; Edinburgh: Clark, 1973) 1.442–54; Daniel R. Schwartz, *Agrippa I. The Last King of Judaea* (Tübingen: Mohr-Siebeck, 1990).

[3] *Flacc* 54.

with the kind of whip usually used on Egyptians, rather than with the flat blade used on Alexandrians. Flaccus then had his soldiers search the houses of the Jews for arms. The violence was finally interrupted when Flaccus was arrested and taken off to Rome. There, we are told, the leaders of the Alexandrian mob, the very people Flaccus had sought to conciliate, appeared to accuse him before the emperor.

At this point the focus shifted to Rome. Both Jews and Alexandrians sent delegations to Caligula, but neither got much satisfaction. The Jewish delegation was led by the philosopher Philo, who has left us an account in his *Legatio ad Gaium*.[4] The Alexandrian delegation included the grammarian and Homeric scholar Apion.[5] The emperor did not even give them his attention. At one point he asked the Jewish delegation about their civic rights but then did not allow them to answer.[6] The Jews were relieved when he finally dismissed them as "unfortunate rather than wicked" and foolish for refusing to believe in his divinity.[7] They must have been further relieved when Caligula was assassinated. At this point, Josephus tells us that the Jews in Alexandria took heart again and at once armed themselves.[8] The new emperor, Claudius, however, took the matter in hand. He instructed the prefect of Egypt to restore order, and ruled on the issues in dispute in a letter to the Alexandrians.[9]

As Erich Gruen has recently emphasized, this calamitous incident lacked all precedent.[10] There had been a substantial Jewish com-

---

[4] For commentary see E. Mary Smallwood, *Philonis Alexandrini Legatio ad Gaium* (Leiden: Brill, 1961).

[5] Josephus, *Ant* 18.257.

[6] *Leg* 363.

[7] *Leg* 367.

[8] *Ant* 19.278.

[9] The letter is preserved on papyrus (*CPJ* 153). The edict preserved by Josephus in *Ant* 19.280–85 is quite different from the authentic letter found on papyrus. See Miriam Pucci Ben Zeev, *Jewish Rights in the Roman World* (Tübingen: Mohr-Siebeck, 1998) 295–327. Pucci Ben Zeev defends the authenticity of the edict, arguing that it was issued before the renewal of hostilities. The resumption then provoked the letter, which was less sympathetic to the Jews. But as Tcherikover remarked, every attempt to defend the authenticity of the edict in *Ant* 19.280–85 "encounters numerous difficulties." (*Hellenistic Civilization and the Jews* [Peabody, MA: Hendrickson, 1999, reprint of 1959 edition by the Jewish Publication Society] 414). It is not apparent why the Jews should have renewed hostilities if Claudius had already issued a favorable edict.

[10] Erich Gruen, *Diaspora. Jews amidst Greeks and Romans* (Cambridge, MA: Harvard, 2002) 67

munity in Alexandria for more than 300 years, and they had never
been subjected to attack like this. There are to be sure literary works
that describe threats of violence to Diaspora Jews. The oldest of
these, the Book of Esther, comes from the eastern Diaspora, but in
one recension of the Greek translation Haman is called a Macedonian.[11]
3 Maccabees recounts a threat to the Jewish community in the time
of Ptolemy IV Philopator, allegedly arising from the King's promo-
tion of the cult of Dionysus. Josephus has a very similar story, but
sets it in the time of Ptolemy VIII Physcon (*Ag Ap* 2.49–56). The
story is evidently legendary, and no historical reconstruction can be
based on it.[12] Stories such as Esther and 3 Maccabees are significant
insofar as they reflect the fears of Jewish communities in the Gentile
world, but even in these stories the calamity is always averted.

There were also precedents for actual attacks on Jews by Gentiles.
In Egypt, we have the case of the Jewish community at Elephantine,
whose temple was destroyed by the local Egyptians at the end of
the fifth century.[13] This incident, in fact, bears some similarity to the
one in Alexandria. A local mob prevailed on the governor to allow
them to demolish the Jewish temple. The governor was subsequently
removed. In this case the Jewish practice of sacrificing lambs was
most probably offensive to the local priests of the ram-god Khnum.
There was also resentment on the part of Egyptian nationalists towards
the Jews, because of their loyalty to the Persians. But while the situation in Elephantine is analogous to that in Alexandria to some
degree, there was no real continuity between the two events. There
were also significant differences in the situations. The attacks in
Alexandria were directed much more broadly against a larger Jewish
population, and the specific issues were different. The anomaly of
the events in Alexandria remains.

---

[11] Addition A 17, at Esth 3:1. Carey A. Moore, *Daniel, Esther and Jeremiah. The Additions* (AB 44; New York: Doubleday, 1977) 174.

[12] See further John J. Collins, *Between Athens and Jerusalem. Jewish Identity in the Hellenistic Diaspora* (Grand Rapids: Eerdmans, 2000) 122–31; Erich Gruen, *Heritage and Hellenism* (Berkeley: University of California, 1998) 222–36; John M. G. Barclay, *Jews in the Mediterranean Diaspora from Alexander to Trajan (323 BCE–117 CE)* (Edinburgh: Clark, 1996) 192–203.

[13] Pierre Briant, *From Cyrus to Alexander. A History of the Persian Empire* (Winona Lake, IN: Eisenbrauns, 2002) 603–7; "Une curieuse affaire à Éléphantine en 410 av. n. è.: Widranga, le sanctuaire de Khnûm et le temple de Yahweh," *Méditerranées* 6(1996) 115–35; Joseph Mélèze Modrzejewski, *The Jews of Egypt from Rameses II to Emperor Hadrian* (Princeton: Princeton University Press, 1995) 21–44.

It is unfortunate that we have only one account of the actual events, Philo's treatise against Flaccus, and it makes no pretence of objectivity. Philo treats the life of Flaccus as a moral fable: Flaccus himself supposedly recognizes that his eventual downfall is punishment from the Most High for his crimes against the Jews.[14] It is difficult to believe that the Jews were as passive as Philo portrays them. The arrest of their leaders, and the search for arms in the Jewish community, strongly suggests that there was resistance, and Josephus refers explicitly to Jewish arms when the violence was resumed after the death of Caligula. The action that precipitated the violence was the installation of images in the synagogues. Jewish sensitivity to pagan images was well known to all involved. It was a measure that was sure to please the emperor, who promoted the idea of his own divinity, and who, almost contemporaneously, ordered that his statue be installed in the temple in Jerusalem, precipitating a crisis that was only resolved by his assassination.[15]

The emperor, however, was not the prime mover in the conflict in Alexandria. This point is amply shown by his cavalier disregard for the envoys when they came to him in Rome. It is also clear that the governor Flaccus was not motivated by personal hostility towards the Jews, but was attempting to save his own skin by placating the Alexandrians. On Philo's account, Flaccus was a good governor while the emperor Tiberius lived. But he lost his friends at court when Caligula came to power. He had opposed the claims of Caligula, and was one of those who had accused Caligula's mother, who had been executed by Tiberius. He had good reason to fear if any accusation were brought against him before Caligula. His early relations with the Alexandrian leaders had been strained. He had dissolved the drinking clubs that were the power base of such people as Isidorus, who had to flee from Alexandria to avoid arrest.[16] Flaccus's attempt to appease the Alexandrian leaders was futile. They eventually came to Rome to accuse him before the emperor. But it seems clear that his actions against the Jews arose from fear of the Alexandrians rather than from any Roman agenda.[17]

---

[14] *Flacc* 170–75.
[15] *Ant* 18.261–309.
[16] *Flacc* 145.
[17] Sandra Gambetti, "The Alexandrian Riots of 38 CE and the Persecution of the Jews: A Historical Assessment," (Diss. Berkeley, 2003) argues that Flaccus was

Philo vacillates in his description of the antagonists of the Jews in Alexandria. He often refers to them as "Alexandrians" and mentions some Alexandrian leaders, Dionysius, Isidorus and Lampo, by name (*Flacc* 20). Yet much of his invective is specifically anti-Egyptian. The Egyptians, we are told, have "we might say innate hostility to the Jews" (29). They are prone to sedition (17). In the context of the setting up of images in the synagogues, he refers to "those who deified dogs and wolves and lions and crocodiles and many other wild animals on the land" (*Leg* 139). The disposition of Caligula was due, in part, to the influence of his servants: "The majority of these were Egyptians, a seed bed of evil in whose souls both the venom and the temper of the native crocodiles and asps were reproduced" (*Leg* 166). He makes much of the influence of Helicon, an Egyptian slave (*Leg* 166–77). We must bear in mind that it was easier to pour invective on Egyptians, who were universally reviled, than on Greeks. Moreover, in the matter of civic status Philo and his like wanted desperately to be associated with the Greeks and distinguished from Egyptians.[18] To refer to Alexandrians as Egyptians was to insult them. Roman polemicists referred to to Cleopatra as a "mulier Aegyptia".[19] Josephus is at pains to insist that Apion was of Egyptian origin. He further argues that "the real promoters of sedition, as anyone can discover, have been citizens of Alexandria of the type of Apion. The Greeks and Macedonians, so long as the citizenship was confined to them, never rose against us, but left us free to enjoy our ancient worship. But when, owing to the prevailing disorders, their numbers were swelled by a host of Egyptians, sedition became chronic" (*AgAp* 2.69). The implication of Josephus's tirade seems to be that the principal agitators were people of Egyptian origin who had infiltrated the ranks of the Greeks in Alexandria, and become citizens.[20] Besides Apion,

---

only implementing a mandate from Rome, restricting the rights of the Jews to those that could be documented. In that case, however, the involvement of the Alexandrian mob is difficult to explain. I am grateful to Ms. Gambetti for making her dissertation available to me.

[18] Philo's attitudes towards Greeks and their culture were complex. In the words of Maren Niehoff, "more than half of Philo's references to things Greek . . . lack a sense of the Greek as Other," although he could assume a sense of superiority towards Greek writers and philosophers. See Maren Niehoff, *Philo on Jewish Identity and Culture* (Tübingen: Mohr Siebeck, 2001) 137–58. (The quotation is from p. 139).

[19] Dio Cassius XLVIII.24.2; L.3.5; 6:1; 24:3 etc.

[20] Compare K. Goudriaan, "Ethnical Strategies in Greco-Roman Egypt," in Per Bilde, ed., *Ethnicity in Hellenistic Egypt* (Aarhus: Aarhus University Press, 1992) 86–93.

Chaeremon, another member of the delegation to Claudius, is variously described as a Stoic philosopher and an Egyptian priest.[21] These Graeco-Egyptians were presumably a very small element in the Egyptian population. The Egyptian rank and file were still sharply distinguished from the Alexandrian citizens, as can be seen from the episode of the different kinds of whips in *Flacc* 78. But by the Roman era there were enough Alexandrian citizens with Egyptian blood to warrant the use of anti-Egyptian rhetoric on the part of Philo and Josephus, even if the adversaries were Alexandrians.[22] In any case, the conflict presented to the Roman emperors was one between Alexandrians and Jews. Regardless of who did the actual pillaging, the ringleaders of the pogrom were clearly Alexandrian citizens, not common Egyptians. The Alexandrian delegates who pleaded their case in Rome included people of Egyptian extraction, such as Apion and Chaeremon, but they were respected Alexandrian intellectuals, just as Philo was on the Jewish side.[23]

II

The issues in dispute

The explanations given for the anti-Jewish outburst in Alexandria are basically of two kinds. Some scholars argue that the hostility arose from social and political circumstances peculiar to the situation in Alexandria in the early Roman era. Others posit widespread and deep-rooted anti-Jewish sentiment on the part of both Greeks and Egyptians, dating back to the beginning of the Hellenistic era. These explanations, of course, are not mutually exclusive and can be viewed as complementary, but the emphasis placed on one or the other can reflect different views of the conflict.

---

[21] See Pieter Willem van der Horst, *Chaeremon. Egyptian Priest and Stoic Philosopher* (Leiden: Brill, 1984).

[22] On the rising prominence of Jews and Egyptians from the middle of the second century BCE, and the growth of a class of Greco-Egyptians, see P. M. Fraser, *Ptolemaic Alexandria* (Oxford: Clarendon, 1972) 1.88–92. Fraser remarks that "the Egyptian strain, though present racially, had little social significance any longer for this group" (91). See also now Gambetti, "The Alexandrian Riots," 118–28.

[23] On Apion's scholarly credentials see now Pieter W. van der Horst, "Who Was Apion?" in idem, *Japheth in the Tents of Shem. Studies on Jewish Hellenism in Antiquity* (Leuven: Peeters, 2002) 207–221.

The evidence that pertains most directly to the conflict of 38 CE and its aftermath suggests that the status of the Jews was a major issue in the conflict. Philo expresses outrage that Flaccus declared the Jews to be "foreigners and aliens" (*Flacc* 54) and treated the members of the gerousia who were flogged in the theater as if they were Egyptians (*Flacc* 78). Caligula asks the Jewish delegates about their *politeia*, but does not give them a chance to respond (*Leg* 363). We may infer that their *politeia* was one of the subjects at issue. Even the placing of statues in the synagogues, which ignited the conflict, must be seen in light of Apion's famous question: "why, then, if they are citizens, do they not worship the same gods as the Alexandrians?" (*AgAp* 2.65). The question implies that the Jews claimed to be citizens, and that Apion disputed the claim. The Letter of Claudius warns the Jews "not to aim at more than they have previously had," and reminds them that they enjoy an abundance of good things "in a city which is not their own."[24] The latter phrase recalls the ruling of Flaccus that the Jews were foreigners and aliens; it indicates clearly that the Jews as a body were not citizens of Alexandria. It is clear that the Jews were agitating for something. Gruen suggests that "under the circumstances, the Jewish delegates most likely sought guarantees of security, perhaps a pronouncement that would deter future prefects of Egypt from stripping them of civic privileges as Flaccus had done."[25] But this would be merely a reaffirmation of what they already had. Claudius clearly implies that they were aiming at higher status. Of course the difference here is a matter of different perspectives. From their own point of view the Jews may have only been arguing for the restoration of the privileges stripped by Flaccus. The issue was whether Flaccus had ruled correctly that the Jews were aliens. Claudius ruled that he had, and so that the Jews were agitating for privileges to which they were not entitled.

The understanding of the situation that has been most widely accepted over the last half century was articulated by Victor Tcherikover. Ptolemaic Alexandria had allowed for a range of classes, some of which enjoyed privileges even though they were not full citizens.[26]

---

[24] *CPJ* 153. Trans. Modrzejewski, *The Jews of Egypt*, 182.
[25] Gruen, *Diaspora*, 80.
[26] For example, "Alexandrians" were apparently distinct from, and inferior to, demesmen, or full citizens. See P. M. Fraser, *Ptolemaic Alexandria* 1.38–92, especially 49.

The Romans drew a sharper line between citizen and non-citizen. The difference was underlined by the *laographia*, or poll-tax, from which Greek citizens of Alexandria were exempt, but which was levied on Egyptians and other non-citizens.[27] Ever since the work of Tcherikover,[28] it has been assumed that the *laographia* entailed a loss in status for the Jews of Alexandria. In the words of Modrzejewski, "they had been 'Hellenes;' now, they had suddenly become 'Egyptians'."[29] This led to increased efforts on their part to obtain citizenship. One way of doing this was by infiltrating the gymnasium and becoming ephebes.

Gruen disputes the assumption that Jews were subject to the *laographia*.[30] The basis for this widely held assumption is two-fold. Since Jews, as a group, were evidently not citizens of Alexandria, there is no apparent reason why they should be exempt, and there is no reliable evidence that they were.[31] Second, a papyrus preserves the petition of one Helenos son of Tryphon, whose exempt status had apparently been denied by an administrator.[32] Helenos began by calling himself an "Alexandrian," but the word is crossed out and replaced with "a Jew from Alexandria." Helenos claimed that his father was an Alexandrian and that he himself had received the appropriate education as far as his father's means allowed. It is a reasonable inference that the petitioner thought that his case would be stronger if he were "an Alexandrian" rather than "a Jew from Alexandria." We do not know whether the correction was made by

---

[27] Tcherikover-Fuks, *CPJ* 1.59–62; E. Mary Smallwood, *The Jews under Roman Rule* (Leiden: Brill, 1976) 231–2; Modrzejewski, *The Jews of Egypt*, 161–3; Barclay, *Jews in the Mediterranean Diaspora*, 49–50. Citizens of Naucratis and Ptolemais were also exempt. There was also a third class, of Greeks outside the cities, which paid at a reduced rate. A special class was created in 4/5 CE, for people who were graduates of the gymnasium, descendents of military settlers or inhabitants of the chief towns (*metropolitai*).

[28] *Hellenistic Civilization*, 311–12; *CPJ* 1.59–62.

[29] Modrzejewski, *The Jews of Egypt*, 163.

[30] Gruen, *Diaspora*, 75–77.

[31] Gambetti, "The Alexandrian Riots," 47, claims that the Jews living in Alexandria were exempt. The basis for this claim is a statement attributed to King Agrippa in the Acts of Isidorus that: "no one has levied taxes on the Jews." (Herbert A. Musurillo, ed., *The Acts of the Pagan Martyrs* (Oxford: Clarendon, 1954) 26. The historical value of the *Acts*, however, is very questionable, and in any case the passage could be taken to mean that there was no precedent before the Roman era for imposing such a tax on the Jews. The passage is discussed further below.

[32] *CPJ* 151. See Modrzejewski, *The Jews of Egypt*, 164; Tcherikover, *Hellenistic Civilization*, 312.

the petitioner or by an official who denied his claim to the status of Alexandrian.

The issue of the poll-tax is also raised in the *Acts of the Pagan Martyrs*, which are fictional compositions, dramatizing the fate of Alexandrian leaders at the hands of the Roman emperors, and are presumably indicative of popular Alexandrian sentiments.[33] In one passage, Isidorus engages in a dispute with Agrippa about the Jews:

"I accuse them of wanting to stir up the entire world . . . They are not of the same temperament as the Alexandrians, but live rather after the fashion of the Egyptians. Are they not on a level with those who pay the poll-tax?" Agrippa retorts that "the Egyptians have had taxes levied on them by their rulers . . . But no one has levied taxes on the Jews."[34] Gruen infers that "it follows that Jews are *not* subject to it."[35] A safer conclusion would be that their liability was in dispute. Isidorus argues that the Jews are akin to the Egyptians. If this argument were accepted, Jews should presumably be subject to the tax. Agrippa argues to the contrary that there was no precedent for such a tax on the Jews. (It should be remembered that the whole dialogue is fictional in any case). The issue of the poll-tax is not as clearcut as scholars after Tcherikover have supposed, but it is very likely to have been an issue nonetheless.[36] In any case it is clear that some reduction in the civic status that the Jews had enjoyed under the Ptolemies was at issue in the disputes of 38–41 CE.

The actual aspirations of the Jews of Alexandria are likely to remain controversial. Some individual Jews certainly became citizens of Alexandria. Philo's nephew, Tiberius Julius Alexander, went on to become prefect of Egypt and crushed Jewish resistance in Alexandria in 66 CE, at the time of the outbreak of the rebellion in Judea. Full citizenship, however, would have been difficult to maintain without participating in the pagan cults. Some individuals may have been able to finesse this issue; Philo may well have been a citizen and Paul was a Roman citizen. But presumably it would have been more difficult for a whole community to avoid the civic cults.[37] Philo may

---

[33] For a lively account of the Acts, see Modrzejewski, *The Jews of Egypt*, 173–83.

[34] Musurillo, *The Acts of the Pagan Martyrs*, 26. *CPJ* 156.

[35] *Diaspora*, 77.

[36] So also van der Horst, *Philo's Flaccus*, 21–22.

[37] The argument that Jews did not seek Alexandrian citizenship is made especially by Aryeh Kasher, *The Jews in Hellenistic and Roman Egypt* (Tübingen: Mohr, 1985).

have articulated the aspirations of many when he wrote, in the Life of Moses, that "strangers, in my judgment, must be regarded as suppliants of those who receive them, and not only suppliants but settlers and friends, who are anxious to obtain equal rights with the citizens, and are near to being citizens because they differ little from the original inhabitants."[38] Josephus's formulation of the Edict of Claudius has the emperor acknowledge that "the Jews in Alexandria, called Alexandrians, were fellow colonizers from the very earliest times jointly with the Alexandrians and received equal civic rights (*isēs politeias*) from the kings."[39] Such terms as "Alexandrians" and even "citizens" admitted of an imprecise, non-technical sense, and Philo and Josephus exploited the ambiguity. What they wanted were privileges similar to those of the citizens, without having to participate in the civic cults. Access to gymnasium education and exemption from the poll-tax are examples of the kind of privileges that were at issue.[40] Jews saw no reason why they should not continue to enjoy the status of quasi-Hellenes, as they had under the Ptolemies. But distinctions were more sharply drawn under the Romans. Apion and his fellow-Alexandrians were infuriated by the Jewish claim, of privilege without full participation in the life of the city. The prominence of gymnasiarchs in the conflict lends some support to the view that access to the gymnasium was one of the points at issue.

The situation was also colored by the reduced status of the Alexandrians under Roman rule. They were a conquered people, ruled by foreigners. While the Jews had their own ethnarch, at least for a time, and a senate or *gerousia* thereafter, the Greeks were not allowed to have a city council. Hence their resentment and mockery of the Jewish king, Agrippa, and Flaccus's humiliation of the Jewish senate in his efforts to appease them. From the Alexandrian perspective, the Jews were still over-privileged, and Jewish professions of loyalty to the Romans did nothing to endear them to the Greeks or Egyptians. The Greeks knew better than to rebel against Rome, but they could at least get some satisfaction from asserting their superiority over the Jews.

---

[38] *De Vita Mos.* 1.34–36.
[39] *Ant* 19.281.
[40] It should be noted that a gymnasium education, and completion of the *ephebeia*, did not automatically qualify people as citizens. See D. Delia, *Alexandrian Citizenship During the Roman Principate* (Atlanta: Scholars Press, 1991), 88.

In light of this situation, it is apparent that the violence against the Jews did not arise spontaneously from innate hatred on the part of the Greeks, or even of the Egyptians. It was a product of very specific circumstances in the pressure-cooker that Alexandria became under Roman rule, where status and privilege were scarce commodities, and one party's gain was viewed by the other as loss.

III

A tradition of hostility

This is not to suggest that there was no hostility towards the Jews in Egypt before the Romans came. A papyrus from the first century BCE contains a request for lodgings in Memphis for a priest (who is presumably Jewish) because "they" (the people of Memphis) "loathe the Jews."[41] We should not assume that the Jews were exceptional in this regard. There was plenty of racial animosity to go around in Hellenistic Egypt.

The argument for widespread anti-semitism in the Hellenistic world depends on the dossier of evidence presented by Josephus in his treatise *Against Apion*. Josephus seems to have collected every reference to the Jews that he could find, both positive and negative. Part of his agenda was to show that Judaism was of great interest to Greek writers.[42] The material is taken out of context, however, and often gives an exaggerated impression of the interest of a given author in the Jews.

Much of Josephus' energy is devoted to refuting distorted accounts of Jewish origins.[43] The earliest of these are attributed to the Greek ethnographer, Hecataeus of Abdera, and the Egyptian priest Manetho, both of whom wrote at the beginning of the Ptolemaic era.[44] Both

---

[41] *CPJ* 141. Modrzejewski, *The Jews of Egypt*, 154–5.

[42] On the character of the treatise see Louis H. Feldman and John R. Levison, ed., *Josephus' Contra Apionem. Studies in its Character and Context* (Leiden: Brill, 1996).

[43] These accounts have often been reviewed. See John G. Gager, *Moses in Greco-Roman Paganism* (SBLMS 16; Nashville: Abingdon, 1972); Claude Aziza, "L'Utilisation polémique du récit de l'Exode chez les écrivains alexandrins (IVᵉᵐᵉ siècle av. J.-C.–Iᵉʳ siècle ap. J.-C.)," *ANRW* II.20.1 (Berlin: de Gruyter, 1987) 41–65; Gruen, *Heritage and Hellenism*, 41–72 ("The Use and Abuse of the Exodus Story"); Peter Schäfer, *Judeophobia. Attitudes towards the Jews in the Ancient World* (Princeton: Princeton University Press, 1997) 15–33.

[44] For Hecataeus, se Menaham Stern, *Greek and Latin Authors on Jews and Judaism*

of these associate the settlers of Judea with people who were expelled from Egypt because of pestilence, which is specified as leprosy by Manetho. Manetho's account is more complex, as the initial settlers of Judea are identified with the Hyksos, who had been driven out of Egypt, but these later invaded and pillaged Egypt again at the invitation of the lepers. The lepers had settled for a time in Avaris, the deserted city of the Shepherds, which was also associated with Seth-Typhon. Their leader, Osarseph, established a law that they should neither worship the gods nor refrain from eating the sacred animals. The passage concludes: "It is said that the priest who framed their constitution and their laws was a native of Heliopolis, named Osarseph after the god Osiris . . . but when he joined this people he changed his name and was called Moses."[45]

Hecataeus's account is not anti-Jewish. The foreigners driven from Egypt settle in Greece as well as in Judea, even if the more outstanding among them go to Greece. He goes on to give a remarkably positive account of Moses' legislation, including the prohibition of images. He notes, however, that 'as a result of their own expulsion from Egypt, he introduced "a somewhat unsocial and inhospitable mode of life'" (*apanthrōpon tina kai misoxenon bion*).[46] The word *misoxenon* is often translated as "intolerant" or "hostile to strangers." As Katell Berthelot has shown, however, it should be understood as the opposite of *philoxenos*, hospitable.[47] The basis of the remark is the common refusal of Jews to participate in table fellowship, which was often in the context of sacrifice. Even this behavior, which seemed strange to Hecataeus as a Greek, is excused in part by the experience of Moses and his followers in Egypt. It does not imply that the Jews hated humankind. But while Hecataeus himself cannot be accused of bias against Jews, his characterization of their mode of life would lend itself to a more hostile interpretation by later authors.

The attitude of Manetho towards the Jews is more controversial. The account of the Hyksos is based on old Egyptian tradition, which

---

(Jerusalem: The Israel Academy of Sciences and Humanities, 1976) 1.20–44; Manetho, ibid., 1.62–86.

[45] AgAp 1.228–52. Stern, *Greek and Latin Authors*, 1.78–83.

[46] Hecataeus in Diodorus Siculus, *Bib Hist* 40.3; Stern, *Greek and Latin Authors*, 1.26–29.

[47] Katell Berthelot, *Philanthrôpia judaica. Le débat autour de la 'misanthropie' des lois juives dans l'Antiquité* (Leiden: Brill, 2003) 80–94.

originally was not concerned with the Jews at all. Some scholars have thought that the reference to settlement in Jerusalem was added secondarily.[48] The story that Jerusalem was built by the Hyksos was not necessarily hostile to Judaism. Erich Gruen has even argued that it was invented by Jews.[49] Much more ominous is Manetho's story about the lepers, which attributes to Moses hostility to Egyptian religion. Here again, the story was not originally concerned with the Jews,[50] and many scholars have questioned whether the references to Jerusalem and Moses were inserted by Manetho or by a later author.[51] The identification of Moses with Osarseph at the end of the second account is especially suspicious, since Osarseph is mentioned earlier in the passage without the identification.[52]

Like Gruen, I think it unlikely that either Manetho or Hecataeus knew the story of the Exodus in its biblical form, or indeed that either had more than an incidental interest in the Jews. Manetho drew on traditional Egyptian polemic against invaders from Asia, which had its roots in the experience of the Hyksos but which was revived in more recent times by the invasions of the Persian kings, Cambyses and Artaxerxes III. But the association of the Jews with this tradition, however, incidental, would have highly negative associations for the Jews. They could henceforth be identified with the followers of Seth-Typhon, archetypical enemies of Egypt.[53] The Jews were neither the only nor the primary people who were so identified in the Hellenistic period.[54] They did not pose a threat to Egypt in

---

[48] See Berthelot, *Philanthrôpia judaica*, 96–7. She is sympathetic to that view.

[49] Gruen, *Heritage and Hellenism*, 63–64, Berthelot, *Philanthrôpia judaica*, 97, finds the argument convincing.

[50] For echoes of the Amarna age in this story see Jan Assmann, *Moses the Egyptian. The Memory of Egypt in Western Monotheism* (Cambridge, MA: Harvard, 1997) 23–44.

[51] Berthelot, *Philanthrôpia judaica*, 97–99. Again, she favors the view that the association with the ancestors of the Jews is secondary.

[52] Gruen, *Heritage and Hellenism*, 64, also thinks that the identification of Osarseph with Moses was the work of a Jewish redactor. I find this unlikely. See my comments in "Reinventing Exodus: Exegesis and Legend in Hellenistic Egypt," in Randal Argall, Beverly Bow and Rodney Werline, ed., *For a Later Generation. The Transformation of Tradition in Israel, Early Judaism and Early Christianity* (Harrisburg, PA: Trinity Press International, 2000) 52–62, especially p. 61. The essay is reprinted as chapter 3 in this volume.

[53] Jan-Willem van Henten and Ra'anan Abusch, "The Jews as Typhonians and Josephus' Strategy of Refutation in *Contra Apionem*," in Feldman and Levison, ed., *Josephus' Contra Apionem*, 271–309.

[54] See especially Ludwig Koenen, "Die Adaptation ägyptischer Königsideologie

the way that the Seleucid kings, for example, did. But nonetheless, association with the Hyksos and with Seth-Typhon had negative implications, that could be exploited by polemicists.

When we survey the dossier of anti-Jewish polemic presented by Josephus, however, what is striking is how little evidence he presents for such polemic in Egypt or Alexandria. The only Alexandrian author cited who can plausibly be dated between Manetho and Apion is Lysimachus, if indeed he is to be identified with the Alexandrian mythographer and historian who lived around 100 BCE.[55] Lysimachus repeats the story of the lepers but adds that Moses instructed them "to show goodwill to no man, to offer not the best but the worst advice, and to overthrow any temples and altars of the gods which they found."[56] Moreover, Jerusalem was originally called Hierosyla because of the sacrilegious propensities of the inhabitants. The over-throw of temples was a standard part of the traditional Egyptian account, but the determination to show goodwill to no one was a new development. The implication is that the Jews rejected the laws of Buzyges, and so could be genuinely accused of hatred of human-kind.[57] Lysimachus evidently had some animus against Jews, but even here we do not know whether his account was anything more than a passing gibe against a foreign people, or whether his animus against Jews was any greater than his contempt for Asiatics in general. Apion's fellow-emissary, Chaeremon, appears to have embellished the story of the lepers with some motifs from the myth of Osiris, casting the lepers in the role of Seth. But the fragment cited by Josephus has little by way of anti-Jewish polemic, except that the leaders of the lepers were Moses and Joseph.[58] Even in the case of Apion, Josephus cites only a brief version of the account of Jewish origins.[59] Moses was a native of Heliopolis, who erected prayer houses open to the air, all facing eastwards. This account may be confused, but it is not especially hostile. Apion does add a malicious story that

---

am Ptolemäerhof," in W. Peremans, ed., *Egypt and the Hellenistic World* (Studia Hellenistica 27; Leuven University Press, 1983) 174–90.

[55] Berthelot, *Philanthrôpia judaica*, 106–7. The main fragment is found in *AgAp* 1.304–311; Stern, *Greek and Latin Authors*, 1. 382–86. Stern lists him as "date unknown."

[56] *AgAp* 1.309; Stern, *Greek and Latin Authors*, 1.384.

[57] Berthelot, *Philanthrôpia judaica*, 107–9.

[58] *AgAp* 1.288–92; Stern, *Greek and Latin Authors*, 1. 419–21. Schäfer, *Judeophobia*, 30, comments on "the almost complete absence of any open hostility to the Jews."

[59] *AgAp* 2.8–27; Stern, *Greek and Latin Authors*, 1.389–97.

relates the origin of the sabbath to a disease of the groin, allegedly called *sabbatosis* in Egyptian.

According to Josephus, Apion drew much of his material from Greek authors who were not Alexandrians, such as Mnaseas, Posidonius and Appollonius Molon.[60] Mnaseas, from Lycia in Asia Minor, lived in the early second century BCE.[61] He is the earliest source cited for the legend that Jews worshipped an ass's head in the Jerusalem temple, and he mentions this in connection with a conflict between Jews and Idumeans.[62] A related, though less offensive, story appears in Diodorus, in a passage that is sometimes thought to derive from Posidonius.[63] Allegedly, Antiochus Epiphanes entered the innermost sanctuary of the temple, and found there a statue of Moses as a bearded man seated on an ass, with a book in his hands. This passage also reports the advice given to Antiochus VII Sidetes by his advisers when he was besieging Jerusalem. They rehearse the story of the expulsion of the lepers from Egypt, and urge the king to wipe out the race of the Jews, "since they alone of all nations avoided dealings with any other people and looked upon all men as their enemies." But the king, we are told, being a magnanimous and mild-mannered person, dismissed these charges. It would seem from this story that some quite vitriolic anti-Jewish propaganda circulated in the Seleucid realm, some of it designed to justify the actions of Antiochus Epiphanes in persecuting the Jews. The allegation that Jews annually practised the ritual murder of a Greek is also told in connection with Antiochus's desecration of the temple.[64] The story of ass-worship is often thought to have originated in Egypt, because the ass was associated with Seth-Typhon.[65] Such colorful slanders may have circulated widely. Their currency is better attested in other parts of the Hellenistic world than in Egypt.

---

[60] *AgAp* 2.79, 112.

[61] Stern, *Greek and Latin Authors*, 1.97–98.

[62] AgAp 2. 112–14; Stern, *Greek and Latin Authors*, 1.99–101. On the story see Bezalel Bar-Kochva, "An Ass in the Jerusalem Temple—The Origins and Development of the Slander," in Feldman and Levison, ed., *Josephus' Contra Apionem*, 320–26.

[63] Diodorus, *Bib Hist* 34–35.1.1–5; Stern, *Greek and Latin Authors*, 1.181–85. On the derivation from Posidonius see Berthelot, *Philanthrôpia judaica*, 127–28, and her article "Poseidonios d'Apamée et les Juifs," *JSJ* 34(2003) 160–98, especially 177–87.

[64] *AgAp* 2.89–96.

[65] Bar-Kochva, "An Ass in the Jerusalem Temple," 318–25; van Henten and Abusch, "The Jews as Typhonians," 287–8.

Most of the people cited by Josephus were Hellenistic intellectuals of some prominence. Apollonius Molon was a famous orator who lived on Rhodes and counted Cicero and Caesar among his pupils. The most distinguished of the lot was Posidonius, the Stoic philosopher, who wrote a history of the period 145–85 BCE, approximately, continuing that of Polybius. This history has not survived, but it is often thought to have been the source for two passages concerning the Jews: the passage from Diodorus cited above and a passage found in Strabo of Amaseia.[66] The account of Jewish origins in Strabo is very different from the usual story of the expulsion of lepers. Moses and his followers left Egypt because they objected to the Egyptian animal cults, and they also rejected Greek anthropomorphism. They held that people should worship God without an image, and live self-restrained and righteous lives. This has been described as "a remarkable piece of idealizing ethnography."[67] Strabo goes on to say that later "superstitious men were appointed to the priesthood, and then tyrannical people," who harrassed both their country and their neighbors. This latter allusion has sometimes been explained as a reaction to the expansionistic policies of the Hasmoneans, with whom Posidonius was contemporary.[68] The passage from Diodorus contains much more hostile sentiments towards the Jews, but they are attributed to the advisers of Antiochus Sidetes. Diodorus, and presumably Posidonius, if he is indeed the source, rather approved of the magnanimity of the king in disregarding the charges.

The implication of Posidonius in anti-Jewish propaganda is of some importance for the question of anti-semitism in the ancient world, since it is sometimes argued that Stoic universalism was a factor in the perception that Jews were misanthropic.[69] (Chaeremon was also a Stoic philosopher, and Seneca referred to the Jews as "an accursed race").[70] Jewish particularism was practically the antithesis of the Stoic ideal of cosmopolitanism. Even the benign account preserved in Strabo disapproves of the superstition and aggressiveness of con-

---

[66] Strabo, *Geog* 16.2.34–36; Strabo, *Greek and Latin Authors*, 1.294–311. Berthelot, *Philanthrôpia judaica*, 113–23.

[67] John G. Gager, *The Origins of Anti-Semitism* (New York: Oxford, 1983) 73.

[68] Berthelot, *Philanthrôpia judaica*, 122; "Poseidonios," 175–77.

[69] Berthelot, *Philanthrôpia judaica*, 174–79.

[70] Seneca, *De Superstitione*, in Augustine, *De Civitate Dei* 6.11. Stern, *Greek and Latin Authors*, 1.431.

temporary Jewish leaders. Nonetheless, it is unlikely that Stoic philosophy animated the mob in Alexandria. Whatever Posidonius may
have thought about the characterization of Judaism by the advisers
of Antiochus, he surely did not approve of their proposal to extir-
pate the Jews.[71] As we have seen, Chaeremon is not especially polemical. While Seneca regarded the Jews as superstitious, he did not
accuse them of misanthropy. Judaism did not conform to the Stoic
ideal, but the evidence for Stoic involvement in anti-Jewish polemic
is very slight.

While the evidence is limited, it seems that the charge of misanthropy was known in both the Seleucid and the Ptolemaic realms
by the late second or early first century BCE, if not earlier, and
derogatory stories about ass-worship and the like circulated widely.
Nonetheless, there is little or no evidence of violence against Jewish
Diaspora communities in this period.[72] There were occasional disputes over Jewish rights, such as the right to send money to Jerusalem,
but no major conflict is reported in the Diaspora, apart from
Alexandria, until the time of the Jewish revolt against Rome. At that
time violence against Jews became widespread in the Hellenistic cities
of Palestine and in Syria. According to Josephus, Antioch, Apamea
and Sidon were the only Syrian cities that refrained from killing or
imprisoning Jews.[73] In Antioch, violence subsequently broke out at
the instigation of a Jewish renegade. Conflict in Alexandria was also
renewed at this time. The revolt against Rome created a new situation, and provided new reasons or pretexts for antagonism towards
the Jews. How far the feelings of hatred or fear (*JW* 2.478) to which
the Gentiles gave vent on this occasion had been building up, and
how far they were triggered by the war, is difficult to say. We hear
of no similar conflicts in Asia Minor.

Anti-semitism in antiquity?

It has become customary to refer to this tradition of anti-Jewish
polemic as evidence for "anti-semitism" in antiquity.[74] The term

---

[71] This is recognized by Berthelot, "Poseidonios," 198.
[72] See the survey by S. Applebaum, "The Jewish Diaspora," in S. Safrai and
M. Stern, ed., *The Jewish People in the First Century* (CRINT 1.1; Assen: van Gorcum,
1974) 117–83.
[73] *Ant* 2.479. Applebaum, "The Jewish Diaspora," 140.
[74] E.g. Gager, *The Origins of Anti-Semitism*; J. N. Sevenster, *The Roots of Pagan Anti-
Semitism in the Ancient World* (Leiden: Brill, 1975).

"anti-semitism" was coined in the 19th century, in the context of a growing interest in the characteristics of different races.[75] Strictly speaking, anti-semitism is directed against all semitic peoples, not just the Jews, but it has come to mean an irrational hatred of Judaism, which found its ultimate expression in the Nazi campaign of extermination. To describe ancient attitudes towards the Jews as anti-semitic is to imply that they attest to the same phenomenon as modern anti-semitism, or in the words of Tcherikover, that "the inner quality of anti-Semitism" is always and everywhere the same."[76] It also implies that hostility to the Jews in the ancient world was qualitatively different from prejudice against other peoples.

There are obvious problems with this use of the term "anti-Semitism."[77] The racial theory of modern anti-semitism has no basis in the ancient world. Moreover, much of the prejudice against Jews in western history was grounded in, or legitimated by, Christian supersessionism, which obviously was not a factor in the attitudes of the Greeks and Romans.[78] Scholars persist in using the term, for various reasons. In some cases there is an apologetic overtone, insofar as the original sin is shifted away from Christianity or modern Europe to ancient paganism. In many cases the usage arises from a Judeo-centric view of antiquity, to which Christians as well as Jews are prone. Most scholars who work on ancient Judaism have little interest in other peoples in antiquity and are eager to believe that the Jewish experience was unique. Moreover, the primary evidence, such as the *Against Apion* of Josephus, was compiled by Jews and transmitted by Christians for apologetic purposes.[79]

In my opinion, this usage is unfortunate and unhelpful, and only impedes the understanding of Gentile attitudes to Judaism in the

---

[75] The term was apparently coined by Wilhelm Marr in 1879. See Zvi Yavetz, "Judeophobia in Classical Antiquity: A Different Approach," *JJS* 44(1993) 1–22; Shulamit Volkov, *Jüdisches Leben und Antisemitismus im 19 und 20 Jahrhundert* (München: Beck, 1990) 27.

[76] Tcherikover, *Hellenistic Civilization*, 358.

[77] See, for example, Shaye Cohen, "Anti-Semitism in Antiquity: The Problem of Definition," in David Berger, ed., *History and Hate. The Dimensions of Anti-Semitism* (Philadelphia: The Jewish Publication Society, 1986) 43–47.

[78] See e.g. Rosemary Ruether, *Faith and Fratricide. The Theological Roots of Anti-Semitism* (New York: Seabury, 1974).

[79] Gideon Bohak, "The Ibis and the Jewish Question: Ethnic Bias in the Greco-Roman World," in M. Mor, A. Oppenheimer, J. Pastor and D. R. Schwartz, ed., *Jews and Gentiles in the Holy Land in the Days of the Second Temple, the Mishnah and the Talmud* (Jerusalem: Ben Zvi, 2003) 27–43.

ancient world. One of its by-products is endless quibbling as to what actually constitutes anti-semitism, or when "mere" anti-Judaism becomes anti-Semitism.[80] Almost invariably, the answer is a matter of degree. A certain amount of ethnic animosity is normal, but in the case of anti-Semitism it is carried to excess. Peter Schäfer has rightly objected to this kind of casuistry, but he still speaks of the charge of misanthropy as crossing the line from the "justifiable" to the "unjustifiable," from "anti-Judaism" to "anti-Semitism."[81] In fact, if the racial factor in anti-Semitism is left out of account, the only basis for a distinction is the scale and severity of the prejudice. Rather than quibble over the point at which to draw the line, it would be better to leave the word "anti-semitism" for its proper, racial, usage, and try to understand ancient conflicts in their own cultural context.

For Schäfer, "the crucial historical questions are (a) whether there was always the same kind of hostility against and hatred of the Jews throughout history, and (b) whether there is something unique about this hostility directed at the Jews which distinguishes the Jews from other ethnic groups."[82] To my mind, the answer to the first question is clearly no. The riots in Alexandria cannot be compared to Hitler's Final Solution. The enormity of the German project cannot be diluted by claiming that it was only an instance of a perennial phenomenon. Hitler's *Endlösung* was indeed a unique kind of hostility in the experience of the western world, at least. But was the hostility towards the Jews in the ancient world unique in its own context?[83]

To answer that question properly we should have to do a thorough comparative study of ethnic prejudice in the ancient world. To my knowledge, such a study has never been attempted on an adequate scale.[84] The Jews were certainly not the only people in the ancient world who had defamatory stories told about them. Think

---

[80] See Schäfer, *Judeophobia*, 197–206, with reference to Gavin Langmuir, *Toward a Definition of Anti-Semitism* (Berkeley: University of California, 1990).

[81] Schäfer, *Judeophobia*, 206.

[82] Ibid., 197.

[83] Van der Horst, *Philo's Flaccus*, 25, recognizes that "anti-semitism" is anachronistic, and opts for "Jew—hatred." He does not discuss whether this "Jew-hatred" is qualitatively different from other ethnic prejudice.

[84] See now, however, the major study of B. Isaac, *The Invention of Racism in Classical Antiquity* (Princeton: Princeton University Press, 2004), which appeared after this article had gone to press. See also Bohak, "The Ibis and the Jewish Question," and his "Ethnic Stereotypes in the Greco-Roman World: Egyptians, Phoenicians, and Jews," *Proceedings of the Twelfth World Congress of Jewish Studies, Jerusalem, 2000*, Division B, 7*–15*. Some useful material can be found in A. N. Sherwin-White, *Racial*

for example of the cursing of Canaan for looking on his father's
nakedness in Gen 9:20–27, or the incestuous begetting of Moab and
Ammon by Lot's daughters in Gen 19:30–38. No people endured
more ridicule in the Hellenistic world than the Egyptians.[85] The ways
of the Egyptians, like those of the Jews, were different from those
of the Greeks and Romans.[86] Some of the gibes against them were
topoi that could be applied to all barbarians. Others were more
specific. The charges against them included xenophobia[87] and *apan-
thropia*.[88] They were the most superstitious of all people.[89] The animal cults provided endless cause for derision. Moreover, according
to Philo, Egyptians were "a seedbed of evil in whose souls both the
venom and the temper of the native crocodiles and asps were reproduced" (*Leg* 166).

Prejudice against Jews was not more widespread than prejudice
against Egyptians in the ancient world. Was it different in kind? The
most distinctive charge against the Jews, that of misanthropy, of
actively hating the human race, is exceptional. It is documented from
the late second century BCE in the words of the advisers of Antiochus
Sidetes and in Lysimachus. Apion echoes their charges.[90] After the
Jewish war, this charge gained credence in Rome.[91] Even this, however, can be viewed as an intensification of the ethnic antagonism
that pervades this literature. Such charges were in circulation for
centuries, but they did not lead to pogroms in the Seleucid or
Ptolemaic kingdoms. As we noted at the beginning, the actions against
the Jews in Alexandria lacked precedent. Stereotypes, even misanthropic ones, did not of themselves lead to violent action.

In the corpus of anti-Jewish literature, one passage stands out as
reminiscent of Hitler's Final Solution: the advisers of Antiochus Sidetes

Prejudice in Imperial Rome (Cambridge: Cambridge University Press, 1967); J. P. V. D.
Balsdon, *Romans and Aliens* (London: Duckworth, 1979). S. Davis, *Race-Relations in
Ancient Egypt* (New York: Philosophical Library, 1952) relies heavily on the Jewish
evidence.

[85] See, for example, Maren Niehoff, *Philo on Jewish Identity and Culture* 45–74 ("The
Egyptians as Ultimate Other").

[86] For references, see Bohak, "The Ibis and the Jewish Question."

[87] W. Helck, "Die Ägypter und die Fremden," *Saeculum* 15(1964) 103–116; Bohak,
"The Ibis."

[88] Philo, *Spec Leg* 2.146.

[89] Lucian, *Pro Imag* 26; Tacitus, *Hist* 4.81.1.

[90] *AgAp* 2.121: Jews allegedly swore an oath to show goodwill to no alien.

[91] Berthelot, *Philanthrôpia judaica*, 156–71. See especially Tacitus, *Hist* 5.5.1–2,
Stern, *Greek and Latin Authors*, 2.26.

urge the king "to make an end of the race (*genos*) completely, or fail-
ing that, to abolish their laws and force them to change their ways."[92]
The king did not act on the advice, and neither did any other ancient
ruler. Antiochus Epiphanes tried to change Jewish customs, but he
certainly did not contemplate genocide. No such proposal is recorded
in the conflict in Alexandria. We do, however, find genocide con-
templated in a Jewish text. In the Hebrew text of Esther, Haman
says to the king: "There is a certain people scattered and separated
among the peoples in all the provinces of your kingdom; their laws
are different from those of every other people, and they do not keep
the king's laws, so that it is not appropriate for the king to tolerate
them. If it pleases the king, let a decree be issued for their destruction" (Esth 3:8–9). Haman does not say that they hate humankind,
nor does he mention their refusal to worship the gods of the Persians.
(The charge of misanthropy is introduced in the Greek translation,
3:13d–e). As far as we know, this story is fantasy, not history, but
it points to the most basic, persistent feature in the conflicts involving Jews in antiquity, and probably in all ethnic conflicts: their laws
and their ways were different.[93] The most basic reason reason why
the Jewish people has been repeatedly involved in conflict over the
centuries is that more than any other people it has maintained a
distinctive identity and resisted assimilation. To say this is neither to
praise nor to blame, but to observe that difference is an essential
ingredient in ethnic conflict.

But difference does not always breed conflict. The Jews in Alexandria
were no more different from their neighbors than the Jews of Asia
Minor, and no more different from the Alexandrians of the Roman
era than from their Ptolemaic forebears. Ultimately, the causes of
conflict must be sought in specific social and historical circumstances,
as we have seen in the case of Alexandria under Roman rule. To
speak of anti-semitism as if it were some kind of ahistorical virus is
only the obverse of the genuinely anti-semitic tendency to find the
cause of conflict in the Jewish, or semitic, character.[94] It is also to
fail to appreciate the contingent character of history.

---

[92] *Bib Hist* 34–35.1.5. Stern, *Greek and Latin Authors*, 1.183.
[93] Compare the remark of Salo Baron, that the root of the negative attitude
towards the Jewish people over the centuries was "dislike of the unlike" (Feldman,
Jew and Gentile, 124). Tcherikover, *Hellenistic Civilization*, 358, says that the alien character of the Jews is the central cause of the origin of anti-semitism.
[94] For examples, see Feldman, *Jew and Gentile*, 124.

CHAPTER TWELVE

THE JEWISH WORLD AND THE COMING OF ROME

In 1 Maccabees 8, we are told that after the defeat of Nicanor in 161 BCE "Judas heard of the fame of the Romans, that they were very strong and were well disposed toward all who made an alliance with them, and that they pledged friendship to those who came to them and that they were very strong" (1 Macc 8:1–2). Accordingly, he dispatched Eupolemus, whose father had negotiated Jewish rights with Antiochus III, to Rome "to establish friendship and alliance." According to 1 Maccabees, the Romans responded by making an alliance with the Jews, that required each party to come to the aid of the other in case of war. Thus began the fateful relationship of Rome and the Jews. It was initiated by the Jews, with a view to freeing themselves from the yoke of the Greeks. In time, the yoke of Rome would prove far heavier than anything imposed by the Seleucids, and result in destruction on a scale comparable to that wrought by the Assyrians and Babylonians. Rome, the erstwhile supposed protector, eventually became the archetypical enemy of the Jews.

The alleged treaty between Rome and Judas Maccabee had little significance in its time, and some have questioned whether it was a formal treaty at all.[1] Judas was killed shortly after the embassy to Rome; treaties normally lapsed with the death of the ruler with whom they were made and Judas was not even formally ruler of the Jewish people. Nearly twenty years later, Jonathan Maccabee sent ambassadors to Rome to confirm and renew their friendship (1 Macc 12:1–4). Again, the Romans responded positively, but they took no action when Jonathan was kidnapped and murdered by the usurper Tryphon. When Simon Maccabee assumed the High Priesthood, he too sent ambassadors to Rome, with a gift of a golden

---

[1] A. N. Sherwin-White, *Roman Foreign Policy in the East: 168 BC to AD 1* (Norman: University of Oklahoma, 1984) 70–9, argues that there was no formal treaty between Rome and the Jews in the second century BCE See also E. R. Gruen, *The Hellenistic World and the Coming of Rome* (Berkeley: University of California Press, 1984) 2. 745–51.

shield (1 Macc 14:24). But again, Rome took no action when Simon was murdered, and promises of aid were similarly empty when John Hyrcanus was attacked by Antiochus VII Sidetes. Hyrcanus appealed for help again later in his reign when he was attacked by Antiochus IX. This time a *senatus consultum* ordering Antiochus to desist seems to have had the desired effect.[2] As Erich Gruen has observed, the Roman responses to these Jewish advances "expressed no more than polite courtesies,"[3] but they allowed the Jews to view Rome as a benevolent power that might provide a useful counterweight to the Seleucids. The Romans had crushed the power of Antiochus the Great and were the Kittim who had humiliated Antiochus Epiphanes in Egypt, as noted in the Book of Daniel, chapter 11. And yet the Jews were not unaware of the exercise of Roman power. The same passage in 1 Maccabees that reports the embassy of Judas notes how the Romans crushed Antiochus the Great and imposed heavy tribute on his heirs, and how they had plundered and enslaved the Greeks. But, it adds, "with their friends and those who rely on them they have kept friendship" (1 Macc 8:12).

Pompey

The first serious intervention of Rome in Judea came almost a century after the embassy of Judas Maccabee. The context was a civil war between the Hasmonean brothers, Aristobulus II and Hyrcanus II. The Roman general Pompey, having defeated Mithridates in 66 BCE sent his lieutenant Scaurus to Syria. Both Aristobulus and Hyrcanus pleaded for his support. Aristobulus sent a lavish grapevine of gold, worth 500 talents, to Pompey, in hope of winning his favor. Subsequently three Jewish delegations appeared before Pompey in Damascus—one from Aristobulus, one from Hyrcanus and one from the Jewish people that was critical of both. Pompey deferred his decision, but when Aristobulus impatiently withdrew, the Roman general marched against him. Aristobulus surrendered, but was unable to deliver Jerusalem to Pompey. There the followers of Hyrcanus opened the gates to the Romans, but the followers of Aristobulus

---

[2] E. M. Smallwood, *The Jews under Roman Rule* (Leiden: Brill, 1976) 10.
[3] Gruen, *The Hellenistic World*, 746–7.

entrenched themselves on the temple mount and a siege ensued. The siege lasted three months, but ended in a blood-bath in which some 12,000 Jews were said to have died, including priests at the altar. Pompey, notoriously, entered the Holy of Holies, where only the High Priest was allowed to go, but he left the temple treasure untouched. His treatment of Jerusalem was severe. He had the leaders of the resistance executed, and imposed a tribute. Hyrcanus was left as High Priest without royal title. Aristobulus was forced to walk before Pompey's chariot in the celebration of his triumph in Rome. Thousands of Jews were deported to Rome as slaves, where they eventually were set free and swelled the ranks of the Jewish community in Rome.[4]

One Jewish reaction to Pompey's invasion is recorded in the Psalms of Solomon:

> Foreign nations went up to your altar, in pride they trampled it with their sandals" (Pss Sol 2:2).

The defilement was just punishment for the defilement of Jerusalem by its inhabitants, not least by the Hasmonean rulers. But the assassination of Pompey in Egypt, in 48 BCE, is also viewed as divine punishment for the arrogance of the Roman general:

> He did not consider that he was a man, nor did he consider the end. He said, I will be lord of land and sea and he did not recognize that God was great (2:28–29).

We might compare this view of Rome to Isaiah's view of Assyria, the rod of Yahweh's anger, which would itself be punished for its excess.

Another reaction is found in the Pesher on Habakkuk in the Dead Sea Scrolls, which identified the Romans, or Kittim, with "the Chaldeans, a cruel and determined people," of whom the prophet spoke. The pesherist is clearly impressed by their power: "fear and dread of them are on all peoples" (iii 4), but he has no illusions about their moral character: "all their thoughts are to do evil, and with cunning and treachery they behave towards all the nations . . . All of them come to use violence . . . to devour all the nations, like an

---

[4] Josephus *Ant* 14.1–79; *JW* 1.120–58. E. Schürer, *The History of the Jewish People in the Age of Jesus Christ* (rev. and ed. G. Vermes and F. Millar; Edinburgh: Clark, 1973) 1.233–42.

eagle, insatiable." The pesher goes on to note that "they gather their wealth with all their loot like fish of the sea" (vi 1). Yet it also affirms that God is not to destroy his nation at the hand of the peoples, but will place the judgment over all the peoples in the hand of his chosen ones (v 3–4).

Herod

Rome, however, would have a more lasting impact on Judea than did Assyria. In the following years the Jews would get the flavor of Roman rule in the east.[5] Aulus Gabinius, who had been a legate of Pompey, was assigned control of Syria in 57–55 BCE and had to put down a rising by Alexander, son of Aristobulus. Gabinius was frequently denounced by Cicero for corruption and extortion, and was eventually convicted of extortion in Rome. His successor, Crassus, appropriated the temple treasury, and also stripped gold from the temple building, to support his campaign against the Parthians. This provoked another abortive revolt, led by one Pitholaos, which resulted in the enslavement of more Jewish prisoners of war. During the civil war between Pompey and Caesar, Aristobulus and his son Alexander were put to death by supporters of Pompey. When Caesar gained control of Palestine, he enhanced the status of the High Priest Hyrcanus, but essentially renewed the settlement that had been imposed by Pompey. Most significantly, he awarded Roman citizenship to the Idumean Antipater in recognition of services rendered, and gave him responsibility for supervision of taxation.[6] Antipater's son Herod would rule Judea for most of the remainder of the century as a client king of Rome.

Herod's rule was arguably the most brilliant that Jerusalem had seen since the legendary Solomon, whom Herod emulated by his temple building project.[7] Like Solomon, Herod was also liberal in his support of pagan temples, although he confined them to the non-Jewish cities in his kingdom. His building projects undoubtedly brought

---

[5] Schuerer, ibid., 245–6.
[6] Smallwood, *The Jews under Roman Rule*, 39.
[7] On Herod see Schürer, *A History*, 1.287–329; A. Shalit, *König Herodes. Der Mann und sein Werk* (Berlin: de Gruyter, 1969); P. Richardson, *Herod. King of the Jews and Friend of the Romans* (Columbia, S. C.: University of South Carolina Press, 1996).

a measure of splendor to Palestine.[8] Whether, or how far, these projects were supported by heavy taxation is disputed. Applebaum argued
that they were, and pointed to Josephus' statement that Herod spent
more than he could afford.[9] Against this, however, it has been pointed
out that Herod had many sources of income besides taxation. He
controlled trade routes, and had income from royal estates such as
Jericho and from copper mines in Cyprus which he leased from
Augustus. The harbor he constructed at Caesarea was a boon to
trade in Palestine, and his building projects provided much employment.[10] There is no doubt that some people prospered during his
reign, but the fate of the general populace is less clear. Herod is
credited with reducing taxes by one third in 20 BCE and by a quarter in 14 BCE,[11] and with providing relief with his own funds in
time of famine,[12] but the fact that tax relief was needed and that
the famine took place suggest that the situation of the common people was precarious. In any case, Herod was widely reviled by the
end of his reign. In part, his disrepute was due to the incessant
palace intrigue and blood-letting. In part it arose from religious
resentment of the symbols of paganism that abounded during his
reign. Shortly before his death, two teachers, Judas and Matthias
incited people to tear down a golden eagle from the temple gate.
Herod had the leaders burned alive.[13] Such action could only increase
popular resentment. That some resentment was also due to economic
issues is shown by the demands of the populace after his death:
reduction of taxes, abolition of duties and release of prisoners.[14]
According to Josephus, Jewish delegates besought Rome to rid them
of Herodian rule and assume direct control, "for he had tortured
not only the persons of his subjects, but also their cities; and while
he crippled the towns in his own dominion, he embellished those of

---

[8] See Duane Roller, *The Building Program of Herod the Great* (Berkeley: University
of California Press, 1998).
[9] *Ant* 16. 154–6. S. Applebaum, "Economic Life in Palestine," in S. Safrai and
M. Stern, ed., *The Jewish People in the First Century* (CRINT 1/2; Philadelphia: Fortress,
1976) 664–66.
[10] All of this is acknowledged by Applebaum. See the discussion by E. P. Sanders,
Judaism. Practice and Belief. 63 BCE–66 CE (Philadelphia: Trinity Press International,
1992) 164.
[11] *Ant* 15.365–7; 16.64. Schürer, *A History*, 1.315.
[12] *Ant* 15. 299–316.
[13] *Ant* 17. 149–67; *JW* 1.647–55.
[14] *JW* 2.4.

other nations, lavishing the lifeblood of Judaea on foreign communities. In place of their ancient prosperity and ancestral laws, he had sunk the nation to poverty and the last degree of iniquity."[15] Of course this diatribe was not an objective assessment of the situation. It entailed a romantic view of the past and resentment of Herod's expenditures on Gentile cities. But it certainly was not the voice of a contented populace.

The First Century CE

Herod ruled at the pleasure of Rome, as he well knew. His death was followed by rebellion, which was put down harshly by Varus, the governor of Syria.[16] Herod's son Archelaos was installed as eth-narch, but was deposed after two years because of Jewish and Samaritan complaints. Judea was now annexed as a prefectorial province. The client kingship would be restored briefly under Claudius, with Agrippa I as king (41–44).[17] Thereafter it would revert to provincial status, ruled by Roman procurators. After two decades of turbulence under the procurators, Judea would erupt in revolt.[18] There was a roughly parallel development in the Egyptian Diaspora, where Roman rule was also welcomed at first, but the situation of the Jews gradually deteriorated. In Egypt, the catastrophic revolt came a little later, in the early second century, under Trajan.[19]

What caused this deterioration in Jewish affairs under Roman rule? Inevitably, we are dependent on the account of Josephus, whose reli-

[15] JW 2.84–93.
[16] JW 2.1–100; Ant 17.206–323; Schürer, A History, 1.330–35.
[17] D. R. Schwartz, Agrippa I. The Last King of Judaea (Tübingen: Mohr, 1990). On the fortunes of Herod's descendants see N. Kokkinos, The Herodian Dynasty (Sheffield: Sheffield Academic Press, 1998).
[18] Schürer, A History, 1. 330–483; Smallwood, The Jews under Roman Rule, 144–292; E. Paltiel, Vassals and Rebels in the Roman Empire. Julio-Claudian Policies in Judaea and the Kingdoms of the East (Brussels: Latomus, 1991); J. S. McLaren, Power and Politics in Palestine. The Jews and the Governing of their Land. 100 BC–AD 70 (Sheffield: Sheffield Academic Press, 1991) 80–187.
[19] See the classic account of this history in V. Tcherikover and A. Fuks, ed., Corpus Papyrorum Judaicarum (3 vols.; Cambridge, MA: Harvard University Press, 1957–64) 1–111; Smallwood, The Jews under Roman Rule, 220–55; J. M. Modrzejewski, The Jews of Egypt: From Rameses II to Emperor Hadrian (Princeton: Princeton University Press, 1995).

ability is often open to question, and who must be read critically.[20]
Martin Goodman distinguishes five major explanations of the conflict
between the Jews and Rome, all based on Josephus' work: the incompetence of the Roman governors, the oppressiveness of Roman rule,
Jewish religious susceptibilities, class tensions, and quarrels with local
gentiles.[21] He adds another factor, division within the Jewish ruling
class, and the failure of that class to fulfill its role as mediator between
Rome and the Jewish people. While all of these factors deserve serious consideration, I will focus here on the two that seem to me most
fundamental, Jewish religious susceptibilities and the oppressiveness
of Roman rule. Many of the other issues—the incompetence of the
governors, class division, tensions within the ruling class and even
friction with the local gentiles were all, I believe, grounded in, or at
least exacerbated by the pressures created by Roman rule.

Jewish Religious Sensibilities

Josephus lays much of the blame for the conflict on the so-called
"fourth philosophy" which resisted Roman rule for religious reasons.[22] After the deposition of Archelaus, we are told, "a Galilean
named Judas incited his countrymen to revolt, upbraiding them as
cowards for consenting to pay tribute to the Romans and tolerating
mortal masters" (*JW* 2.118). This "philosophy" according to Josephus
"filled the body politic immediately with tumult, also planting the
seeds of those troubles which subsequently overtook it" (*Ant.* 18.9).
The sentiments attributed to Judas are repeated later by Eleazar,
the commander of Masada: "A long time ago, brave comrades, we
firmly resolved to be subject neither to the Romans nor to any other
person, but only to God, for only he is the true and lawful Lord of
men" (*JW* 7.323). The sentiment is an old one—compare the misgivings about the introduction of the monarchy in Israel in 1 Samuel.[23]

---

[20] See S. Schwartz, *Josephus and Judaean Politics* (Leiden: Brill, 1990); J. S. McLaren, *Turbulent Times? Josephus and Scholarship on Judaea in the First Century CE* (JSPSup 29; Sheffield: Sheffield Academic Press, 1998).

[21] Goodman, *The Ruling Class of Judaea*, 7–14. Cf. McLaren, *Turbulent Times?* 150–8.

[22] See especially M. Hengel, *The Zealots. Investigations into the Jewish Freedom Movement in the Period from Herod I until 70 AD* (Edinburgh: Clark, 1989).

[23] 1 Sam 8:7: "they have not rejected you but have rejected me from being king over them."

It is undoubtedly true that many of the flashpoints of conflict involved religious issues—the incident with the golden eagle at the end of Herod's reign, the introduction of Roman insignia into Jerusalem under Pontius Pilate, the demand that a statue of Caligula be placed in the Jerusalem temple. There was a tradition of Jewish resistance to foreign rule, dating to the Maccabean revolt, and this tradition had always entailed religious zeal.[24] Moreover, Jewish religion was exceptional in the ancient world in its exclusiveness, and in its sensitivity to iconic representations. This exclusiveness, no doubt, was difficult for some pagans to comprehend, and was often an occasion of conflict.[25]

Yet religious differences can hardly be placed at the root of the conflict with Rome. Roman policy (like that of the Greeks and Persians before this) generally affirmed the right of people to live according to their ancestral laws. This right was granted to Greek cities as well as to Jewish communities: "Whatever laws, whatever right, whatever custom existed . . . the same laws and the same right and the same custom shall exist."[26] The reason for this was simply that it was the easiest way to keep peace. This policy often worked to the benefit of Jews, as it guaranteed their rights even in Greek cities. Allowances were made for Jewish sensibilities- notably exemption from military service, permission to send offerings to the temple in Jerusalem and permission to offer sacrifices for the emperor instead of worshipping him. Of course other people too offered sacrifices on behalf of the emperors, and some emperors (Augustus, Tiberius, Claudius) sometimes refused divine honors offered by eastern peoples.[27] The emperor cult was not monolithic, at least in the first century, and each community was free to honor the emperor in its own way. There were occasional lapses in Roman tolerance

[24] W. R. Farmer, *Maccabees, Zealots and Josephus. An Inquiry into Jewish Nationalism in the Greco-Roman Period* (New York: Columbia University Press, 1956).
[25] P. A. Brunt, *Roman Imperial Themes* (Oxford: Clarendon, 1990) 528 argues that Jewish religion was the peculiar factor that distinguished the situation in Judea from other parts of the empire. On Roman perceptions of the Jews see K. L. Noethlichs, *Das Judentum und der römische Staat. Minderheitenpolitik im antiken Rom* (Darmstadt: Wissenschaftliche Buchgesellschaft, 1996) 44–69.
[26] A sample inscription cited by M. Pucci Ben Zeev, *Jewish Rights in the Roman World* (TSAJ 74; Tübingen: Mohr, 1998) 461; see also 413–4. On the extent and limits of Roman tolerance see also Noethlichs, *Das Judentum und der römische Staat*, 27–43.
[27] Pucci Ben Zeev, *Jewish Rights*, 476–77.

in this matter—notably in Caligula's demand that his statue be worshipped—but the exceptions prove the rule. Even after the destruction of Jerusalem we find that Titus refuses the request of the people of Antioch that the Jews be expelled from their city and insists that their rights remain as they were before (*JW* 7.100–111).

Moreover, few Jews are likely to have held to the philosophy that submission to human masters was incompatible with the rule of God. The scriptures provided numerous injunctions to the contrary. Jeremiah had affirmed that the kingship of Nebuchadnezzar was granted by God and that all people should obey him (Jer 27:6–11). Josephus has the Jewish delegation that requested direct Roman rule instead of the ethnarchy of Archelaus promise that "the Jews would then show that, calumniated though they now were as factious and always at war, they knew how to obey equitable rulers" (*JW* 2.92). In fact, Jewish resistance to Roman rule was sporadic, and was triggered by other factors besides opposition to foreign rule as such. This is not to deny that most Jews would have regarded foreign rule as ultimately unacceptable, and hoped for eventual restoration of native rule. But this was not always a matter of great urgency, and for some upper-class Jews Roman rule was probably quite beneficial for the present.

In this regard, it is interesting to note that Rome plays a very limited role in the Dead Sea Scrolls, which provide our main corpus of Jewish documents from the land of Israel around the turn of the era.[28] (It may be that most of the Scrolls were written before the arrival of Pompey, but it is clear that some, at least, date after that time). Rome is never mentioned by name in the Scrolls. Only one Roman is mentioned by name—Pompey's lieutenant, Aemilius Scaurus, in 4Q324a, a calendrical text. The Kittim in the pesher on Habakkuk are clearly to be identified as the Romans, as we have already seen. It is generally assumed that the Kittim are also the Romans in the War Rule, although it is possible that the Kittim of Asshur and the Kittim in Egypt, in 1QM 1, were originally references to the Seleucids and the Ptolemies.[29] The Kittim here are the

---

[28] H. Lichtenberger, "Das Rombild in den Texten von Qumran," in H.-J. Fabry, ed., *Qumranstudien* (Göttingen: Vandenhoeck & Ruprecht, 1996) 221–31.
[29] J. J. Collins, *Apocalypticism in the Dead Sea Scrolls* (London: Routledge, 1997) 106–107.

eschatological enemy, the opponents in the final war. But what is perhaps most striking about the portrayal of the Kittim in the War Rule is the lack of specific information about them. They are simply "the other"—no more defined than Gog from the land of Magog in Ezekiel or the somewhat garbled Gog and Magog in the Book of Revelation. Such texts bespeak a general hostility to the Gentile world that is deeply rooted in biblical traditions about the Day of the Lord. For the Qumran sect, as for Judas the Galilean, foreign rule was ultimately unacceptable as such, and its destruction was assured. Unlike Judas, however, the Qumranites were resolved not to requite evil to anyone until the Day of Wrath, and so they must have reconciled themselves to Roman rule until the time was right, a time which they may have believed to have come in 66 CE.

The relatively restrained rhetoric of the Scrolls with regard to Rome may be contrasted with the bitter outpourings in the apocalyptic writings after 70 CE.[30] In 4 Ezra 12 the messianic lion reproves the Romans, who are represented by an eagle: "He will denounce them for their ungodliness and for their wickedness, and will display before them their contemptuous dealings." The fifth Sibylline Oracle, written perhaps a little later around the time of the Diaspora revolt is more vindictive: "Alas, city of the Latin land, unclean in all things, maenad, rejoicing in vipers, as a widow you will sit by the banks and the river Tiber will weep for you, its consort. You have a murderous heart and impious spirit" (Sib Or 5. 168–71). Most eloquent of all is the Book of Revelation, where Rome is portrayed as the whore of Babylon. All of these portrayals, however, were written after the destruction of Jerusalem. No doubt, negative feelings about Rome had built up over the first century and ran high on the eve of the revolt. But the animosity reflected in the apocalyptic texts is not simply a rejection of Roman rule in principle but a reaction to a century of misrule and oppression.

---

[30] J. H. Charlesworth, "The Triumphant Majority as Seen by a Dwindled Minority: The Outsider According to the Insider of the Jewish Apocalypses, 70–130," in J. Neusner and E.S. Frerichs, ed., 'To See Ourselves as Others See Us.' Christians, Jews, Others in Late Antiquity (Chico, CA: Scholars Press, 1985) 285–315.

Roman Oppression

In fact, while Jewish relations with Rome had their distinctive character, and this character was colored by religion, they were not atypical of relations between Rome and other subject peoples. In the words of Stephen Dyson, "one of the most persistent phenomena related to the extension of Roman conquest and control in the Western Empire was the sudden, widespread native revolt."[31] Dyson discusses five major examples, in Britain, Gaul, Germany and Pannonia-Dalmatia. We know of these revolts primarily from Roman sources, but where we get glimpses of their motivation a fairly consistent pattern emerges. Native peoples resented Roman depradation, and the erosion of their traditional way of life. Disregard for native religion was sometimes a factor. (In Britain, the Romans attacked and desecrated a Druid center off the coast of Wales).[32] A relatively early formulation of native reactions to Rome is attributed to Mithridates of Pontus, in an attempt to enlist the support of the Parthians:

> For the Romans have never had but one reason for making war on all nations, peoples and kings—an insatiable desire for power and wealth.[33]

An oracle preserved in Sibylline Oracles Book 3, sometimes associated with the campaign of Mithridates,[34] sometimes with that of Cleopatra,[35] expresses an easterner's desire for revenge, and reflects the typical grievances of the conquered peoples against Rome:

> However much wealth Rome received from tribute-bearing Asia,
> Asia will receive three times that much again
> From Rome and will repay hear deadly arrogance to her.
> Whatever number from Asia served the house of Italians

---

[31] S. L. Dyson, "Native Revolts in the Roman Empire," *Historia* 20(1971) 239–74 (239).

[32] Dyson, "Native Revolts," 260.

[33] Sallust, *Epistulae et Orationes VI, Epistula Mithridatis*. See further H. Fuchs, *Der Geistige Widerstand gegen Rom in der antiken Welt* (Berlin: de Gruyter, 1938), 16–17.

[34] J. Geffcken, *Komposition und Entstehungszeit der Oracula Sibyllina* (Leipzig: Hinrichs, 1902) 8; H. G. Kippenberg, "Dann wird der Orient Herrschen und der Okzident Dienen," in N. W. Bolz and W. Hübner, ed., *Spiegel und Gleichnis. Festschrift für Jacob Taubes* (Würzburg: Königshausen & Neumann, 1983) 45.

[35] W. W. Tarn, "Alexander Helios and the Golden Age," *JRS* (1932) 135–59; J. J. Collins, *The Sibylline Oracles of Egyptian Judaism* (SBLDS 13; Missoula: Scholars Press, 1974) 57–61.

Twenty times that number of Italians will be serfs
In Asia, in poverty, and they will be liable to pay ten-thousand fold."
                                        (Sib Or 3:350–55).[36]

It is surely significant that the initial rebellion of Judas of Galilee
was sparked by a census for the purpose of introducing a poll-tax.[37]
Other rebellions against Rome were ignited by the introduction of
regular tax assessment, in Gaul in 12 BC and in Cilicia in 36 CE[38]
There is an ongoing debate as to whether taxation in Roman Judea
was excessive. On the one hand, scholars like Applebaum have argued
that the Jewish peasantry was "crushed with merciless exactions under
Pompey and his successors and no less under Herod."[39] On the
other, E.P. Sanders has argued that Rome took local conditions into
account, and that taxation was not especially oppressive before the
revolt.[40] (The tax imposed by Vespasian was admittedly punitive).
Sanders' argument, however, is largely a relative one—the burden
on people in other parts of the empire was just as heavy. Indeed.
And it sometimes led to revolts, even if not on the same scale as
the one in Judea. What may have seemed like reasonable, moder-
ate taxation to the Romans did not necessarily seem so to those who
paid the tax. Julius Caesar had granted Judea certain exemptions,
from tribute in the seventh year and from the requirement of bil-
leting troops (*Ant* 14.202–10). Nonetheless, Tacitus records a com-
plaint against the tax burden in 17 CE (*Ann* 2.42). Pontius Pilate took
money from temple treasurey to pay for an aquaduct, admittedly a
worthy cause (*JW* 2.175; *Ant* 18.60). The procurator Florus confiscated
temple funds for "the imperial service" (*JW* 2.293). There was a
general increase in Roman taxation under Nero and an extraordinary levy under the procurator Albinus in the early sixties (*JW*
2.273). In the end, even Sanders admits that "the people were hard
pressed."[41] The phenomenon of brigandage throughout this period,

---

[36] J. J. Collins, "The Sibylline Oracles," in J. H. Charlesworth, ed., *The Old Testament Pseudepigrapha* (2 vols.; New York: Doubleday, 1983, 1985) 1.370. On resistance to Roman rule see further R. MacMullan, *Enemies of the Roman Order* (Cambridge, MA: Harvard, 1966).
[37] Smallwood, *The Jews under Roman Rule*, 150–53.
[38] Goodman, *The Ruling Class*, 11, n. 38.
[39] Applebaum, "Economic Life in Palestine," 661–2.
[40] Sanders, *Judaism*, 157–69.
[41] Sanders, *Judaism*, 168.

but especially in the years before the revolt, is most readily explained against a background of economic hardship. It should also be noted that there was famine in Judea under Herod, who famously provided relief from his own funds, and again under Claudius, when relief was provided by Queen Helena of Adiabene (*Ant* 20.101). Moreover, there was more at stake than simple ability to pay. Taxation by a foreign power had implications for status, and symbolic significance. The resentment of the *laographia*, or poll-tax by the Jews of Alexandria seems to have been largely a matter of status, vis-à-vis the Alexandrian Greeks.

By all accounts, Roman rule in Judea became more oppressive after the re-annexation of the province under Claudius.[42] The procurators who followed the brief reign of Agrippa I were not impressive people. Even if we view Josephus' account of their maladministration with some suspicion, we must note that Tacitus says that Felix "practised every kind of cruelty and lust, wielding the power of a king with all the instincts of a slave," (Hist 5.9) while his statement that the patience of the Jews lasted until Gessius Florus (Hist 5.10) accords with the view of Josephus that Florus was the last straw. But the problem lay deeper than the personalities of the procurators. In the increasingly centralized Roman system, procurators lacked authority, and often had little experience and low social standing. One, Felix, was an ex-slave. The governor of Syria could intervene at any time in Judean affairs. The combination of exacting imperial demands and poor administration created the pressure that exacerbated other problems such as social divisions.

The Romans, of course, did not view themselves as oppressive. On the contrary, they prided themselves on their humanity and justice.[43] Roman law, when properly administered, was perhaps the main cultural legacy of the empire. But by definition, the interests of Rome came first, and policy was directed to the advancement of the wealth and power of the empire. The glory of the empire was enhanced by the construction of cities and buildings. The archeological remains brought to light in recent years show the splendor of Herod's constructions at Caesarea and elsewhere and indeed

---

[42] See Paltiel, *Vassals and Rebels*, 261–301.
[43] Cf. the speech attributed to Titus in *JW* 6.333–36, where he ironically suggests that the Jews were driven to revolt by Roman *philanthropia*.

the luxury of the wealthier residents of Jerusalem.[44] Yet the Jewish experience of Roman rule is all too vividly symbolized by the story of Herod's temple. Here was a splendid project that enhanced the glory of Jerusalem and of Judaism. It provided employment in Jerusalem for decades, and was finally brought to completion a few years before the revolt. Less than a decade later, there was scarcely left of it a stone upon a stone. The prosperity that attended Roman rule for a time, at least among the upper class, was swept away in the brutal suppression of the revolt. The Jewish experience was ultimately similar to that of the Gauls and the Germans, and other peoples who were brought under the yoke of Rome. I can think of no better articulation of that experience than the indictment of Rome attributed to the Briton Calgacus by the Roman historian Tacitus: "These plunderers of the world, after exhausting the land by their devastations are rifling the ocean: stimulated by avarice, if their enemy be rich; by ambition, if poor: unsatiated by the East and by the West; the only people who behold wealth and indigence with equal avidity. To ravage, to slaughter, to usurp under false titles, they call empire; and when they make a desert, they call it peace" (Tacitus, *Agricola*, 30).

[44] N. Avigad, *Discovering Jerusalem* (Jerusalem: Shikmona, 1980); L. Levine, *Judaism and Hellenism in Antiquity. Conflict or Confluence?* (Seattle: University of Washington Press, 1998) 48–51.

INDEX OF AUTHORS

INDEX OF PASSAGES

New Testament

Matthew
11:3   70

Mark
13:8   93

Luke
7:19   70

1 Corinthians
7:1   118
7:39   119
15   135

15:44   171
15:50   133, 171

2 Corinthians
6:14   118

1 Peter
3:1   119

Revelation   89, 133, 155
12   90
19   154
20   211

Apocrypha

Ben Sira   29, 100, 143, 144, 158–160, 179
4:14   145, 159
7:97   165
24   157
24:23   106
33:15   21
42:19   162
42:24   21
48:25   162

4 Ezra   155
7:28–31   133
12   90, 211
12:22–30   93
13:5–11   93
14:5   96

Judith
8:26–27   99

1 Maccabees   32, 35–37
1:11–15   27
1:29   35
1:34   35
1:41   36
1:44   36
2:52   99
8:1–2   202
8:12   203
8:17   30
12:1–4   202
14:24   203

2 Maccabees   27, 30–32, 37
4:11   32
4:13   3
4:18–20   30
4:39–42   35
5:11   27, 35
5:27   35, 36
6   36
6:2   34
6:6   39
6:8–9   36
7   131
11   37
11:22–26   38
13:4   37

3 Maccabees   79, 183

4 Maccabees   26, 131

Wisdom of Solomon   3, 18, 24, 131, 139, 143–159, 163–167, 170, 173, 174, 178, 179
1   148
1–5   145, 148, 157
1:1–6:21   143
1:13   165
1:14   148
1:15   164
1:16   165
2   149, 160
2:1–24   143
2:2   147

Dead Sea Scrolls

Hellenistic Jewish Authors

Talmud

Other Rabbinic Texts